There's Nothing
in This Book
That I Meant
to Say

PAULA

POUNDSTONE

There's Nothing in This Book That I Meant to Say

THREE RIVERS PRESS • NEW YORK

Published in the United States by Three Rivers Press, an imprint of the
Crown Publishing Group, a division of Random House, Inc., New York.
www.crownpublishing.com

Three Rivers Press and the Tugboat design are registered trademarks
of Random House, Inc.

Originally published in hardcover in the United States by Harmony Books,
an imprint of the Crown Publishing Group, a division of
Random House Inc., New York, in 2006.

Library of Congress Cataloging-in-Publication Data
Poundstone, Paula.
There's nothing in this book that I meant to say /
Paula Poundstone.—
1st ed.
1. Poundstone, Paula. 2. Comedians—United States—Biography.
3. American wit and humor. I. Title.
PN2287.P573A3 2006
792.702'8092—dc22   2006012897
[B]

ISBN: 978-0-307-38228-3

Printed in the United States of America

Design by Lynne Amft

10 9 8 7 6 5 4 3 2 1

First Paperback Edition

To the one person who thought adopting three kids was a good idea and to my three brilliant ideas, Toshia, Alley, and Thomas E, who proved beyond a shadow of a doubt that that one person was right. Oh, yeah, and to Moe, Larry, and Curly, too.

Acknowledgments

I can still remember asking Shaye Areheart, my wonderful publisher at Harmony Books, "What if I can't finish the book in a year?" when we had our first meeting. It seemed such an unlikely event, I don't think she even answered me. She might have chuckled. That was eight and a half years ago. I must be the luckiest writer in the world to have gotten eight and half years of enthusiasm, support, and encouragement from Shaye Areheart.

I'm really glad that Shaye called Peter Guzzardi to ask him to edit my book. I think it worked out well for both of us. I got the benefit of his expertise and he got a sharp reminder to screen his calls more carefully. I also appreciated Kim Meisner's help.

My literary agent, Colleen Mohyde, has been a mentor, an inspiration, and so much fun to work with, I was almost sorry to finish the last page. Almost. I appreciate the hard work, kindness, and "will do" attitude of my assistant, Carmen Cannon. We have called my friend Gordon McKee for technical support so many times, I'm surprised he never figured out that we break that stupid computer on purpose just because we love to have him come over. Without my nanny, Heather Kang, I

Acknowledgments

could not have squirreled away a minute to write so much as one run-on sentence; she has done a wonderful job for eleven years, and *Mary Poppins* is my favorite movie, so my nanny standards are very high. Dave Snyder and my other agents at William Morris have been kind, productive, and loyal for the many long years of our relationship and, let's face it, ten percent of my fees doesn't really cover that.

I don't know how to thank my manager, Bonnie Burns, for all she has made possible for me. She makes me feel funnier than I actually am.

In the course of writing this book, my own mistakes have brought me through an extremely dark tunnel of personal crisis. The people that I gratefully acknowledge here not only helped me to write this book, but also stuck with me throughout, and there truly are no words that can express my appreciation.

Contents

Foreword

PAULA POUNDSTONE is my friend, though we live on separate coasts and rarely have a chance to see each other. I have no idea what we have in common other than a shared respect for truth, a fondness for irony, and a dedication to humor—mostly mine, I think!

This book reveals a woman who is strong, yet vulnerable, having been through a few battles that she'll share with you. I know this: Paula is steadfast in her love for the children who are her family, and they are her strength and inspiration.

Her flawless comedic musings on life, her own chief among them—which is good, it being an autobiography and all—spring from stories she tells about her heroes: Joan of Arc, Abraham Lincoln, and Helen Keller, to name a few.

This book is layered with wisdom (and I don't go seeking wise friends as a rule), but Paula's writing makes it easy to embrace its author. It is funny, thoughtful, and fluid. I was delighted and surprised at the way she takes sudden turns and meanders down less-traveled avenues of thought.

Enjoy this book—I know I did. I feel like I know my friend a little bit better now, and I want you to, too.

—*Mary Tyler Moore*

There's Nothing in This Book That I Meant to Say

1

Joan of Arc: Called by God and Driven by Drink

Canonized as a saint 508 years after her death, Joan of Arc led the armies of France when she was seventeen years old. At nineteen she was captured by the British, tried by the Church, and burned at the stake as a heretic. At seventeen I left high school because there was a parking lot that needed to be hung out in, and I didn't want the brainy kids to have to take a shift. At nineteen I became a stand-up comic, turning my back on a successful table-bussing career, and at forty-one I was arrested, putting off my canonization indefinitely.

Joan of Arc was born to Isabele and Jacques d'Arc in Dom-remy, France, in 1412. I don't understand French names. Apparently Joan of Arc was never called "Joan" in France; she was Jeanne d'Arc. Two different authors I read said they were calling her "Joan" because that was how Americans knew her. Well, who started calling her "Joan" in America? You can't just do that. If it's Jeanne, then it's not Joan. It's not even like it saves your tongue time. It's the same amount of sounds. Why not save ink and call her "d"?

Joan or Jeanne was raised in a manner considered proper in that time and place. Her father said he would rather have had her brothers drown her than allow her to lose her virtue. I'd have been pretty water-safe back then. My mother told me that she learned to swim when someone took her out in a boat to the middle of a lake and threw her overboard. I said, "Mom, they weren't trying to teach you to swim."

The youngsters in Joan Jeanne Joan's community had the responsibility of taking each family's sheep, goats, and cows to pasture and watching them while they ate. There is a bit of controversy in the record as to whether Joan Jeanne Joan regularly took her turn driving the livestock to pasture, but if she did it drunk we'd have something in common. In June 2001 I was arrested on a felony child-endangerment charge, for driving drunk with my children in the car, a misdemeanor child-abuse charge, the details of which I am not permitted to discuss because they are sealed by the court, and four charges of lewd acts with a minor, which were later dropped. I pled guilty to the child-endangerment charge and the misdemeanor child-abuse charge because those things were true. There is nothing I care about more in the world than my children, but in fact I was drunk when I drove them to the Baskin-Robbins one day, and it was reported to the police. I have no one to blame but myself—which, I've always said, takes the joy right out of blaming. I wish Dick Cheney could have been involved somehow.

I did have a drinking problem. I don't know if you heard. It was kept kind of hush-hush out of deference to me: I was actually court-ordered to Alcoholics Anonymous on television. That pretty much blows the hell out of the second "A," wouldn't you say? Not only have I not been granted the world-famous anonymity, but when I arrive at those secret clubhouses, there are big blinking WELCOME, PAULA signs. Looking back, I can see that there were red flags I should've noticed. In my defense I'll say that I was drunk. That's the good news and the bad news about drinking; there are red flags, but they're kind of blurry and they zip on by. I guess I was in denial. For a while I thought I had an ice cream problem.

I should have known. About three weeks before I went into rehab I got really drunk, went into a pet store, and bought a dog. It would have been no big deal, but we had nine cats. Believe me, the cats started hiding the alcohol after that. We now have ten cats, a big stupid dog, two tadpoles, a bearded dragon lizard, and a bunny. I'm going to be honest with you. I'd been drunk in that pet store before, and I don't want to play the victim here, but I believe they knew and I believe they took advantage. Does anybody else's pet store have a wine section? It seems unusual to me.

I was very drunk when I got my first bunny. I sobered up by the next day and bought another bunny to prove I would have gotten the first bunny even if I wasn't drunk. That should have been a huge red flag. Most people in AA have bunnies. They don't say it when they stand up. They say their names and identify themselves as alcoholics, but most don't have the courage to admit openly to bunny ownership.

My dog was a cute little puppy when I got him. However, about three weeks later, having had no success at quitting drinking on my own, I went into a rehab for 30 days and got stuck there for 180 days. In one of the kindest gestures ever bestowed upon me, a woman I had never even met took my puppy the whole time I was away. Six months later, when I couldn't possibly share in a circle one more time and my dog had ingested all of her furniture, this woman dropped off in my front yard, in what I liken to a drive-by shooting, one of the biggest, dumbest animals I've ever seen. I don't really even have any proof that it was the original dog, but it didn't seem polite to question it. As it turns out, my dog Cal is part black Lab, part German shepherd, part pit bull, and part chow. I believe there was at least some alcohol involved in his conception. He has eaten everything. Some bleeding-heart dog people have told me he was teething. Sharks eat everything, are they teething? I believe his German shepherd/black Lab/pit bull/chow mother got really wasted one night, went down to the beach, and had sex with a shark. The most diabolical plan of the maddest mad scientists couldn't have come up with this combination. I read in a dog-training book that during his "chewing phase" I should put anything I don't want chewed out of his reach. He eats the side of the house. I'm not sure which high shelf to put the house up on.

As I fly by my neighbors at the end of his leash, they sometimes shout after me, "Why don't you get rid of that dumb dog?" Sometimes, after exercising the dog, while popping my arm back into its socket, I think about getting rid of him, but he's an important part of my punishment. It should have been part of my sentence—five years probation, random drug and alcohol testing, and keep the dog-shark.

When she was twelve, Ms. d'Arc heard voices that she believed were sent by God. The voices eventually told her that she had been chosen by God to restore the kingdom of France. She was instructed to dress as a man, crop her hair, take up weapons, lead the French troops to victory, and assist King Charles in reclaiming his kingdom.

I thought I heard God speak to me once. He said, "You're wearing that?"

I bought a black chiffon spaghetti-strap shirt and jacket once. The salesperson told me I couldn't wear it with corduroy. There was a sense of danger in her voice. It didn't sound like merely a "fashion don't," but rather a word of serious caution, as though the combination of the two fabrics might result in an explosion. She repeated the warning as she bagged the garment. She was troubled by an uncanny sense that I owned a lot of corduroy. The military must have bunkers full of carefully separated corduroy and black chiffon secreted away somewhere in Nevada. It's one of those tigers we hold by the tail, like the A-bomb. I never wore the black chiffon shirt and evening jacket. Too risky. I buy impulsively sometimes, totally forgetting what I look like and how I spend my time. Amazingly, the fantasy of going out someplace kind of fancy, on a night when I wasn't wearing corduroy and had shaved, lasted long enough for that shirt and jacket to make the cut through three moves and countless closet cleanings.

Much of history's record of Jeanne's extraordinary life comes from her own testimony during her heresy trial, although I can't imagine that they got it all written down accurately. My criminal court case in Santa Monica was rescheduled three times in a row, weeks apart, in part because the court clerk wrote the wrong time down on my lawyer's official document.

Once, at the appointed day and time, the district attorney wasn't there and the judge had to go to a doctor's appointment. In an effort to cheer me up, my lawyer told me, after he rescheduled with the clerk, "It'll be next month on the nineteenth and the clerk says this'll be good because the judge can be there that day." I realize that, as a criminal, my thoughts on the legal process don't carry much weight; still, for whatever help it may have been to my lawyer in his own personal relations, I explained to him that people are supposed to plan things for the times they are available to do them, and that one does not score points for scheduling a court hearing for a time when they can be in court—especially when they are the judge. It's hard to believe that all of what Joan Jeanne Joan said in court got written down exactly as she said it.

Jeanne claimed to have heard voices and seen accompanying apparitions several times each day for five years. She said they were Saint Michael, Saint Catherine, and Saint Margaret, and were often flanked by hundreds of unidentified angels. I keep picturing Michael Landon and Della Reese surrounded by those little white decorative soaps shaped like angel heads, but I'm sure that's inaccurate. Who would crop her hair short and cross-dress because little soaps told her to?

Joan Jeanne Joan said she never sat for a portrait, but there are many artists' renderings of her. Since she rather famously cut her hair, it's clear that the images of her with long, flowing red hair are inaccurate. Jeanne was a farm girl who labored in the sun, and she came from thick, short, muscley farm people, so it's not likely either that she was tall and thin, with soft pale skin, as she's often depicted. My face started to wrinkle this year. I don't see what function it serves in nature, but it's amazing. My face is folding in on itself. It's no wonder I'm tired a lot—that has to be a draining process. I recently bought wrinkle cream. I tried to slip it surreptitiously into the basket at the Rite-Aid, but my daughter Alley saw me and kept asking, "What's that?" in a really loud voice. I was so embarrassed. I had always hoped that I'd be willing to age gracefully, but sometimes you panic. "Wrinkle cream," I muttered. But Alley wouldn't let it go. She looked at me wide-eyed and said, "But, Mom, you don't even believe in stuff like that."

"Yeah, but what if I'm wrong?" I answered.

I dyed my hair because HBO wanted me to. Not when I subscribed to cable, but when I did a show on their network. It was a series. Well, it was four shows. We taped them in two nights, and they decided not to make any more midway through my "we love it" hug from the executive on the second night. It was a good show, though. My hair was dark. I did three shows of a series for ABC once. The third one didn't air in the L.A. area because it was preempted by the Malibu fires. It was a good show, though. My hair was dark.

I started to make a pilot for Fox once, but it got turned into a "presentation" partway through, which is to television what a show in the Little Rascals' barn was to theater. It was one of the worst show-business experiences I've ever had, and I've hosted a pie-eating contest brought to you by Zim's family restaurants. I should've seen that one coming. I shouldn't have even put in a rinse. When I met the head of that network, before I could re-coil effectively, he had immobilized me with his python-like embrace and oozed, "I'm an executive who hugs." Not too many sentences later he told me, "We're like a family here." I should have run. He got fired a couple of years later. I guess Grandpa let him go.

A couple of years ago, after Bob Costas and then Greg Kinnear had left the position, *Later* invited me to host their one-on-one interview show for a week. It was sort of an unofficial audition for a permanent position. With coaching and practice, I have done a good job as an interviewer in the past. I actually got a CableACE Award for my work as an interviewer on my extensive four-episode HBO talk show. I beat out Larry King and Charlie Rose, and Larry King became bitter and had me on his show and didn't show up to do the interview. The whole thing was a fluke, of course, because nobody is a better interviewer than Charlie Rose, but my point is I have done that job before. So, *Later* lined up a week of interviews for me beginning with Betty White, who I love. Betty White was great. I was nervous and I could not stop talking. If I read the "We'll be right back after the commercial" cue at all, I still wasn't able to stop talking afterward. In fairness to me, I think I talked mostly about Betty White. So I was on topic. That's something. I could probably be heard just faintly behind an ad with some woman happily cleaning and disinfecting a stubborn stain in just one easy swipe exclaiming, "With Pine-Sol every day is fresh . . . Did someone say something about Betty White? . . . What's that noise? . . . Who's talking while I'm trying to clean and disinfect? . . . Anyways, I'm sorry . . . Buy this stuff. Really."

The producer came into my dressing room afterwards and said I'd done a good job. He said I had gone too long, but that meant there would be lots to choose from in editing. However, the following day, the same guy called and said they felt I had purposely tried to sabotage their show. I couldn't believe it. Not that I didn't perhaps suck. I sometimes do, but this was beyond simply not liking me, or the classic "we've decided to go in another direction." Apparently I was so bad that it appeared I had planned to be bad, as if it had been a studied, skillful execution of a plot of mine, or perhaps of a rival network against the *Later* show. It wasn't an honest blooper, it was a conspiracy. I didn't simply lack talent; I was part of a terrorist organization aimed at disrupting the American way of life by bringing down the *Later* show. I know nothing about the history of France except what I've recently read about Joan Jeanne Joan. Oh, and I've also seen *Beauty and the Beast,* both the video and the hit Broadway musical when it came to L.A. In fact, my daughter Toshia was in a kid's production of the play and I saw that a few times. Still, there are gaps in my working knowledge of the history of France. Toshia played a wolf and a peasant. I asked her what her favorite part of the show was. She said, "The bow." That is so-o-o my daughter. Come to think of it, with the exception of the making of *The Wizard of Oz,* I know almost no history.

Once, in Washington, D.C., I bought a timeline of world history in a three-poster set that equaled twelve feet across. I had it with me on my way home at the D.C. airport. My flight was delayed and I went into a bar to kill time. The bartender handed me a drink and told me the guy at the end of the bar had bought it for me. I didn't want to hurt the guy's feelings and I was too shy to say "no thank you," so, stupidly, I accepted the drink and the guy moved to the barstool beside me. I assume the neon I'M STUPID sign went on over my head; I heard a click. The guy kept trying to make conversation and, just trying not to be rude, I answered his questions. Then he suddenly reached across and grabbed my crotch, crushing my poster. He said he was trying to make sure I was a woman. What a waste of good manners on my part. Gee, I'm embarrassed to get caught reading a name tag at a social gathering. Anyways, I broke up with him. What I do know about the history of the world is that it is twelve feet long and the United States doesn't even begin until the last four inches. My arrest isn't even mentioned, and there's a mysterious bend in the middle.

When Jeanne got her instructions from God, France was in the midst of the Hundred Years' War with England. That's a long war. That'd be just under half of our nation's history, or about a third of how long it has taken me to write this book. I guess France had been bothering Scotland, and England had taken issue with that. Charles was the heir to the throne of France, but he had not, at that time, actually sat in the big chair. There were many Charleses back then, and they were all kings. It's like Briannas at my kids' school. There are so many that even the use of the last initial can't keep them all straight. They have to use a complicated numeric system as well. Toshia may have Brianna G.57 as a reading buddy next year. There's a Brianna Club at school, and this year they had a highly competitive "What Being a Brianna Means to Me" essay contest.

If I ever give birth, I'm gonna name my kid "Yikes." I've never had any interest in giving birth before. I was a foster parent for eight years and I fostered eight children, in various combinations within that time. In three strokes of luck, which I could never deserve, I was able to adopt my foster children Toshia, Allison, and Thomas E Poundstone. Part of my sentence was that I can no longer adopt. I had hoped to adopt the two foster children who were in my care at the time of my sad mistakes, but they were taken from me permanently. Toshia, Allison, and Thomas E went back into foster care. For a year I had to have a monitor with me while I picked them up from their foster home at 6:00 a.m. every day. I took care of them until I brought them back at bedtime, and I didn't leave them until they were asleep. I taped labels with the numbers 1 through 365 all over our house, and each day the kids searched for the right number to rip off of the wall, lizard tank, playhouse, stilts, Harpo Marx photograph, jukebox, etc., in a sort of life-size Advent calendar. By December 2002 we were reunited and quite happy to put it all behind us. Now when I see a blue adopt-a-highway sign on the side of the road, I think, "Sorry, can't." I'll have to give birth to my own highway.

So, France had been taken over by England and they didn't like it at all. It's probably what caused them to begin battering and frying foods. As weapons were quite unsophisticated back then, and the English couldn't cook, naturally they'd eat at French restaurants; the French probably figured they'd jack up British cholesterol levels and, boom, they'd keel over from heart attacks before they could get the skirts on their horses for battle. I got a sandwich at a Wawa convenience store in Pennsylvania recently. They had a little deli section. I looked up at the menu board behind the counter and then told the lady there that I wanted a pork Hot Hoagie. She pointed to a row of touch screens in front of the counter and said I had to order with those. I looked confused, so she came around the counter to help me. HOT SANDWICHES came up on the screen and the lady said to push that and then the computer showed the choices among the Hot Hoagie genus. I said, "I want a pork Hot Hoagie," and she said I had to push it on the screen. She could have made me two or three Hot Hoagies in the time it took her to show me how to use the screen, but clearly this was the public-education phase of Wawa's plan to wean the public from human contact during their sandwich purchase. The condiment selection appeared on the screen next. There was an oval that said MAYONNAISE, and one that said A LITTLE MAYONNAISE. Soon they'll have one where you spread imaginary mayonnaise across the screen to show them how close to the edge of the bread to get it. After I finished, she went back around the counter to receive my order by computer and then she made my pork Hot Hoagie, which I ate without the aid of technology.

Jeanne had a plan to enlist the help of a cousin's husband, Durand Lassois, who lived near Vaucouleurs, which was a place that had a French governor guy who could hook her up with the Charles she needed in order to rescue France.

The story gets a bit thick with French names and titles here, so with all due respect to France, I'm going to blow through some of this quickly. Against the backdrop of more English sieges of French territory, Jeanne Joan Jeanne pursued a "six degrees of Kevin Bacon" trail toward Charles. Those she told her story to were skeptical, but she kind of wore them down and enlisted their cooperation. She was pretty ballsy, they were extremely superstitious, and France was in a pickle. They didn't have much to lose by going along with her. At that time I guess it wasn't so unusual for someone to say God spoke to them. God was chatty back then. I never hear about God showing up and speaking to people now. You'd think God would e-mail.

I hate e-mail, but everyone swears by it. I used to write for *Mother Jones* magazine and they had an e-mail address, so when readers sent an e-mail to me at the magazine, *Mother Jones* would print it out and mail it to me. So I have received e-mails before. The great thing about regular mail is the natural editing process that takes place. One doesn't just dash off an angry thought that would be better kept to oneself, because fifty percent of the people who happen to have a pen on them have to borrow a piece of paper, or vice versa, and that takes time. Even those anal enough to have immediate access to both a pen and paper when the urge to correspond is upon them can't escape the compulsory envelope search, which is critical to the editing process of a well-written letter. How many poorly conceived resignations and humiliating, flowery admissions of undying love have been reconsidered during the envelope search? It could get dicey once the letter is in the envelope, because our memory tells us it's well written and well deserved, but again, the sheer brilliance of the post saves us from ourselves. The stamp. Sure, some overachievers have stamps in their top desk drawer, but not even Ben Franklin himself knows the postal rate. I've got a wax-paper kind of a bag with a U.S. Postal Service logo on it, teeming with E stamps, F stamps, and D stamps, with flower stamps, flag stamps, and Laurel and Hardy stamps, but I don't have a clue how many I need to mail a letter. I write a lot of letters, but I don't mail that many. If the letter happens to make it past every other barrier and the intended re-cipient has moved, it gets returned to me, I open it, reread it, think about how I've grown since I wrote that, and rewrite it. People who e-mail rarely get the chance to think about how they've grown. I used to get e-mails that said, "Is this really your address?" No one has ever mailed me a letter for the sole pur-pose of marveling that they could.

Jeanne Joan Jeanne claimed to be a virgin when she told the governor guy that she had instructions from God to dress as a man, take up arms against England, lead the French troops, and put the Charles guy on the throne. He assembled a team of women to examine her and verify that she was indeed a virgin. Makes the crotch-grabbing guy in the D.C. bar seem well within his rights.

This virgin thing was big with these people. Her followers referred to her as "the virgin." I am not, at this time, a virgin myself, but I don't like sex, so I abstain, which should certainly be at least a cousin to virgin, perhaps deserving something in an honorary title. Should I become a beloved hero in my time, my followers could refer to me as "the virginish."

I'm a single working mom with nine cats, a dog-shark, a lizard, and a bunny. I don't go to bed, I pass out. The idea that I'd get to my bed and there'd be someone in there with whom I was supposed to have an activity is horrifying to me. It's a safe bet that I'm not good at sex, that I do it wrong. In fact, there's probably something horribly wrong with me, and if I went to a sex therapist several times a week to spend endless hours talking about it, took medications, watched educational films, and worked with plastic figurines, I could probably be miraculously cured, but I can't imagine any feeling, sexual or otherwise, that'd be so satisfying, so pleasurable, that it'd outweigh the appeal of sleep.

The virgin was deeply religious. When a letter about her intentions reached the Charles guy, he sent a messenger to accompany the young visionary 350 miles across France to the court. She never complained to the governor's soldiers who escorted her about the difficulties of the trip; however, she pestered her companions repeatedly about stopping to hear Mass.

I once chaperoned a backpacking trip through New Hampshire with students from my former high school. These kids had to stop every tenth tree clump to apply lip balm. They would frantically pass around a tub of Blistex, each dipping a finger into the mint-scented grease and smearing it urgently onto their lips. Lip balm is addictive. It soothes your lips, then peels them off. There's a whole section over at the Betty Ford. Not one of those kids realized they had a problem. I'm not exaggerating. We almost lost a shiny-lipped Harvard-bound girl when the Blistex tub slipped out of her hands and over a cliff and she tried to follow it. We could have run out of food and toilet paper and the group would have pressed on, but when the lip balm was gone, the trip was cut short. Somewhere in New Hampshire there's a squirrel whose lips are peeling. I'm not sure what the original idea was behind lip gloss. Is it supposed to simulate drool?

My friend Nicole does a great job on my hair and makeup, but for a while—I guess it was the latest fashion—she would put my lipstick on about an eighth of an inch beyond where my lips ended. I don't get that. If it doesn't stop at the lip line, where does it end? I don't mind a little lipstick so my lips show up better, but I don't see any upside to deceit about the amount of lip that I have.

Once, I got lured onto a stool at a department store makeup counter. I was incredibly awkward. The saleswoman rubbed, patted, fanned, and sprinkled my face with a series of "must have" oils, creams, enhancers, and powders. She was covered in makeup herself because, while she waited to sell the makeup, she rubbed, patted, fanned, and sprinkled her own face with a series of "must have" oils, creams, enhancers, and powders. If I had been given three wishes in that moment, I would have wished first, as always, that everyone had food; second, that everyone had a home; and, third, that I had not sat down on that stool. I felt uglier and more embarrassed by the minute. I mumbled sheepishly, "I never wear makeup," and the saleswoman, in her desperation to sell a top-of-the-line face fixer, blurted out, "Neither do I." Her black-flocked eyelashes lowered to reveal eyelids the color of fresh avocados. The look on my face must have indicated that I'd caught her in a fairly stupid lie. She backpedaled. "Uh, well, I only wear it at work." I must not have been able to hide my disbelief, because she stammered, "Or when I go out . . . or in."

"But not when you scuba-dive?" I offered.

"Right. Never," she answered.

So Joan Jeanne Joan was real religious. I'm an atheist. The good news about atheists is that we have no mandate to convert anyone. So you'll never find me on your doorstep on a Saturday morning with a big smile, saying, "Just stopped by to tell you there is no word. I brought along this little blank book I was hoping you could take a look at."

The third step of the twelve-step program, the backbone of Alcoholics Anonymous, is that you turn your will and your life over to God, which is why it's unconstitutional for the courts to order people to AA. People in AA are quick to counter that it doesn't have to be God, just a higher power. They'll say stuff like, "It could be the ocean." It could be, but it isn't. I guess the alcoholics in Nebraska are screwed.

Jeanne Joan Jeanne wore men's clothing for the trip across France. Jean de Metz, one of the governor of Vaucouleurs' soldiers, was devoted to her. He mixed and matched with his servant's armor and provided an outfit for her. I borrowed a pair of socks from the wife of the treasurer of California on a campaign trip before he was elected. He has served a couple of terms now. I think he's doing well, which goes to show you can be a good treasurer even if your wife has given her socks away. His name is Phil Angelides, and when I met him I think he was the head of the California Democratic Party and we were campaigning for Bill Clinton at a rally at UC Berkeley. A man wearing only something to partially obstruct the view of his private parts kept moving through the crowd shouting unintelligible things. He was given a fairly wide berth. The head of the AV department at UC Berkley must have been a Republican, because instead of a microphone and speakers, we were only provided a megaphone. Whatever the almost naked man was saying, he was passionate about it; he was louder than the megaphone.

Calli Couri spoke before me. She wrote *Thelma and Louise,* which I hated. It was considered a breakthrough film for women at the time. I hope we've crawled back into our hole and covered ourselves over since then. The Geena Davis character comes away from holding a guy up at gunpoint and tells the

Susan Sarandon character that she "never felt so alive," which may well be the case for her, but for most of us, feeling dead will simply have to do. Once, after I had endured two hours of questions, mainly about my drinking debacle and subsequent court nightmare from the tenth therapist I had been court-ordered to, she concluded that I needed antidepressants because I appeared depressed. Perhaps, perhaps not, but, given the subject matter, at what point should I have burst into song? Should I have been more upbeat?

"You know what's the best part about being accused of child molesting? . . . When your kids are removed from your home, you never have to turn off the vacuum and say 'What?' . . . The Lifetime network is going to be all over this."

One guy who did a psychological evaluation of me for the court would close his eyes, shake his arms, and raise his face to the ceiling for lengthy periods while forming his questions, as if the questions were whispered to him by decorative angel soaps instead of recalled from a fairly standardized list that he has used time and again. It wasn't a quick "it's on the tip of my tongue" squint. It was a prolonged gesture, and he did it repeatedly, which left me with that increasingly awkward feeling, wondering if there was something I should do for him, like when someone chokes or when a friend stays in your bathroom way too long. It looked like a seizure except he'd stop and ask me a question and go back to it. He may have been channeling. This was the guy who was writing the report to the court about my mental stability. It was a bit disturbing. Maybe it was part of the psychological testing: if I noticed his arms wiggling about with his eyes shut, then I was way screwed up; if I didn't notice, then I was an incurable threat to society.

I was court-ordered to fifty-two therapy sessions with a graduate student. She got a "C" on me. I could tell I was her term project because she spent one session making a modeling-clay figure of me. I think she liked me. She asked if the year-book photographer could get a shot of us doing therapy together. Of course she didn't want to breach my confidentiality, so she said I didn't actually need to be doing therapy in front of the photographer, but if I could look like I was sharing something deep, that would be great.

At one point I was seeing four therapists a week to satisfy the court. Even Sybil didn't see four therapists. If I was that fucked up, I couldn't hold the pencil to schedule all of those appointments. If I needed four therapists, I shouldn't be out and about. I should be strapped into one of those Hannibal Lecter things and kept in a dark room. One psychiatrist said I was bipolar, which is also called manic-depressive. Maude had that. Remember? It was toward the end of the *Maude* series, the Norman Lear spin-off of *All in the Family*, with Bea Arthur, Adrienne Barbeau, etc. Maude became very enthusiastic about running Henry Fonda for president. She even made posters. Her husband Walter and her daughter Carol, the Adrienne Barbeau character, called a shrink and lo and behold, it turned out Maude was suffering from manic depression. This was before the Reagan presidency, when the suggestion that an actor might run for president was considered a symptom of manic depression.

This psychiatrist I was stuck seeing firmly believed that the fact that I sometimes stayed up late cleaning was a dangerous symptom of manic depression. It can also be a symptom of having five kids, nine cats, a dog-shark, a bunny, two tadpoles (whose plastic pond replica needs to be drained and refilled every other day), and a love of original grout luster and coloring. I'm gonna guess this guy doesn't have kids if he thinks staying up late cleaning is a symptom of a mental health disorder. Kids are sticky. That's why there are dark tunnels in most amusement park rides, so that people don't see how many kids were zipping by and just adhered to the wall. At the end of the summer, a cleaning crew goes through the rides with a powerful steam cleaner, and there are always a couple of kids still attached to the wall, clutching boxed juices.

Whoever invented boxed juice either didn't have kids or had a deep and abiding hatred for all life on earth. They're made of some kind of weird unrecyclable waxy paper, with a little bit of foil where the plastic straw goes in after you remove it from the little plastic envelope that kids can't open. The box is filled with tooth-rotting, ant-attracting, obesity-linked juice that no kid can possibly drink without squishing it out of the wholly inadequate container.

There was a French place called Orleans that the English had taken over. I assume New Orleans is named after that Orleans. I was invited to perform at the Farm Aid concert at the Superdome in New Orleans once. Willie Nelson was gonna be there. The Neville Brothers were gonna be there. I was incredibly flattered to be invited. It seems obvious now that telling my little jokes in between bands to an audience of 30,000 and kegs of beer, toward the end of a six-hour show, wouldn't go that well. I had a hint that I was in trouble when I watched comedian Paul Rodriguez kill about two hours before I went on. He told the crowd that he'd gone out drinking on their main street the night before and that he had been sexually harassing women, punctuating his monologue with hand gestures that looked as if he were squeezing a woman's breasts, and they roared—roared. Right then I decided to open up with the piece about the cat bathing the baby's head. I followed Kris Kristofferson with my whimsical observational humor, trying to talk over the blang-bling-thump-testing-1-2-3-4 sounds of Neil Young's band tuning up behind me. Then I was sure I was in trouble. It didn't go well. The crowd viewed me as an obstacle to their enjoyment of Neil Young's band's warm-up. Several individuals shouted "Neil!" repeatedly. Some, I know, were anxious to see Neil Young, but some absolutely thought I was Neil Young, but they liked his old stuff better. The noise level in the Superdome rose. I was bombing in the classic sense of the expression. I felt like a substitute teacher. It was bad. Bob Zmuda, who had booked me into the Farm Aid show, hid in the bathroom after the show to avoid me. Old MacDonald went to the phone to beg the bank to foreclose on his farm.

Joan made her way toward her king, who promptly assembled a group of women to examine her to make sure she was a virgin again. This, remember, is before they had videotape. Assured of the virgin's virginity, Charles VII set her up with a small staff. She got to have a confessor. I would kill to have a confessor. Whenever I felt the need, I could just crook my finger and whisper discreetly, "Confessor? Could you come here a minute? . . . I haven't shaved for a month. Thank you."

"Confessor? Psst." I'd motion him over with my head. "I ate Pop-Tarts in bed last night . . . Come back, come back, there's more. It wasn't the first time."

Paula Poundstone

She also got a couple of servants, a couple of heralds, and a page. I wasn't there. I read this. I looked up the meaning of the word *herald*. My dictionary says it's "an official crier or messenger." The third definition is "announcer," but Joan also had a page, which is defined as one employed to deliver messages. Couldn't the page announce, too, like the herald? Or were they specialists? Did they only deliver messages, or could they receive? Could they be set on "vibrate"?

Every time I insist my daughter Toshia look up a word, I accompany her painfully slow word search with a well-worn speech about how important it is that she learn to work independently, and that means using the dictionary instead of asking me. Invariably she looks up the word only to find it defined with another form of itself. I sheepishly read her the definition and then explain it myself.

"I'm not always going to be around when you're reading, so you need to be a big girl and look it up by yourself . . . There it is . . . 'Redundant: dundant more than once'—see?" Maybe I read it wrong. Maybe a page is a herald and the author was just trying to mix it up a bit so as not to be dundant again.

There was very little agreement among the dozen therapists/counselors/psychiatrists who evaluated me for the court, so the district attorney concluded not that some of the diagnoses might be inaccurate, but that I was in the grip of every malady that any of these guys suggested. Hence, in the DA's affidavit, I'm bipolar, depressed mildly, depressed severely, borderline personality disordered, drug and alcohol dependent, alcoholic, obsessive-compulsive, manic-depressive, compliant, noncompliant, defensive, paranoid, prompt, late, city mouse, and country mouse. The more people I see in the helping profession, the sicker I get. What does that tell us? The graduate student told me, in a desperate attempt to get me to "share" with her, that everyone has something deep down inside that they don't like about themselves and that once they "deal with" whatever it is, they can drink as much as they want. I told her that that idea conflicted with some of what I'd been told by my other court-ordered experts. She seemed so disappointed that I finally said, "Here's something that must have impacted me terribly. I was raised by my Aunt Polly and one summer night I wanted to go to the county fair and she wouldn't let me so I snuck out a second-story window and climbed down a tree to get out and on my way back in I fell out of the tree and my legs were paralyzed."

"Miss Poundstone, that sounds a lot like *Pollyanna*."

"Oh, really, I never saw that film, did you? Here's something else that must have been significant. For a while my family lived in Austria and the Nazis were after my dad and one night after a concert we had to sneak out the back and hike across the Alps. That was painful. Of course, we had our music."

Joan joined the army, and on March 22, 1429, she dictated a letter to the king of England and some of his cohorts demanding that they return the keys to the towns they had taken. I once saw an ad for the Custom Key Company in the Yellow Pages. I thought they were all supposed to be custom. Isn't that the genius behind the whole key concept? There's a place called the Progressive Shoe Store in Beverly Hills. They had some of the first upright customers. Joan was in the right place at the right time, up until the time she was jailed and burned at the stake. The fighting had become a bit lackluster, I would guess.

Could they have been really trying after one hundred years? I imagine that every so often an English guy looked out over the wall of the town he'd stolen from France, saw a French guy climbing it, shoved him off, and went back to his muffin. The cops climbed over the gate when I was arrested while I was in rehab June 2001. It seemed odd because the gate swings open. If I could wish for only one thing in my entire life to have been different, it might be that that gate had swung open while the cops were on it.

My dog-shark has figured out that he can jump over the fence at the house we're renting. He tried to eat the neighbor's cat a couple of days ago. I guess we're not going to be first on the block party committee phone list. Although the child-molesting charges were dropped, the press didn't feel the same zeal about their duty to inform the public of that, so real-estate values didn't exactly soar when I carried my cleaning products over the threshold of the house we recently rented. I'm a very important part of my neighborhood watch right now. The eyes in the signs follow me like those of the older couple in *American Gothic*.

Anyways, if my dog-shark had eaten my neighbor's cat, I think that'd pretty much cancel the "welcome to the neighborhood tea," and I'd have to keep the sugar fully stocked, because clearly I wouldn't be borrowing any. Man, he took off after that cat. At one point the cat was several feet in the air above the dog. Then the cat ran through the crawl space under the house, and the dog-shark scrambled through after it. I stuck my head through the hole. The barking and yowling seemed to move into the heating duct. I considered just leaving them there, but

I had visions of them rocketing out of the heater during the first cold snap. I don't go under the house. That's for plumbers and rat catchers and other ne'er-do-well tradesmen who come out all dirty and lie to you about what needs to be done and you pay them without question because there's no way you're going under the house. I had a plumber once who came out from under the house and handed me a Polaroid photograph of pipes. He said they were my pipes. I acted like I recognized them.

"Oh, that's a nice shot. Let me show you one from a few years ago. It's here in my wallet. We had this done for Christmas cards that year. See the tinsel?"

Anyways, I went under the house. The pipes were adorable. I wished I had my camera. I got the dog-shark out. The cat will probably never come out.

We'll probably leave in a couple of years. I think I can avoid eye contact with my neighbor until then. It wasn't entirely the dog's fault. I think there was some history between the dog and the cat. I saw the dog eat a pile of cat poop one day, so clearly he had lost a bet with the cat.

The trainer told me to spray the dog-shark with vinegar when he chases our cats. It works, only now he freaks out at those fancy restaurants where they make the salad at your table. I worked at a salad-bar restaurant, and I was in charge of refilling the big bowls of vegetables in the salad bar. I would stack up the empties to refill them in the kitchen, and often a disappointed-looking all-you-can-eat salad-bar customer would point to the remaining two or three bowls and ask, "Just chickpeas and alfalfa sprouts today?" They must have had some very unfair dining experiences in the past, like finding they had to penetrate a defensive line to get to the spaghetti after paying for the all-you-can-eat Howard Johnson's spaghetti buffet.

When I first moved to San Francisco from Boston in 1980, coincidentally there was a place not far from my apartment called Boston Style Subs. As it happens, subs were an important part of my Boston experience. So I went to Boston Style Subs and ordered a roast-beef sub. Quite properly the guy behind the counter asked me, "Do you want everything on it?"

"No onions," I replied.

Soon I got the roast-beef sub, and there were black olives on it. There were black olives on my roast-beef sub. I said to the guy, with a bit of outrage, "There are black olives on my roast-beef sub." I thought maybe it'd fit into a pattern of local crimes that he could recognize. I expected him to say, "Oh, Jesus, I'm sorry. He's done it again. How did that guy get in here? Some guy has been putting black olives all over town. Let me get those off of there for you. Would you like me to rinse the meat?" Instead he said, "You said you wanted everything on it."

I was incredulous. "Yes, but it didn't occur to me that I had to list every hideous, disgusting food that belongs nowhere near a roast-beef sub. No grapefruit, no coconut . . . if you use Necco wafers, not the black ones."

I once ate at a pizza place in Chicago. The waitress brought over a very complicated menu for pizza. It had an elaborate list of toppings, including cheese and tomato sauce. I consulted the waitress at length, trying to understand why you had to order cheese and tomato sauce when ordering a pizza. Isn't that what pizza is? "If I were to order a mushroom pizza at this establishment," I asked, "would I get a crust with mushrooms resting atop it? Not even secured?"

"Yes," she said, as if that were obvious, how it always was and always would be. I finally established that I wanted a pizza with cheese, tomato sauce, and mushrooms. After it arrived and cooled, I took a bite and bit into a walnut. I called a waitress over to tell her there were walnuts in my pizza. She wasn't surprised at all.

"Yes, we put walnuts in our pizza."

"Let me get this straight," I said. "I have to order cheese and tomato sauce specifically, but walnuts come on your pizza automatically?" She acted as if it were as normal as apple pie with sliced apple.

I happen to hate nuts, but I also really object to the favoritism they enjoy. How many times have you bought a baked good that listed raisins, coconut, and/or chocolate chips on its label, only to bite in and find a nut? Nuts are so awful they have to be snuck into foods without the customer's approval. Raisins would never get such privilege. I eat raisin toast almost every night, because it's as close to a grape as I'm allowed to get anymore. One night I happened to read the packaging on my Sun Maid raisin bread while I waited for four slices to toast. In small yellow print up near the opening of the bag, it said, "Fifty percent more raisins than the government requires." I think it's a strange brag for a raisin bread company that the government has to require them to put raisins in their raisin bread. Any company could make that claim anyways. Chevrolet could tape a raisin to each truck steering wheel and claim they have one hundred percent more raisins than the government requires.

Joan sent a herald to deliver her letter to the English. The English captured the herald. Joan sent two more to get him back. It's not uncommon for me to lose a dollar in a soda machine and put another in right away—and lose it. I exude hope. I can always risk another dollar for a soda. I drink over sixteen diet sodas a day. The only time I don't have to pee is when I'm being tested at the probation office. I was sentenced to five years of random drug and alcohol testing, which means whenever I'm told to, I go to the probation office at the Santa Monica courthouse and pee in a cup in front of a woman, with the title of deputy, whose job it is to stand there and watch. It's as humiliating as you'd think it is. Occasionally, however, I look up from my squat and think, "At least I'm not her." Imagine having that job. Did she apply for it? Or did she just apply for a job with the city and this was what she got?

"We've found a job that you're uniquely qualified for. The good news is that we're gonna make you deputy. The bad news is you're gonna be the pee watcher. Deputy Pee Watcher!" The "deputy" title has to be the perk they use to get someone to do that job. They'd have to make me the police chief to get me to do that job, and even then I'd negotiate a lot of breaks. Sometimes I've seen Deputy Pee Watcher eat right there in the bathroom. I swear it. The city feels it has to have someone do that job because otherwise people might smuggle in clean pee, when theirs is contaminated with drugs and/or alcohol, and, with some sleight-of-hand with the sample cup, substitute clean pee. There is no reason for any level of unemployment in the United States of America; in this country you can sell your clean pee. Well, I guess I couldn't. That's my point, I can't pee under pressure. I go in with a tank full of soda in me, dying to pee, dying to get out from under the withering gaze of the lunch-eating pee watcher, and I can't pee a drop. It gets very quiet in that bathroom, unless Deputy Pee Watcher is eating chips. There's a line of other criminals forming outside the door, waiting to pee in a cup, and I'm a dust bowl. Sand comes out. Cobwebs form. Sometimes, kindly, the other criminals make water sounds.

My dog makes a big deal of stopping at a bush occasionally and lifting his leg and then not peeing. He just stands there delicately balanced, his brown eyes darting back and forth with that worried look dogs get. I tell him, "It's okay. I know you haven't been drinking." He sleeps in a cage in the living room. Unless the cats are sneaking in a flask to him, he's clean.

A guy at the rehab I was at got popped for storing drugs inside the back of his radio. It was a dead giveaway when the disc jockeys started slurring their words. Occasionally, "clients" at the rehab would arrange to have someone toss liquor or drugs over the wall to them. Darn shame for the second-string heralds that Joan's original letter-bearing herald hadn't used that method. Wouldn't it suck to be the herald sent to demand the first herald back? That incident was probably the inspiration for the singing telegram. If you dress up like a banana and sing the message, no one will keep you. I was a bicycle messenger in downtown San Francisco in 1981. I can say with some pride, given the backdrop of history, that I was never captured. I wasn't very good at it, though. I was hit by trucks twice, and it was my fault both times. Looking back, I marvel that I ever did the job at all. I'm too wimpy to ride up hills and I'm afraid to ride down. There were no deliveries to Kansas, so I didn't last long. I ride a bike like Alice from *The Brady Bunch*.

Lo and behold, the English didn't honor the requests in Jeanne's letter. You can't trust anyone. One of the court-ordered psychiatrists that I was seeing recommended to the court that I see a cognitive behavioral therapist and then he told me he never made that recommendation. I know he did. I saw the letter. Maybe he didn't just lie to me, maybe it was some modern form of psychological testing. I've been subjected to a lot of that. I took a Rorschach test where you look at inkblots as well as a Horshack test, where you shoot your arm in the air and say, "Oh! Oh!" when you think you see a penis. I have no idea what the Rorschach test is supposed to mean. I can't believe any insight has ever been gained by asking people to interpret pictures of inkblots.

You've no idea of the stress caused by taking a Rorschach test when you've been accused of child molesting. Maybe they were supposed to look sexual to the normal brain. Maybe they weren't. Honestly, they could have shown me an eight-by-ten of a penis and I would have said, "Uuh . . . I don't know . . . a teakettle? . . . an anvil? . . . a puffy pink cloud?" Anyways, I went to the cognitive behavioral therapist. He was $210 an hour, plus $10 for parking in his building in Beverly Hills. He said we needed to make a list at the beginning of each session of what we were going to talk about. I didn't tell him, but that was one of my problems: I couldn't stop making lists. I used to make daunting "things to do" lists. I loved the satisfaction of crossing things off. Sometimes I would set the bar low by writing things like "get up" or "eat a snack."

Occasionally, desperate for self-esteem, I'd write down stuff I'd already done and cross it off. I went several times to the $210-an-hour list-maker. His list was about as successful as mine. I've never gotten through a list. I might get two or three things done, but the bulk of the list simply rolls over to become a part of the next day's list. I still have to clean out my high school locker. The only concrete thing the list-maker told me was that there was a behavioral technique, named after the guy who developed it, where you postpone a pleasurable activity during your day until after you've completed work on the task you are finding difficult to achieve. I don't want to put a halt to all of the breakthrough work going on in cognitive behavioral research, but I thought of that technique myself when I was a kid, and I have never even been in a laboratory. Probably the lab rats themselves came up with that without the aid of the higher thinking of great doctors of cognitive behavioral psychology. For as long as I can remember, I have vacuumed the entire house before opening a new package of underwear. I don't need to pay $210 an hour to anybody to be told that. The parking attendant could have told me that for $12 and he would have parked my car.

I asked my attorney to request relief from the judge from the financial burden and bother of so much therapy. In court that day, the judge, my attorney, and the DA went into the judge's chambers for a long time. I thought I smelled pot when they finally came out, but it was probably just my imagination. My attorney handed me a business card with the name and phone number of a therapist scribbled on the back of it. He said, "Call and make an appointment with this guy. The court is going to pay for it. The judge says this'll be good because he knows this guy, so he trusts him."

When I looked more closely at the business card, I realized it was that of the judge. I didn't know judges had business cards. I guess that's so if a dispute breaks out at the cigar bar or the dominatrix dungeon, they can pick up a little extra judge work on the side:

"Your Honor, Mr. Jones promised to pay two hundred dollars for thirty lashes with a whip, and he has paid only one hundred."

"Mr. Jones, I find you guilty of nonpayment for services and order you to pay the dominatrix the one hundred dollars in full, and as further punishment, you may no longer be beaten."

When I went to the psychologist from the back of the judge's business card, I asked him how the judge knew him, and he answered cheerfully, "I'm his neighbor." Great, my mental health and legal problems can be discussed over the barbecue:

"Paula Poundstone's really fucked up, isn't she? Do you think these coals are hot enough?"

"Ya, tell your wife to get that meat. Oh my God, you're not kidding. I showed her a picture of a penis and she thought it was an anvil. Your apron is on fire. She wants you to return her kids, she says they're suffering."

"Oh, she does, does she? Fuck, burned right through my apron, and that was a wedding present, too. Doris, you wanna bring that meat? . . . Honey, that doesn't please the court, now bring the meat."

I went to the judge's psychologist neighbor five times. He was supposed to charge only the court, but he billed me five hundred dollars and billed the court three hundred. Then he denied having billed me in an interview with a social worker. So I sent a letter of complaint to the psychologists' board of ethics, along with the bill, the canceled check, and the letter from the judge instructing him to give me back my money. I hope it ruins the block party. Maybe if he loses his license he can pick up some jobs mowing lawns around the neighborhood. The judge will hire him. He knows him.

The French troops were inspired by Joan. They defeated the English at Orleans. Joan's prophecies were coming to pass, including that of her own battle injury, which she had predicted to both her king and her confessor. She took a sword in the chest, right through her armor. I could have predicted that, by the way. You didn't have to be a soothsayer to figure out that charging into a group of people who oppose your approach and are holding swords might get you poked. Whenever my son picks up a stick, someone gets hurt, and he doesn't have a cannon or a steed. I've predicted injuries. Time and again I've told my kids if they jump on the furniture they're going to fall and get hurt and I haven't once been wrong when I've said, "This wrestling game always starts out fun, but someone's gonna end up in tears."

Because of budget cuts, my kids' elementary school only has a nurse three days a week. On Tuesdays and Thursdays they tell them to be careful. Mondays, Wednesdays, and Fridays they throw caution to the wind. They bungee off the monkey bars. They train for the running-with-scissors relay. There are so many safety precautions for kids nowadays. How can kids possibly get hurt? The playground at my kids' school has soft pavement. Still no cure for the common cold, but science may yet eliminate the bruise. Kids have to have helmets to ride bikes now. Why? We didn't when we were growing up. How come it was okay for our heads to smack into the cement? I think kids are wimpier than they used to be. I have some buckets that came emblazoned with big, black international "no" signs over the image of a little kid leaning into a bucket. The print beneath warned not to let your child play with the bucket because they might fall in and drown. How is that even possible unless the child was a perfectly balanced, gymnastically inclined, suicidal flathead? If someone leaned into a bucket and began to drown, wouldn't they flail a bit? Wouldn't the bucket tip? Who are these bucket children?

I bought some Silly Putty for Toshia a couple of years ago. It now comes in the cute little egg with a scroll of cautions. It says not to use it for earplugs. Well, who used it for earplugs and ruined it for everyone? It was probably the bucket children. They had Silly Putty stuffed in their ears and couldn't hear their mothers' panicked cries of "Get away from the bucket!" Kids didn't use Silly Putty for earplugs when I was a kid. We put it on comic strips and stretched Little Lulu's face and enjoyed it very much, thank you. I did put a piece of candy from a candy necklace up my nose once. It wasn't labeled.

Toshia asked me if she could bring a water bottle to school. She said her teacher said the students could keep them at their desks. Are kids drier than they used to be? The school has running water. They have two recesses a day and the fountains are just a hop, skip, and a jump over the soft pavement. Why does my unbelievably easily distractible daughter need a water bottle at her desk? She may or may not have ADD, but I can tell you this: a water bottle on my kid's desk will cut her academic day in half. Next week they'll ask for fondue pots in case they need a cube of bread dipped in melted cheese.

Afraid of the renewed, peppier French army, the English turned the keys over to a few more towns. Jeanne pressured the rightful Charles, who was very wimpy and reluctant, into being crowned in Reims. I'm sorry Jeanne d'Arc had to go to all that trouble, but happy for the French if this reluctance to lead remains a trait among French leaders. It would make it a lot easier for citizens to protect their democracy if their leaders were reluctant to take office. They're less likely to cheat. I don't know whether our elections are fraudulent or not, but they often appear rigged. We had the hanging-chad debate and then we got touch-screen voting machines with no paper trail, which seems highly questionable. At my polling place they give out stickers that say, "I think I voted." You can also get a little mayonnaise on your ballot. Reims is the town where they kept the small bottle of holy oil that had to be put on the king when he got crowned in order to make him the king. I'm going to have to remember that when I play checkers.

I give mineral oil to Daisy, my bearded dragon lizard, every day. He's constipated. My friend who knows about lizards told me that my lizard accidentally ingested the indigestible sand at the bottom of his tank each time he ate his crickets or his chopped vegetables. Now he's full of sand. He's like a Beanie Baby at the bottom of his tank. He could be an animated paperweight. I was advised to give him mineral oil and a twenty-minute warm bath twice a day. I'm lucky if I get a five-minute shower once a day. The lizard is going to have to get his towel and wait in line.

Even after Charles got crowned, there were still more towns to relieve from English occupation. Against Joan Jeanne Joan's will, Charles kept trying to make deals with the Duke of Burgundy (which is the color of our van) from the English side, despite their really poor record of trustworthiness.

One day on her way off to a battle, she got a letter from the Count of Armagnac, to which she dictated an unfortunately hasty reply. If I answer the phone when I'm running out the door to pick up the kids at school, I'm always pissed at the caller, as if they could have any idea of my schedule or had somehow forced me to answer the phone. I have an answering machine. I don't have to answer the phone if I'm busy, but I can't help it. If the phone rings, I pick it up. It doesn't matter when. By the way, I always lie if someone asks if I was asleep when they woke me with the phone. I hate the question. The phone could ring at 3:00 a.m. and the caller always says, "Were you asleep?" I think, "Is that what you called to ask? Is this a survey? Are Sominex salespeople cold-calling?" That's not what I say, though. I say, "No, I'm up. Why?"

I narrowly avoided going to jail based on some really poor instruction from my attorney. When I fired him he wanted to know why, and I reminded him of his lousy advice. He said, "Well, I was busy, I shouldn't have even taken your call, and now you're throwing that up in my face." That was the best argument he could mount to me? I can't help wondering if his $30,000 criminal defense of me was as compelling and brilliant. I'm lucky he didn't use his "oh, throw that up in my face" argument in court. Get your criminal attorney now. This person holds your life in their hands. I know nothing about the law, and it's likely that you don't either. I didn't join a gang or case a joint or plan the perfect crime. I didn't plan to be a criminal, and once you're in jail it's hard to wait for just the right attorney to apply for the job.

While seeking my first job, I filled out twenty-one minimum-wage job applications. One of the last questions was always what my hobbies were. Why would they care?

"Thank you for your application. We're looking for someone to mop the floors and clean and stock the bathrooms. I see you're available anytime we need you and you're willing to work for minimum wage with no benefits. That's great, but I see that in your spare time you enjoy working with beads, so we're going to have to pass on you."

Do they think someone's going to divulge something that makes them somehow unacceptable? Hobbies, uhm . . . counterfeiting, glue sniffing, graffiti, and I love to disorient the elderly.

So Joan made a misstep when the Count of Armagnac sent his messenger to ask her to ask Jesus which of the three popes then claiming the title should be followed. She dictated a reply saying she'd get back to him after a couple of battles. This was later used against her in her heresy trial. I guess she wasn't supposed to speak on a subject of the Church's domain. She was in a bit of a time crunch because she was rushing off to war and a nearby group was threatening to throw the messenger in the river.

I would not have done well in the fourteenth century. Joan of Arc says God told her to cut her hair, dress as a man, go to battle to rescue France and crown the king, and she's a celebrated hero, but when asked by a nobleman to ask God what pope to follow, she way oversteps a boundary. At that time people believed everything anybody did was because of God or the Devil. That's before they invented the inner child. I have a restraining order that prevents me from having contact with my inner child.

I'm not good with protocol. When introduced to someone, I forget their name almost instantly. Of course, the longer I know the person, the more uncomfortable I feel asking their name. This happened with me and my dad. Very uncomfortable.

I often don't remember to offer food or drinks to guests in my home until they are leaving. I have considered having some sack lunches and to-go containers right by the door so they can grab something on their way out. I would have been burned at the stake at a very young age. It would have been a very short stake, maybe a croquet stake.

Along about this time, Joan Jeanne Joan's voices started telling her that she was going to get captured and die. Her battles weren't going so well. It was a down time. I had some days a couple of years ago when I actually thought, "I would blow an al-Qaeda guy to get him to shoot me in the head." That's a uniquely low American feeling. Of course, I'm not as young and impulsive as I used to be, so I thought it through. I thought, "If I did blow an al-Qaeda guy to get him to shoot me in the head, you know what people would say? They'd say, 'It wasn't like her to blow someone.' "

The English and the Burgundians were after the French town of Compiegne. Joan saddled up with a small group of followers to go protect that town, which the wimpy Charles was using to attempt a bargain with the Duke of Burgundy. There was a battle outside the walls of the town. Most of the men made it back, but the enemy was following them, so one of the guys with Joan Jeanne Joan ordered the drawbridge raised and the gates closed. She continued to fight while Englishmen and Burgundians crowded around her, pushing and shoving and grabbing for her and her horse. Everyone wanted Joan Jeanne Joan to give herself up to them. I was so disappointed when I missed out on the $25 million the U.S. government was offering for the capture of Zarqawi, the al-Qaeda guy. I had been looking. I travel a lot. I always figured it couldn't hurt to take a peek around. Just a few weeks ago I made sure he wasn't at the Cracker Barrel restaurant near Lansing, Michigan. I still think it's unfair that I didn't get the bounty. There's no proof that my relentless search didn't drive him into the hands of the U.S. military in Iraq.

Alley and Toshia used to love to play hide-and-seek when they were little, but they weren't very good at it. I'd walk through the house and say, "Where's my Alley and Toshia?" in a singsongy little voice, and they'd say, "We're in the closet, come find us!" I could have gotten Zarqawi. When the kids go to camp next summer, I was going to zip over to Iraq and take a little look-see. I might have lucked out:

"Where's Zarqawi?"

"I am here, behind the rock . . . how did you find me?"

Finally poor, brave Joan Jeanne Joan was dragged off her horse by an archer belonging to the Bastard of Wendonne.

Remember when Geena Davis almost made it to the Olympics in archery?

Jeff Goldblum was probably lucky he was so skinny. How do archers not bruise the inside of their elbows? Or volleyball players? How do they avoid the big red ball prints on their arms? I've been told you just get used to it. To what end? I suppose I could get used to being punched in the head, but why?

After one of the first shows I did after my infamous arrest, public humiliation, and 180-day rehab stint, I was returning home on a late-night flight from Las Vegas. I waited uncomfortably for my flight to board at the gate. People stared at me and whispered about me a lot. Truth be known, some of the people were probably saying, "That girl thinks we're staring at her. Who is she?" Still, I felt like a spectacle. As I stood, not hiding behind a post at the gate, but certainly trying not to make any eye-catching moves, the line of passengers began parading out of the plane that had just arrived. Mike Tyson was in the line with a bunch of bodyguards. I noticed him. I noticed he was coming straight toward me as if we had an appointment to meet at that time, at that post. He stood in front of me and shook my hand and said, "Congratulations." I assumed he meant for getting through a difficult time, and I thought it was sweet of him. I thanked him and he left. Anybody who hadn't been staring at me before was definitely staring at me now. The handful of people not thinking, "Isn't that that child-molester comedian?" were thinking, "Holyfield's gained weight."

Jeanne was a prisoner. In her first months of captivity she was treated with some amount of respect. She was cared for by a bunch of women also named Jeanne. There must have been some sort of radio contest to select them: "Good morning, you're with Max and Jamie and Stan the Donut Man here on Z98, we're taking the first three Jeannes that call to watch over the captive Joan of Arc." Her biggest concern initially was for the well-being of the people of Compiegne. Her captors were preoccupied with her masculine apparel. They begged her to give it up, even offering her fabric from which to make a new dress. She said God wouldn't let her. I don't know that it's God, but there's certainly a force that makes me wear thick, high-waisted cottony briefs that I buy in bulk every eight to ten years at Sears. I find, by the way, that the elastic goes out at about seven years, but you can still cut it and tie it and get another two or three years out of it. By the time I stop wearing my underwear it's no longer a garment, just sort of some threads with an idea. It looks, in the end, like one of those dream-catcher things. Clearly there's some unearthly force involved.

After six months of imprisonment with the Burgundians, in a sort of CEO jail, Joan was sold to the English to be tried by the Church. She was transported to Rouen, where she was chained and treated cruelly.

I was advised by Pat, a professional dog walker at the dog park, after she repeatedly witnessed me being dragged to the park by my dog-shark, to get him a choke-chain collar called a "pincher collar." Although I've sustained a number of injuries while caring for the dog, the term "pincher collar" does sound a bit cruel, so I was quite sheepish when I motioned the pet-store manager back behind the wine section to ask her where they kept the pincher collars. In a slightly judgmental voice, she replied, "Oh, we don't sell those." I said, "Oh," and was deeply ashamed. I had the dog with me, so she said, "Let me try to walk him." When she returned from a spin around the store with my dog, she handed me the leash, looked furtively up and down the hamster aisle to ensure our privacy, and said, "They have pincher collars at Petco."

Joan's jailers teased her relentlessly. She was chained by her feet, and some say she was chained to a beam. Others say she had no bed. Still others say she got a bed after she got sick because they didn't want her to die before they finished with her, and of course they sent in a team of women again to determine if she was still a virgin.

A female detective was in charge of my arrest. She brought me to a jailer who "processed" me. Then, as she was about to open the door to the hall with the jail cells, the big, fat jailer guy popped his head out over a podium beside the door several feet from the desk where he had been asking me questions just before. He looked like a giant hand puppet. If he had said, "The great and powerful Oz isn't granting any wishes today," I would not have been blown away. I *was* blown away, however, when he barked at me, "What do you like? Men or women?" I was stunned. Are they allowed to ask that? I looked at the detective, hoping she'd correct him, and she just shrugged like, "Oh, those crazy jailers." I just stared at the guy. He barked, "It's for your own protection. What do you like, men or women?"

My mind was racing now, trying to figure out how that could be for my own protection. Was it because people get raped and assaulted in jail? I don't like to be assaulted by either gender. Could I be put in the "no assaulting" section? How kind of him to think of my safety. Perhaps I'd misjudged him. The big hand-puppet jailer continued to stare at me, demanding an answer, so I tried to decide. I looked at the female detective and thought, *I hate her,* and I looked back at the jailer and thought, *This big fat mean guy turns my stomach. I think I'm gonna have to take this on a case-by-case basis. It wouldn't be fair to eliminate an entire gender based on either of these lousy specimens.*

The tribunal of men that stood in judgment of Joan were

all part of the English side. If she hadn't been found guilty of crimes against the Church, she would have been tried for crimes against England. The trial was long and beside the point. She was headed for the burning stake before the trial ever started, so it's just as well that she didn't pay for legal counsel. I'm still paying off the attorney who rushed up to tell me he'd gotten my probation shortened by getting me the death penalty.

JOAN JEANNE JOAN's presence was requested in the marketplace on May 30, 1431, at 8:00 a.m. First she was excommunicated, dumped by the Church in a little ceremony. Then she was forced up on a scaffold so she'd be in view of the ten thousand audience members. She was bound to a stake and burned to death.

I stayed at the Hyatt in Baltimore at the same time as the National Candle Association convention attendees. When I saw National Candle Association name tags on three women in the elevator, I couldn't help asking what the convention was for. With straight faces they told me their members came from all over the country once a year to talk about wicks, wax, and safety. This year's keynote speaker addressed a troubling issue— "Birthday candles, how many are too many? Are our seniors at risk?"

History tells us that Joan's last word was "Jesus," but she may have muttered "Roll, Dick, roll," and just no one wrote it down. Her death was gory and sad and must have kept some butts in the seats in the Catholic Church for a while.

2

Abraham Lincoln: Penny Wise and Poundstone Foolish

braham Lincoln was one of the greatest leaders the world has ever known. He preserved the union of the United States of America and drove the cancer of slavery from its land. He was self-made and self-taught. He was born in a log cabin with a dirt floor in Kentucky. I was born in Alabama, but I only lived there a month before I had already done everything there was to do. Even as an infant I was bored and crawled to the state line. My parents said they had some packing to do. I said, "Fine, I'll meet you. I've gotta get out of here."

Lincoln had an older sister named Sarah and a father named Thomas. His mother, Nancy, died of milk disease when he was eight. My mother had a headache for a long time. My parents got carried away with the letter *P* when they were naming the kids in our family. There's me, Paula, my sisters Peggy and Patty, and my brother Pjimmy, spelled with a silent *P*.

The Lincoln family moved to Indiana when he was young. I hate moving—not my body parts, but all of my things from dwelling to dwelling. What could Bedouins be thinking? I don't want to seem like one of those people who are always finding out that all of their lives they have suffered from the most recently discovered syndrome, but I have been diagnosed with obsessive-compulsive disorder, which makes moving enough to give me the vapors. The good news is that my Legionnaires' disease seems to have cleared up.

We rented a house in August 2002, and soon after we moved in the landlord came to assure herself that her new tenant—the single working felon with three kids, a big stupid dog, nine cats, a bearded dragon lizard, two tadpoles, and a bunny—wasn't wrecking the house. At four years old there's no way my son Thomas E knew what a landlord was, but for some reason he chose the occasion of her visit to, for the first and only time he has ever done this, burst out of his room and yell, "I'm gonna burn this house down." Let me tell you, this landlord has no sense of humor.

Until my last house I never used a dishwasher in my adult life. I used it to file carry-out menus, warranties, and operating instructions. I like washing dishes by hand. It has always seemed to me that for the amount of rinsing dishes required in order to put them in the dishwasher, one might as well just wash them by hand and enjoy the good feeling that comes from that shining achievement. I clean a lot. I have to. My cat Balou is allergic to cat hair.

By the time I was about thirty-five I had fostered six kids and acquired nine cats and three bunnies. We moved to a bigger house, and my sister Patty, who had never particularly cared for me before, visited a few times and encouraged me to use the dishwasher, as if it might erase the fact that she once tied me to the end of a seesaw, stood on the other end, and jumped off.

I couldn't possibly waste water on a less-than-full dishwasher load, and we didn't have enough *Toy Story* plates for a full one, so I bought some new *Winnie-the-Pooh* plates and plastic sippy cups. My daughters fought over who got to use the new plates. When I bought the plates and sippy cups, I also bought, in one of those "get organized" stores, some trash cans and a laundry bag that hangs on a metal rack on wheels. I had always used boxes for trash and laundry before, and that had worked just fine, but I had never been organized before, either, and it appeared, while I stood in the store, that these receptacles might have been the missing ingredient. I couldn't possibly carry everything to the car, so the salesclerk kindly offered to meet me at the loading dock after I got the car. On my way to the car, I realized it was too small to carry those big boxes. Luckily, I had a convertible, so I just put the top down and smiled inwardly at how, when I stay calm, nothing can really throw me. When I pulled out of the garage it was pouring rain, which my car interior possibly could have withstood, had I not gotten lost looking for the loading dock. I pulled into the turning lane and put the top up, mentally adding "towel off leather seats" to my list of things to do. I finally found my merchandise and the wet clerk on the curb in front of the store. I double-parked and tried to defy logic by shoving large boxes into my small car. Although the boxes were softening in the pouring rain, they wouldn't fit. When I finally removed the items from the boxes, they fit handily into the backseat of the car. The traffic that had backed up began to pull around me. I waved apologetically and called out, "I'm sorry, I'm gonna use my dishwasher," but none of the other drivers were big enough to be happy for me.

It took a couple of days to fill the dishwasher and we ran out of silverware, so I tried to serve mostly finger foods. My foster son was a year and a half old, so, unofficially, even milk was a finger food for him. My daughter Toshia was seven and had never eaten a meal without first skillfully dissecting it with her fingers to extract any objectionable ingredients. She would ask for an oatmeal cookie and then labor over it, removing the oats. She loved chocolate milk except for the yucky brown stuff. On the other hand, my daughter Allison was four and would sit tolerantly in front of a plate of food for one minute before telling me she didn't like it and wanted a snack. So we could actually go a few days without silverware.

Finally, one night after I got the kids to bed, I prepared to run the dishwasher. I wanted to be alone in case I teared up. I loaded in the last *Little Mermaid* plate, wondering if I was contributing to the oppression of girls and women by letting my kids eat off of that little marine trollop. I filled both little soap compartments and locked the dishwasher. I feel silly saying this now, but I was actually excited. I thought, "Really, if I got used to this it could save me time, and it is more sanitary than hand washing." I'm not good with machines, so I had to study on the buttons to be sure which to push. There's a button marked POTS AND PANS. My load included one pan. I didn't want to be caught by my dishwasher in a gross exaggeration, but there was no button marked ONE PAN, *LITTLE MERMAID* PLATE, NEW BIG *WINNIE-THE-POOH* PLATES, CAMPING SILVERWARE, AND *POCAHONTAS*

CUPS. Above the buttons, in very elegant silver script, it said, QUIET CLEAN. I pushed it on. It didn't work. It couldn't have been quieter. I unloaded each of the week's worth of dishes into the sink and washed them by hand, quiet as could be.

I got a repairman the next day. He had a thick Middle Eastern accent and seemed to blame me for something. He labored, sighing occasionally with exasperation, and when he finished he grilled me with dishwasher questions.

"Do you put these in there?" he asked, pointing to some plastic syringes we use for oral medication.

I hung my head. "Yes," I replied.

"Well, don't ever. Not even once, or the dishwasher will break."

He continued with a long list of items that I was forbidden to clean in the dishwasher and he threatened me with an equally long list of mysterious disasters, should I be so foolish and headstrong as to disobey.

"Did you put da *Winnie-dah-Pooh* plate?"

"I tried."

"Well, don't ever. Not even once."

He then told me that this dishwasher had a design flaw. If you push the buttons when it's not locked, even once, it will break. Right away I leaned down, hands on my knees, to explain this to my year-and-a-half-old foster son. "Sweetie, there's a design flaw in the dishwasher . . ." At first blush this may seem too sophisticated for a baby to understand, but I think he did, because he waited a good thirty seconds before he started banging on the buttons.

In December 1816, the Lincolns packed up and headed out

on a grueling trip from Kentucky to Indiana. I used to work a nightclub in Indianapolis. Once I visited the Indy 500 track. I could drive fast enough to be competitive in that race, but knowing me, I'd pull over to ask directions before the last lap and lose my commanding lead. I'm constantly lost. I couldn't find my way from Kentucky to Indiana now, let alone before there were roads. Everything looks the same. It's not much better than in the frontier days. "Make a right at the Starbucks" is the useless equivalent of "bear left at the bush."

At eight years old, Abe first swung an ax to help build the family's log cabin. I wonder if it was really helpful help. I'd be a nervous wreck if my kid was swinging an ax. Thomas E swung a Kermit doll at me the other day, and its plastic googly eyes left a big bruise. I get a knot in my stomach when my kids say they want to help bake brownies from the brownie mix, knowing it will double the mess and the time it takes to make them. More likely, Abe swung the ax a couple of times before Tom and Nancy, anxious to sleep indoors, said, "Thank you, Abie. You are such a good helper. Can you give the ax *gently* to Mommy and Daddy and run over by that big tree and practice posing for the penny?"

You know what's weird? I often think of *The Brady Bunch* when making parenting decisions. I know it's just a television show, and a stupid show at that, but I can't help it. It's weird. It's obvious from the theme song that there are no parallels to our experience. "It's the story of a man named Brady"? Nope. "It's the story of a woman named Paula who was bringing up some kids that she fostered and adopted . . . And then one day she was accused of lewd acts with a minor and she was all alone.

Sometimes I catch myself comparing us to the Brady Bunch, realize how silly that is, and turn to the Partridge Family instead. That's a little more realistic. I think. Shirley Partridge never dated, did she?

Milk disease took Lincoln's birth mother's life soon after they moved. The following month, according to Carl Sandburg, his father took a brief trip to Elizabethtown, Kentucky, and returned married to the widow Sarah Bush Johnston, telling Abe and his sister Sarah, "Here's your new Mammy." I saw a commercial for Life cereal once where they introduced "the new Mikey." You can't do that. Mikey is Mikey. It could be someone with similar characteristics to Mikey who essentially functions in Mikey's same naysayer role, but he can't be Mikey any more than he can be Lincoln's mother.

Abraham Lincoln loved books. He once walked twenty miles to borrow a book, and was known to work hard from sunrise to sunset and then read by flickering frontier light until midnight. Lincoln was self-taught. I didn't graduate from my high school. You could say that I'm self-taught; Lincoln just had a better teacher.

I feel bad for kids who are homeschooled. I remember the joy of running home on the first day of school to tell my brother and sisters what teachers I got. What can home-schooled kids tell their siblings the first day? "I got Dad for gym. I got Grandma for history. I got Mom for revisionist history." Plus their marching band would suck. They could only form punctuation during the halftime show.

I shudder at the notion of homeschooling my children. I have long suspected that Toshia, my oldest, can read and calculate handily, but pretends to function below grade level just to see the veins in my neck stick out. On the other hand, maybe none of my kids is that bright. When they used to play musical chairs, instead of having a neutral party turn the music on and off, Toshia would hum. When she stopped humming, they would fight over a chair.

When he took up the study of the law, Abe did it with a passion that sometimes led to exhaustion. They don't all do that. I've had more than one attorney who seemed to have gotten plenty of rest during law school. Lincoln walked thirty miles to a courthouse to observe the lawyers. The first time I ever pulled up at the Santa Monica courthouse, I came to the gate at the parking lot where you take the ticket, and a guy stuck his head out of the little booth and asked, "Are you a city employee?" I said, "No, I'm a criminal." And he said, "Well, then, you can't park here." I was shocked. The criminals can't park at the courthouse? I said to the guy, "Look, buddy, I don't want to brag, but without us this whole thing falls apart." I asked where we were supposed to park, and he gave me elaborate directions to the Doubletree Hotel parking lot. I said, "You're kidding me. Does the Doubletree Hotel know you're telling the criminals to park there?" Lo and behold, I followed the guy's directions, came up on the elevator from the parking garage, and the lobby of the Doubletree Hotel was full of criminals. Some guy who was up for credit-card fraud rented a room and we all partied for an hour before I went back to court.

Abraham Lincoln was nearly six feet four inches tall by the time he was seventeen. His remarkable ability with an ax, along with the physical demands of farming, developed powerful muscles in his lengthy arms and tall figure.

I look like a guy. In the fourth grade in Mrs. Morrisson's class, we put on *A Midsummer Night's Dream*. I played Peter Quince. Mrs. Morrisson was a genius. She found a way to use my flaw. I'd love to find her. I don't think she's teaching anymore. I think she got fired after one of the Fineman twins was blinded in an overly realistic production of *Equus*. I believe she's an agent now.

I think I always knew I'd be a performer, although I had hoped I'd outgrow looking like a guy. For years I took my dry cleaning to a place that was owned by a Chinese family. The husband, who didn't speak much English, always copied my name off the last laundry slip onto the new one. He also called me "sir." Apparently there was nothing among my clothing that corrected this mistaken impression. I went to this dry cleaner for years. I've been mistaken for a guy many times. I try not to correct people. I tell myself that, so long as I know, that's enough. One day, however, I guess I was feeling especially feminine, so I said to the dry-cleaning guy, "It's Paul*a*, Paul*a*, with an *a*. I'm a woman." He shook his head no, and pointed to my name on the slip. I had a glimmer of hope when I saw that he saw the *a*. "Yes, see? *a*," I continued to insist. "No, that's a initial," he argued. Many embarrassing times I have corrected people who have misidentified my gender. This was the first time anyone actually put up a fight. I never did convince the guy. It's a darned shame my crotch-grabbing suitor in Washington, D.C., didn't make his findings more public.

I look like I should be athletic. Sadly, it's just a look. I love to play basketball, but if I have to play against someone, my game falls apart. If you could get points for wheezing, I'd do a lot better. A couple of years ago some comic friends and I used to shoot hoops in a local schoolyard. I never won a game, but apparently I filled the little schoolchildren with wonder. One day a whole group of them were staring at me from across the yard. They were like a swarm of flies; they'd run up and run away, regroup, and discuss and debate any discoveries they made on their last look at me. It was clear I was the subject of much controversy among the group. There was an intense round of "did not, did too" debates. Finally one of them ran right up to me, as if on a dare, and announced, "Uh, uh, he a girl." It was heartwarming the way the little guy had gone to the mat for me. I may hire him to pick up my dry cleaning.

From sixteen to twenty-two, Abe worked at a variety of jobs—farming and other manual labor. At sixteen I worked at Bickford's Pancake House, at eighteen I worked at the International House of Pancakes, and even now my kids occasionally ask for frozen waffles or mini-pancakes, so I've kept my hand in it.

Lincoln was a clerk in a general store for a time, where he became quite popular telling stories and doing impressions, which seems odd since Jack Nicholson hadn't even made a film yet.

For a time young Lincoln worked on a ferryboat on the Ohio River, and at nineteen he was hired to build a flatboat and carry a cargo of produce a thousand miles down the Mississippi to New Orleans with another young man. We had a small creek behind our house when I was growing up. I recently remembered that when I was in the fifth grade I saw a giant turtle in the creek. It was the size of a frying pan, and I was so scared of it I ran like hell up the hill to our house to tell my mother. Only when I remembered the incident a few days ago did I remember that turtles aren't known for their speed. I guess I could have walked. I don't think turtles chase people, either, or cops would use them. *Cool Hand Luke* would have been a different film altogether.

I'm not much of a runner myself, but I flatter myself that I beat that turtle by a nice margin. I had to take steroids to do it, but I wanted to be at my best. Actually, I am a very slow runner. When I play full-court basketball I can never get anywhere near the ball in play. I end up standing in the center, pivoting back and forth from defense to offense. I can actually get dizzy playing basketball. I think I was in the not-so-bright class in gym in elementary school. We never actually played any games. We spent the entire period counting off "one," "two," "one," "one," "one," "stop, start over."

On the remarkably short-lived ABC *Paula Poundstone Show,* I challenged Carl Lewis to a running race. He was the fastest man in the world at that point, and I wanted to see an aerial shot of what that race would look like. I suspect the margin would have resembled that of my turtle race.

I had planned to begin training for the race on the show, to build up the suspense. In one show I got Jackie Joyner-Kersee to come help me train. She said that Carl Lewis got out of the block slowly, and that if I could learn to get out of the block quickly, it would give me an edge. Unfortunately, the show was canceled before the big race. Now we'll never know.

That's the thing about life. One minute you're up and the next minute you're up and the next minute someone is tying you to a seesaw and jumping off the other end.

Lincoln and a partner bought a general store at one point, but they weren't such good businessmen and it went belly-up and it took Lincoln seventeen years to pay off the debt. Maybe he was walking several miles to deliver groceries the way he toted those books. He wasn't that good with money. That's why he's on the penny. In April 1832, Lincoln volunteered in the Black Hawk War. He saw no action, so it was more like a back-packing trip, really, but it provided him the opportunity to be elected captain of his militia company, which he said was "a success which gave me more pleasure than any I've had since." I've worked with Kermit from *Sesame Street* a number of times, and Harry Belafonte kissed me twice.

Lincoln, Abe, Mr. Tall Hat ran for the legislature in 1832 and lost. I ran for class president in the sixth grade. Amy Hayes won. They offered me the vice presidency, which I felt was throwing me a bone. What were the odds of a sixth grader being assassinated? It was rare back then. Sixth-grade politics are especially challenging because there are no issues. It all comes down to your campaign slogan. To this day I don't fall asleep at night without trying to think of something that rhymes with Poundstone. So far, nothing, but I can tell you this: "It Pays to Vote for Amy Hayes." I'm not good at rhyming, which leaves me at a political disadvantage. My friend Garrison Keillor, who is a national treasure, wrote a children's book titled *The Old Man Who Loved Cheese,* it was lots of pages, he rhymed the whole way, and some of the cheeses have names like Camembert and Muenster. He's got my vote.

I know someone who writes rhyming clues for treasure hunts for their kids. You know, that game where you hand them a written clue that leads them to the next written clue and on and on with the last clue guiding the hunter to a prize. I can't get that clever with my clues, or hiding places, either, because my kids don't look for things. I have to leave simple clues like "It's on your desk" or the not-so-subtle "It's right in front of your nose, for godsakes."

In 1834, at twenty-five, Lincoln took another swing at the legislature as a member of the new Whig party. This time he was successful. He then borrowed two hundred dollars to buy some legislator supplies using sixty dollars for fabric for a suit. I tried to get a loan once. The guy at the bank wouldn't even let me borrow his pen to fill out the form. Lincoln was an ungainly fellow with very big hands. He often felt uncomfortable around women. Once, when introducing me to some distant relative, my mother sought to explain why I don't look any better than I do. "Paula, this is Uncle Billy Bob. Uncle Billy Bob, this is Paula . . ." (Long pause.) "See, she uses her hair in her act."

It's true that I have weird hair, but believe me, I didn't cultivate it deliberately as a prop. The day that what my hair does comes into vogue, it won't do what it does anymore.

Apparently there is no record of this in his writings, but those who knew him well confirm that in 1833 Lincoln fell in love with Ann Rutledge. I went out with a guy in 1998. I was having my hair cut at a hair salon, and as I sat in the haircut chair, one of the guys who holds the hair for the hair cutter walked by me. He was so handsome I actually started to blush. The hair cutter happened to notice and very kindly offered to introduce us. A couple of days later the very handsome hair holder called and we began the very lengthy task of finding a night in common on which we could go out. Along the way I discovered that I was eight years older than he. I thought it wouldn't matter, but throughout dinner and the theater he kept calling me "dude." I wasn't offended exactly, but he couldn't stop calling me "dude" because that's what people his age say. It's like if I had gone out with a guy who was too old for me who kept saying "Va-va-va-voom." Anyway, Ann Rutledge died and Lincoln called off any plans he may have had to marry her, which I think was the right thing to do.

The voters of Illinois sent him to their capital city again in 1836, the year he got his law license. Lincoln and other representatives from Sangamon County created a bill that would move the capital from Vandalia to Springfield. While working at a theater in Springfield, Illinois, a couple of years ago I was reunited with Jay Fitzgerald, a guy I knew in the fifth grade. In trying to explain to me what a down-to-earth guy he always was, he said, "All the other fifth-grade guys liked the pretty girls, but I liked you." It's hard to know if a guy is sincere when he lays it on that thick.

I saw a decorator on *The View* explaining how to make your bedroom more alluring for Valentine's Day. *The View* is that show where five women share their views on the important topics of the day. This was awhile back, when Star Jones could still be viewed sharing her views on *The View*. The decorator explained to her and Joy Behar, another woman who shares her views, that pastel-colored "window treatments" and "inviting throw pillows" are essential for successful lovemaking on Valentine's Day night. Star Jones appeared to be mouthing along, trying to commit to memory as many of the ideas as she could.

I think they went to a commercial break early so she could write them down. Gee, are you supposed to redecorate the bedroom for each holiday? My cats ate the string to the venetian blinds so only one side draws, pinching one end of the slats together up top, exposing a pizza-pie slice of window, and the centerpiece of the decorating scheme of my entire house is the Sit 'n Spin in the living room. I did that for Labor Day a few years ago.

According to Carl Sandburg, Mary Todd Lincoln once said to a gold digger friend of hers, "I would rather marry a good man, a man of mind, with a hope and bright prospects ahead for position, fame, and power than to marry all the houses, gold, and bones in the world." Lincoln met Mary Todd in 1839. She was the daughter of a well-to-do banker in Kentucky. When they met, she was living with her married sister in Springfield and was part of high society there. Miss Todd was well educated and had a quick tongue and an interest in politics and the events of the day. I try to keep up. It's harder now because history is longer. I videotape *The NewsHour with Jim Lehrer* every evening to watch when I go to bed, but to be honest, by the time I've done all of my kids' homework, finished the quiet-clean dishwasher cycle, cleaned up enough fur balls to make a plush toy, received calls from every long-distance phone company asking me to switch (I don't have the slightest idea who I'm with), made the next day's lunches, denied junky snacks repeatedly, signed permission slips, including the accompanying legal forms detailing the steps to be taken should my child or I forget their admission fee or die during their field trip to the museum of interesting textures—by the time I finish, I'm tired. I play the videotape of *The NewsHour with Jim*

Lehrer every night, but sometimes I only get as far as the theme song (da da-da-da da-ah) before I fall asleep. Sometimes as soon as Margaret Warner says whether or not Jim Lehrer is on vacation, I drift right off. Somehow just knowing he's well comforts me.

In 1840, Mary Todd and Abraham Lincoln got engaged. They were on-again-off-again from there. She could be jealous and irrational. He didn't have much in the way of manners. Lincoln was certainly ambitious on his own, but she pushed him to look and act in keeping with his improving station in life. I've asked my children to call me Miss Poundstone. Lincoln could be a bit of a downer. Their wedding day was to be New Year's Day 1841, but Lincoln called it off and took to his bed for a while. My own personal suspicion, although there's no record of it, is that sometime after he broke off the first engagement with her, Abe happened to catch a glimpse of Mary's inviting throw pillows and pastel-colored window treatments. Whatever happened, they tied the knot.

Mrs. Lincoln was a bit high-strung and temperamental. She also had a shopping jones. She shopped compulsively, often spending money she didn't have. Merchants were eager to extend her credit. Her spending binges, which she tried to keep secret from her husband, left her feeling guilty and afraid. When Congress appropriated $20,000 to remodel the White House, she spent more than $26,000. History has placed Mary Todd Lincoln's addiction in a rather bad light, but meanwhile Betty Ford gets her own Center. The Betty Ford Center was the chief rival of the rehab I was in. When occupancy was down at the Betty Ford Center, Betty herself would swing by the driveway where I was and ask if any of us wanted to go for a drink. Had Mrs. Lincoln had the benefits of modern times, surely she would have founded the Mary Todd Lincoln Center for Shopaholics, where the clients would tearfully cut their credit cards and unclench their television remote controls during circle time. One year she bought more than three hundred pairs of gloves.

The guy at the pet store says my brown bunny, Fanny Brice, is of a breed bred for use as glove linings. Of course, that's not what I used Fanny Brice for. I don't need gloves. I live in Southern California. If we have a cold snap, I'll just stick my hand up the bunny's butt if I have to. I've had three bunnies. I use them to poop a tremendous amount and bite me. People think bunnies are easy to care for because they poop little pellets. Yes, but there are thousands of them. Pound for pound I'm sure they're worse than elephants. I started with one bunny and when I decided to get another, everybody said, "Don't get an opposite-sex bunny." Like I'm so undersexed myself I never heard about bunnies. I got two females. Just my luck, they were lesbians and they adopted.

The Lincolns had four sons who survived infancy. One died in the White House and one died a couple of years after his father. I have nine cats and an unfortunate tendency to collect things. So far I have nothing from the Franklin Mint, which I'm proud of. I got my ninth cat, Bagheera, at a big "Pet Expo." I seriously considered buying a farm pig from a woman there who raised them and couldn't say enough good things about them, including, "They'll get right up there in the bed with you." I even considered trying to slip a llama past the zoning laws and into my backyard, until I was told you have to have two or they can actually pine to death, which was something I thought only country-western singers were at risk for.

Lincoln practiced law with a few different partners and was admired by Judge David Davis, who presided over the circuit court where he most often appeared. I receive collector's edition *Perry Mason* videotapes from Columbia House. They used to call it the Columbia House Video Club. I think they stopped having a club when I joined. My sisters used to do that to me. Anyways, I receive the tapes monthly, and each one has two episodes. I wanted to be a lawyer when I was a kid because I loved Perry Mason. It turns out I just wanted to be a fat guy with dark circles under his eyes. Now I love Lieutenant Tragg, the homicide cop. In every episode he becomes convinced that Perry is up to no good. Perry Mason has won every case, not only proving his client's innocence, but also extracting a public confession from the real murderer, and that still hasn't won him the lieutenant's confidence. The writers must have had a supply of paper with "This time you've gone too far, Mason" preprinted at the top of the page that they used for scriptwriting.

In 1858, when the Illinois Republican Convention nominated Lincoln to run for the U.S. Senate against Stephen A. Douglas, Lincoln won national attention with his acceptance speech. In it he declared, "A house divided against itself cannot stand. I believe this government cannot endure permanently half slave and half free. I do not expect the house to fall; but I do expect it will cease to be divided. It will become all one thing, or all the other. Either the opponents of slavery will arrest the further spread of it, and place it where the public mind shall rest in the belief that it is in course of ultimate extinction, or its advocates will push it forward till it shall become alike lawful in all the states, old as well as new—North as well as South." If *The View* had been on back then, they would have shown a clip of the speech, shared their differing views, and then had a decorator show how, if you did have a house divided and it did stand, you could decorate it.

There were seven official historic debates between Lincoln and Douglas that took place all around Illinois. Their view on allowing territories to choose to have slavery was a defining difference between them. My daughters Toshia and Alley fight occasionally. Alley adds an extra "eenie" when she "eenie-meenie-minie-moes." I can understand Toshia's objections on this point. I don't think it's deliberate, but it could be considered unfair.

My cats don't always get along. My oldest cat, Smike, had a bad eye. I've always thought that my second-oldest cat, Balou, poked it. Balou was injured in an earthquake. She ran into the fireplace during the earthquake. Apparently that's what it says to do in the little kitty emergency manual. Anyways, Balou got caught on something inside the chimney and ripped herself from stem to stern and had to wear one of those Elizabethan collars to keep her from aggravating her wound. It looked like a big funnel. One day I was in the other room when I believe the words "Funnel head! Funnel head!" were shouted, and Smike came running out with an eye injury. I have always assumed Balou poked it to retaliate for being cruelly mocked.

I had to take Smike to a cat ophthalmologist. Taking your

cat to a cat ophthalmologist is not unlike walking around with a sign that says, TRICK ME, I'M NOT THAT BRIGHT. While Smike and I sat in the waiting room, waiting to be ripped off, a vet came out to talk to a customer about her dog's contact lenses. Right away I told Smike, "You are not getting contact lenses. You can have a seeing-eye dog if you want, but you may not have contact lenses." In the examining room they gave her an eye test. I expected it would be Smike, with a paw over one eye, looking at a chart. "That looks like a mouse. Then there's a ball with a bell in it. And the last one is a picture of some clean carpeting, which is good because I do feel like throwing up right now." In fact, the vision test was less sophisticated than that. The vet put three briefcases in a row on the floor and held the cat across the room from me and told me to call her. If she crashed into the briefcases, she couldn't see. When the vet asked me to call the cat, she asked, "Will she come when she's called?" I said, "I don't know. She has never had a reason to come when she was called. We live in a one-bedroom apartment. If I ever called her, she'd say, 'What? I'm right here.' "

Abraham Lincoln was elected the sixteenth president of the United States on November 6, 1860. On December 20, 1860, South Carolina became the first state to secede from the Union. That couldn't have felt too good. I've had people walk out of my shows. It feels awful. I've been in the business long enough that my instinct tells me it looks better if I leave first. No one taught me that. I just know it, somehow. It's one of those Frances Gumm born-in-a-trunk kind of things.

The Civil War lasted from 1861 to 1865, or the length of a nine-videotape boxed set. It appears to have been all in black and white. It was long, bloody, tragic, noble, and unendurable. It made the baseball documentary seem almost trivial. The Civil War was an immense burden on President Lincoln, and he felt it deeply. My ninth therapist would have thought for certain his depression was biochemical and prescribed medication. Just not a chipper fellow, that Lincoln—everybody needs a little help sometime.

On January 1, 1863, Lincoln emancipated the slaves. I try not to keep my babysitter out late. In fact, I rush home after work and almost never go out socially. Besides, I hate to be away from my kids. We have fun together. We trick-or-treat several times a year. I always say to them, "Let's go on a night that's not so crowded. It's scarier that way." Sometimes the neighbors are out of candy. We say, "That's okay. We'll take whatever you've got, maybe some leftovers. We'll even take some bridge mix if you don't mind picking the nuts out."

I don't want to leave you hanging, so I'll tell you quickly, the Union army won the war. The commander-in-chief of the Confederate armies, Robert E. Lee, surrendered to the commander-in-chief of the Union armies, Ulysses S. Grant, at the McLean House at the edge of the village of Appomattox, Virginia, on April 9, 1865. It's a good thing, too, because, had the Union not been preserved, South Carolina's Independence Day would have been December 20 and they wouldn't get as many presents because everyone would say, "This is for Independence Day *and* Christmas," when they gave them gifts.

On April 14, 1865, Abraham Lincoln was shot while sitting in his private box at Ford's Theatre in Washington, D.C., during a performance of the play *Our American Cousin.* We saw

Annie at the Pantages Theater in Hollywood. We were in the back, on the aisle. No one got hurt.

John F. Parker was Lincoln's guard that night. However, the play captured his interest, and as he couldn't see it from his post, he stepped away and took a seat in the audience. Sometime later the play lost his interest (clearly the F. didn't stand for "focus") and he wandered away and went out for a drink. Taking advantage of the guard's absence, actor John Wilkes Booth snuck into Lincoln's box and shot him. I hate it when people don't do their job. I signed Alley up for group beginner tennis lessons at 5:00 p.m. on Tuesdays at the tennis court at the end of our block. The teacher called on the Sunday before the first class to say there weren't enough people signed up for Tuesdays and could we go to a different park on Thursdays? We couldn't, so I told her we couldn't. She said she would teach the class on that Tuesday, but if more people didn't sign up by the end of the week, she would cancel after that. I brought Alley to the tennis court at the end of our block at 5:00 p.m. that Tuesday. The teacher said that the other kid who was supposed to come would be going on Thursday and could we go on Thursday to another court? We couldn't, so I told her we couldn't, an exchange she clearly loves. She tossed a basket of balls to Alley, who hit them back. After about twelve minutes, the teacher walked over to me and said she was done and did I want my money back from the city? Or did I want to have a credit and sign up again? Sure. The spring session had gone so well, why wouldn't we rush to sign up for the summer one? Why didn't Mary Todd Lincoln get a credit from John F. Parker? He owed her a few hours of security guarding, and what with Lincoln dead, she could have used the company.

Lincoln died on April 15, 1865. I died once, for a minute. There is no bright light and nobody waving you anywhere unless there's a one-minute waiting period that I'm not aware of, or unless my friends and loved ones are avoiding me even in death: "Psst—Cover the light. Cover the light."

3

Helen Keller: Blind and Deaf and Often Very Tired

Helen Keller was born on June 27, 1880, in Tuscumbia, Alabama. At nineteen months old she fell into a world of silence and darkness when she went deaf and blind from what they called "acute congestion of the stomach and brain."

God, I loved to drink. I'm not suggesting for a moment that it was a good idea. The judge asked me once why I didn't drink anymore. It was an astoundingly stupid question, given the circumstances, so I tried to say something that gave no hint that I suddenly realized that he wore that robe because it's easy to put on him, and that when his assistant is out, she must leave him detailed instructions on how to do so. I wanted to say, "Well, drinking didn't go that well for me, did it, you dumb shit?" just to watch the courtroom artist's crayons fly. The courtroom artist wasn't good. He was a caricature guy. I recognized him from the pier. He kept drawing me with big breasts and slightly crossed eyes because he could only do Barbra Streisand. The judge must've tipped him, because he drew him with big muscles on a tiny bike and a word bubble that read, " 'Cause I said so."

I'm a firm believer in a one- or two-drink high, I just kept overshooting it. Years ago someone gave me a questionnaire about my drinking habits. There were twelve questions, and they said if I answered yes to more than two, it meant I had a drinking problem. I answered yes to ten. I went to a support group for other people who answered yes to ten. We drank. We sat around and trashed the twelve-for-twelvers, who we felt were losers who couldn't control themselves. Our group wasn't anonymous, either, although it wasn't as well known as the anonymous one. We used full names and big, gaudy showbiz introductions.

In her autobiography, Helen Keller said she had memories of light, fields, sky, and flowers. Once enveloped in darkness and silence, Helen mostly clung to her mother's dress as she performed her household duties. "My hands felt every object," she said, "and observed every motion, and in this way I learned to know many things." My mother went back to bed most mornings after she got my older brother and sisters off to school. I spent my mornings watching Jack La Lanne, Virginia Graham's *Girl Talk* show, *Romper Room, Captain Kangaroo,* and *The Three Stooges*. In this way I learned to know almost nothing. Jack La Lanne used to urge his kid viewers to run and get their moms. I used to run upstairs and wake my mother to carry Jack La Lanne's message. I always fell for the notion that the guy on television could see me. I never really liked *Captain Kangaroo,* for example, but I was always careful not to say so in front of the TV.

I have always loved the Three Stooges. To me, instead of

some pandering kids' program, the Stooges were adults doing adult things, just not all that well. I've always loved Moe's hair, and I still think, in photos taken when they weren't being Stooges, Larry was quite handsome in a pin-striped suit. I had a dream once that I was making out with Larry. I often blurt that out when talking with people about dreams. I figured it was like the naked dream, that everyone had some version of it, and that other people sometimes had a recurring heavy-petting-with-Moe dream. I used to have this theory that when we share our experiences with others, we discover how alike we all are and feel a titch less lonely. I was eating some M&M's once years back, and someone said to me, "Look, the red ones are back." I had had no idea that the red ones had been gone. I had had many bags of M&M's without red ones; I thought it was just me. I hadn't wanted to be a burden, so I had suffered alone all that time. It was so unnecessary. It was then that I created the M&M Theory of Life, which is that when we share our peculiarities with others, we find, surprisingly, much common ground. However, the Larry from the Three Stooges dream is a prime example of the drawbacks of the M&M Theory of Life. Every time I've told anybody about that dream, they stare at me kind of funny and scooch a little bit away. I told it to a shrink once, and even she got all uncomfortable and started dusting her furniture, accompanying herself with a faint little whistle. She quickly looked it up in her dream-interpretation omnibus, mumbling as she thumbed through the index: "Here we go, 'Making Out Dreams' . . . 'Making Out Father,' 'Making Out Mother'—oops, back up, L-L-L, here it is: 'Making Out Larry from the Three Stooges.' "

I am not a sexual person. I don't have sex. My manager

does, though, and knowing that has, so far, been enough for me. It's not like she broadcasts the intimate details or I guess I'd tape it, but she just has told me that she did here and there . . . have sex, that is. One time we were driving to a meeting together. I like to let her drive so that my death will look accidental and my kids will get a big chunk of change. Anyways, she once told me that she had gone out with this guy that we both knew. She said it was only their second night out, and after dinner they went back to her house and they were making out on her bed and she thought they might have sex and would have welcomed it, but the guy stopped and said that he really liked her headboard and thought that he would very much like to be handcuffed to it. I screamed with laughter and a dash of outrage when she told me. I asked if she could have just written him out a citation this time and wait till their next date to actually handcuff him. Part of me felt bad for having such an incredibly immature reaction to the story. I know I'm the one who is different here, but I cannot relate at all. I could never tell anybody what I want. I'm too shy. I couldn't even tell someone, "Could you move your foot? You're stepping on my neck."

Helen Keller's natural drive to communicate created some signs that those around her came to understand. She developed about sixty altogether. To symbolize her father, Captain Arthur Keller, she pretended to put on glasses. She was quite curious about what her father did in his chair with his newspaper held up before him, and would sometimes climb into his chair, put his glasses on, and hold the paper before her eyes just as he did. My father used to sleep on the couch with the newspaper over his face. I often wondered about that myself. It was especially curious when he wore shorts. My dad had the whitest legs on the planet. On summer nights, moths would leave the porch light to go bump into my dad's legs for a couple of hours. I hate couches. I won't have one. For years I had no furniture at all, except for a Ping-Pong table. I also had no dishes except for one spoon and a bowl that I'd sometimes wash and use after I fed the cats from it. But I never allowed them to use my spoon or get up on the Ping-Pong table. That would have been gross. If I had my life to live over again, I would take back every minute that I have wasted on a couch, all of the hours of watching bad television in the afternoon throughout junior high and high school. I wish I could get Martin Luther King's "Letter from a Birmingham Jail" stuck in my head instead of the theme song from *The Courtship of Eddie's Father*.

As she grew up in her dark and silent world, little Helen Keller would fly into desperate fits of rage. She became wild and made life in the Keller home quite difficult. They began to see her as a danger when she locked her mother in the closet and left her for hours. Honestly, I've tried to teach my kids to do that, but Mrs. Keller may not have been as tired as I am, in which case I can see how it would've upset her. Let me tell you, my closet would've been organized after an incident like that. Helen caused further upset by knocking the baby out of the cradle in a jealous fury. My girls used to be so jealous of one another. Alley was an only child at one and a half years old, when four-and-a-half-year-old Toshia came into our family. Their lives became miserly comparisons in which each thought she was getting less than her new sibling was. I could have cut Alley's head off with a buzz saw, if I were better with machines, and Toshia would have said, "Alley always gets to have her head cut off, but I never do." They constantly told on one another, and yet they both simply denied anything they were accused of, even if I saw it with my own eyes. Alley pushed Toshia once, right in front of me, so I said, "Alley, it's not okay to push and shove." Alley quickly replied, "I wasn't pushing," and Toshia countered, "No, but you were shoving." I always thought pushing and shoving were pretty much the same thing, but apparently there's a subtle distinction. My girls can parse words like a White House press secretary.

Helen Keller said she knocked the baby out of the cradle because she felt the cradle belonged to her most beloved doll, Nancy. Even as an adult Helen spoke highly of Nancy and the wear and tear she unflappably weathered.

My children have had tons of dolls, but none ever more treasured than Barbie. It's a phenomenon that I can't figure. When they were very little I had a strict "no Barbie" rule, but when Toshia was in the hospital once, some social worker gave her a Barbie without even asking me. It just didn't seem wise to take the Barbie away from the crippled kid in the hospital bed in front of the social worker, so in came Barbie. By the way, Barbie had a big smirk on her face, she knew exactly what she was doing. The next thing I knew, we had twenty-three Barbies. I don't know how. I don't think I bought any. I think late at night Barbie drops a sheet out the window and hoists up her trollop friends.

I was interviewed once for a special on Barbie's twenty-fifth year. For years I had been anti-Barbie because she seemed to have no admirable goals or work ethic. However, the director of this Barbie documentary was so anti-Barbie that it caused me to sort of come to her rescue. The director kept asking me to describe how Barbie had screwed up my self-perception with her perfect body type and turned me into a miserable, unhappy failure. Which I am. However, to blame my misery, unhappiness, and failure on Barbie cheapens it in an unflattering way, I think. In fact, in a beautiful ceremony in Washington, my name was recently entered into the Big Book of Losers, but goofy, stupid Barbie had nothing to do with it. This director had a lot of jealousy toward Barbie. I am not remotely jealous of Barbie. I never had one. I had an off-brand doll named Tammy, who was bigger-boned and did not flex. My sister Peggy had a Barbie doll, though, and even on Barbie's best night she slept in a box in the closet. I am not jealous of that. Historically, real people don't choose to sleep in the closet. Ask Helen Keller's mother. Yes, Barbie wore tight pants, but you had to flip her upside down and smoosh her head to get them on her. Gee, I don't feel jealous of that. Human beings spend their lives in such a wild-goose chase to find the source of their pain that poor, imbecilic Barbie has, mistakenly I think, been identified as the culprit enough times that Mattel cracked and introduced a more realistic-shaped Barbie onto the market. It's a fat Barbie. What child could possibly feel good about receiving a fat Barbie? "Honey, Mommy didn't think you could handle the skinny Barbie."

Helen Keller's behavior led her mother to conclude that she needed to be taught. A number of relatives thought that since she was legally considered an idiot, she should be put away somewhere, which does sound unfair since Pat Robertson continues to travel freely. Her mother wouldn't hear of it, and learned in Charles Dickens's *American Notes* of Laura Bridgman, a deaf-mute woman who had been taught by Dr. Samuel Gridley Howe at the Perkins Institution for the Blind. I can't believe that with two kids and no vacuum cleaner, Mrs. Keller had time to read. I have been forced to read *Cinderella* a punishing hundred times easy, but reading for my own pleasure is a pursuit I exchanged for children. If you want to be a foster parent, your home has to pass an inspection occasionally. They want to make sure you have those little plastic safety plugs in your electrical outlets. When Alley was about a year and a half old, she used to bring them to me. She'd pull them out and say to me, "You know what these are? Windpipe Blockers."

I think that so long as Social Services is inspecting your house, when they see a shelf full of adult books, they should just box them up and put an end to any desire to educate oneself further. In fact, they may as well go into your closets and put some kind of disgusting substance on the shoulders of your nicest suits and shirts, color on the walls, put their muddy feet on the furniture, and smash, tear, or put in the bathtub anything valuable or delicate right then and there. This saves your kids the trouble and puts less strain on your relationship with them. I still make attempts at reading books of my own choice. I'm a dreamer. I've had no success. I always fall asleep before the bottom of the first page, and by the time I get a chance to read again, I forget what I've read and have to start over. The picture on the cover of a book has become very important to me.

My kids, of course, love for me to read to them. I used to be so desperate to get away from Cinderella that I'd try to get them to let me read something more substantive. "Here's one, girls, *One Flew Over the Cuckoo's Nest.* It's about a bird. How 'bout I read this?" I just hate Cinderella. If you ask me, I say she ruined a good pumpkin. She had the chance to wish for anything, and she chose to go to a dance. I tell my girls that if someone makes a choice that stupid, they deserve whatever bad things come their way. For reasons about which I am unclear, Alley and Toshia are completely taken with the idea of marriage. They are thrilled by the ending of the story when Cinderella and the Prince are wed. I often tell them that the reason the story ends there is because what happens after that is too scary for little kids to hear.

I don't know why my kids are so wrapped up in girlie stuff. They love tutus, jewelry, high heels, dresses, and tiaras. My baseball cap and desire to wipe the entire world with a damp cloth and a disinfectant has had no impact on them at all. I sometimes hear people say that girls are naturally like that and that boys naturally gravitate to trucks and sports. Maybe, but we have no way of knowing, since babies are barely out of the womb before the boys are drinking from a bottle with blue trucks on it. Women who breast-feed must have to get a tattoo of a baseball or a wrench on their breast when they have a boy, if it doesn't appear there naturally. I've never given birth, but I'm told that when the baby is placed on the mother it instinctively roots for the breast, except for girls, who don't have a chance because they are immediately snatched up and put in a debilitating pink outfit of some sort. The point is that we have no way of knowing what they might naturally respond to.

We receive tons of toy catalogs in the mail. There is often a section of costumes. There is a boy's section with Spiderman, Batman, and doctor's outfits. A guy could pretend to climb up the side of a building, outwit a criminal, drive the Batmobile, jump off a chair and rescue Gotham City, or run alongside of a gurney and hold back the hand of death from a critically injured patient with the use of surgical skills. In the girls' section there is a wedding dress. What is there to pretend when you're dressed up in a wedding dress? That you're a virgin? You can pretend that you've pissed off your closest friends by having them wear really ugly bridesmaid dresses. You can pretend that your mother is upset that you're not getting married in a church. You can pretend that Uncle Tony is drunk at the reception. What fun! I can't help making note that there's no groom costume among the boys' pages. I guess that's because boys don't naturally gravitate toward that.

When Helen was six years old, Captain Keller took her to an oculist in Baltimore who was known for making breakthroughs with very challenging cases. I can never figure out how those people who do psychic readings stay in business. A friend of mine went to one once. She was blown away that the woman knew that her father had been a fireman. She claimed that this proved it was real. Well, real or unreal, it's still not useful. I don't need anyone to tell me what my dad did for a living. I need to know exactly what day I'm gonna die so that I don't bother putting away leftovers the night before.

The oculist was of no help to the Kellers, but he referred them to Dr. Alexander Graham Bell, whose life's passion was working with the deaf. I love the phone. I know many people, much hipper than me, who say they hate talking on the phone.

They usually say it while talking on the phone with me, which is very flattering. I've always loved the phone, but especially in the last twenty-seven years that I've been a stand-up comic. Every time the phone rings, it could be my big break in the show business. It could be the call telling me I've made it. So far it hasn't been, but every ring is another chance. Currently, most of the calls I receive are from MCI wanting me to buy their long-distance service, or from the *L.A. Times* wanting me to subscribe. I decline as quickly as I can and explain that I'm expecting to make it soon and need to keep the line open so I can take the call. Both MCI and the *L.A. Times* reach me about three nights a week. They use pretty much the same techniques.

"Miss Poundstone?"

"Yes?"

"Good evening, my name is Arthur. I'm calling to offer you a week of the *L.A. Times* at no charge and after that only thirty-five cents a day and you may call and cancel at any time."

"How about now?"

Sometimes the *L.A. Times* calls to offer me the chance to take and cancel the *L.A. Times* Sunday paper. I wish I did read the weekday paper, but the Sunday paper? The Sunday paper has such unimportant information that most of it is printed on Thursday. How to make a cheese-and-egg-free quiche is not time-sensitive material. Even in the most up-to-the-minute publication of the Sunday comics, Cathy is still fat.

I was on a strict Butterfinger diet last month. I ate only Butterfingers for two weeks. I felt great and the pounds fell away. One day I ate twenty-six fun-size Butterfingers for lunch, and then I lost my willpower and ate a turkey sandwich. The turkey sandwich made me sick. My body is just not made to handle that kind of food. When I'm at the airport I often purchase the big, big Butterfinger, which has the nutrition information on the back, but at home I have the fun size and there's no room on the package for the nutrition information, so they give an 800 number to call. I haven't called, but I'd like to. I want to talk to the guy who has that job:

"Hi, I just ate a fun-size Butterfinger. How much iron did I get? I feel great. I bet I got a lot of vitamin A, huh?"

Eventually the Butterfinger diet will make its way to headlines in the Sunday paper, but I invented it. I had been of the opinion that recipes, diets, and comics have no place in the news, but then I looked up *news* in the *Merriam-Webster Dictionary:* "Material reported in a newspaper or news periodical or on a newscast." That covers it. I'd still like to know what the standard is for interrupting programming to report news. One morning a few years back I was watching a report on our troops' mission in Somalia on the *Today* show when those dreaded words "We interrupt this program" sent a shiver up my spine. A newscaster came on and said that Lady Di and Charles were officially separated. They interrupted the Somalia report for that? I guess now, instead of interrupting unimportant programming with serious news, they're breaking into important news with silly stuff. Someday in the midst of the State of the Union address they'll break in with "We interrupt this program to bring you a little clip from *Bewitched.*"

Helen Keller was taken to Washington to see Dr. Bell. They took to each other right away, and remained friends until his death. Dr. Bell put the Kellers in touch with Mr. Michael

Anagnos, head of the Perkins Institution for the Blind in Boston, who chose Perkins graduate Anne Sullivan to go to Tuscumbia, Alabama, to teach Helen.

There was a school for the deaf in the town next to the one I grew up in. We used to pass it on the way to the first pancake house I worked in. It had a BLIND DRIVEWAY sign just before you reached it. I used to think, *What more can happen to those poor kids?*

I lived in Boston as a young adult. I bussed tables in a salad-bar restaurant in Copley Square in Boston. This was back when salad bars were the big new thing, so I felt a measure of prestige in the job. I spent hours happily rubbing the creamy Italian salad dressing off of the Plexiglas sneeze guard that hung down from the salad-bar roof making it difficult to reach the garbanzo bean bowl. That's what that Plexiglas is called—a sneeze guard. It's a law that you have to have one if you're gonna have a salad bar. I worked at least twelve hours a day, seven days a week, and I never saw anyone sneeze anywhere near the salad bar. Still, I guess we can't be overly cautious with the public health. At that salad-bar restaurant, I was the most happily employed I've ever been. I often stayed up all night by myself cleaning the place. For a few months I gave up my apartment altogether because I didn't want to go home and be away from the restaurant. I once scraped a layer of slime off the entire cement kitchen floor with a spoon. One time after cleaning for forty-eight hours in a row, I fell asleep while vacuuming, which was especially strange since I find vacuuming so exciting. When I watch the stars walking down the red carpet at the Oscars, I think, "God, I'd love to go over that twice with an upright."

The restaurant had a bay window in front filled with ferns, spider plants, and a lush assortment of big-leafed plants, plus it had fifty ivies hanging from its high ceilings. One day the waitress whose job it was to care for them ladled out one too many soup du jours, had a breakdown of some sort, and had to leave, probably before doing her sidework. Somehow I ended up with her plant job. I am not good with plants. I did not know this for certain until I did this plant job. Every morning I came in to mist them. I watered them regularly and even dusted their little leaves. No matter what I did, the next day I would find more brown leaves. I didn't want anyone to know I wasn't good at the plant job, so whenever a leaf turned brown I would cut it off. Eventually I had fifty pots of dirt hanging from the ceiling, which can look nice if they're arranged properly. I've never been comfortable with photosynthesis.

When I was little, my father used to photograph me when I cried, which explains why, despite the raw talent, I never pursued a career in runway modeling.

I take lots of photos of my kids because they look so perfect. I have been remiss, however, in videotaping my children. In addition to the fact that I am not good with machines, I never have enough hands to videotape. I see the ideal parents at my kids' school videotaping all the time. My hope is to dub some of their tapes or just get some stock footage of children's developmental milestones.

"There you are taking your first step, honey."

"I look different."

"Well, it was a long time ago."

"I look Filipino."

"Yes, uhh, you were Filipino when you were younger. You outgrew it."

When my son turned one, we had a surprise party for him. We had it ten days before his actual birthday, so he wouldn't suspect. Our friends Caroline and Leslie gave him a baby book. He wasn't allowed to touch pens, because in his hands they caused unnecessary injury, as they do in Mr. Blackwell's. So the task of filling out the baby book falls to me. The book lists all sorts of firsts, and provides a blank beside each to fill in a date. I used the blanks to answer yes or no. First ate solid food: *yes*. I don't know when what happened. I knew he had teeth when, instead of just crushing my finger between his gums, he broke the skin. I worried I would discover he was using words when he came to me one night while I was scrubbing the kitchen floor, on my hands and knees with distilled water, and said, "Mother, I get the feeling you're not hearing me." I hope I haven't destroyed his future by not carefully documenting his past. I've never worked in the corporate world; maybe he'll want to, but the missing piece about when he first held his head up will place that goal beyond his grasp.

"Well, young Poundstone, my friend, you seem eminently qualified to come aboard, join our team, and bring your impressive talents to the table here at the Fortune 500's Fastest Growing and Most Innovative Corporation . . . Well, then, of course you're excited . . . You're welcome, Poundstone, see you Monday . . . Oh, and Poundstone, by the way, we need to know when you first held your head up so we can decide what department to make you the head of . . . Oh, you don't? She didn't? Well, it was nice meeting you. We'll be in touch."

Ms. Keller said she was like an animal prior to the arrival of her teacher, Anne Sullivan, who came to be known as "the miracle worker." I love animals. When I was in the fifth grade I asked my mother if I could marry the dog. Instead of explaining to me that marriage is a partnership that often includes a sexual relationship and that we, traditionally, have tried to keep these types of relationships within our species and then, perhaps, using that as a convenient segue to explain what sex was, she said, "Don't be silly." Talk about your good teachers.

I have always answered my kids' questions about their bodies and where babies come from as honestly and with as much information as I could, which may still leave some gaps here and there in the tale. Once when we went to the zoo, Allison, noticing the kangaroos having sex, yelled, "They're making babies, Mama." Of course, all of the parents in our vicinity stared at me as if it were my fault they had lied to their kids. Even though it was recent, I already can't remember how the kangaroos went about having sex. I try to picture it scientifically, but the tail gets in my way. Imagining alternative kangaroo positions gives me a headache. I was kind of surprised that they were such exhibitionists. You expect that from chimpanzees, but kangaroos seem so much more civilized.

On a photo safari in Kenya years ago, I discovered that I am more like baboons than I had ever noticed, and not just because I can't do my own hair. One afternoon our tour guide dared me to go into a river. To me, a dare is like being forced at gunpoint is to most people. One needn't even double-dare me. It was a few nights later when I saw a sign at a lodge that warned that the leading cause of tourist mortality was crocodiles. If I had known that, I would have tried to seem less like an out-oftowner while in the middle of the river. I didn't know that, but the tour guide did and she went in with me because crocodiles are not the leading cause of tour-guide mortality. They wear a special pass. I was certainly aware that crocodiles lived in the river; I just had no idea that being eaten by one would be so commonplace. It is my wish to die of unique causes, perhaps in a high-speed tricycle crash, a bizarre stapling incident, or as a result of inadvertently sucking my brains out through my ear while trying to untwist the vacuum hose.

When the water was clear, we would study the river bottom carefully before taking a step, looking for crocodiles or big logs that appear to be digesting a tourist, but when the river was too deep or muddy to see the bottom, we would scream and laugh and run like hell. I had the inner knowledge that I had once outrun a turtle, so I was at peace in a scared-shit sort of way. We reached a sandbar in the middle where we felt safe enough to rest (although, in retrospect, I realize that's where crocodiles could have made a buffet of us). In a minute we heard screaming. I leaped up and looked toward the disturbance. There, just a bit upstream from us, was a group of baboons crossing using the exact same method. They stood on the riverbank looking carefully, and then, one at a time, the baboons would tear across the river while the others barked and screamed.

Anne Sullivan's biggest challenge, she felt from the start, was to discipline Helen without breaking her spirit. Helen had been greatly indulged by her family, essentially allowed to do whatever she wanted. Annie talked the family into letting her take Helen to live with her in a small house on the grounds, without their interference, so that she could teach Helen to obey her and depend on her. My kids have a really good swimming teacher. So far they haven't had to move out, which is a good thing because the only spare house on my grounds is the Tyco plastic playhouse in the backyard, with the movable door and plastic phone replica.

I once signed the girls up for swimming lessons with the city program on registration forms the school sent home in their backpacks. From what I could make out on the form, they were "guppies." I signed them up for two weeks of guppy classes, and while I was at it I signed them up for "minnows" for the next two-week session. I took them every day for two weeks to their "guppy" class and on the last day I went up to the swimming teacher and asked her what part of the pool I should bring them to the following week when they'd be minnows. "Oh, I'm sorry," she said, "they'll have to be guppies again." Guppies again? We were working backwards. By the end of the summer they were fully certified beer cans at the bottom of the lake.

I've taken CPR classes six times. I could move in with the teacher for a year, even be handcuffed to him and, although I expect I'd crack and obey him and depend on him in a day or so, I still couldn't be taught CPR. Just don't choke near me. I have the Red Cross CPR training card, but I don't imagine that showing it to a choking victim will open his airway. I got the card because I successfully ripped the plastic CPR practice dummy from the jaws of death. It's good to know, because I like to eat out; if I'm ever seated across from the plastic CPR practice dummy and her date, the seatbelt test dummy, and one of them begins to choke (which is likely because she has no teeth), I'm ready.

Anne Sullivan began spelling words into Helen Keller's

hand using the manual alphabet only moments after they met. The manual alphabet is a method of communication invented by Spanish monks under a vow of silence. I cannot shut up. I couldn't keep a five-minute vow of silence. It's a shame, too, because I'm a gifted mime, but I always wreck it. I press upon an imaginary enclosure about three times before I blurt out, "I'm in a box!" People won't pay to see that after a while.

In the seventh grade, my Home Ec teacher, Mrs. Kastler, made a bet with me that I couldn't be quiet for a whole class. Fortunately, it was during the sewing unit, so I secretly sewed my lips together and won. Not surprisingly, it was my only success in Home Ec.

Helen learned very quickly, especially after the famous W-A-T-E-R miracle, when the understanding that everything has a name first dawned on her. Four months after Anne Sullivan began teaching her, Helen wrote her first letter. It was to her mother. It was in pencil on paper fitted over a grooved writing board. Helen formed the letters in the grooves, guiding the pencil with the forefinger of her left hand in a script called "square hand." They don't teach kids how to hold a pencil anymore. I have a callus on my middle finger from years of handwriting, as do most people my age. My daughter Alley has a bump on her pinky finger that she wondered about the other day, and I had no idea where it might have come from until I watched her strange lobster-claw pencil grip during homework that night. I said, "Oh, that's where the bump on your pinky came from. You'll probably have one behind your ear as well, and you may need shoulder surgery soon if you're not careful."

We learned about letter-writing in the fourth grade. To

practice, we each had to write to a celebrity and see what we got back. I wrote to Mike Andrews of the Boston Red Sox. There were some big names on the Red Sox back then: Carl Yastrzemski, Reggie Smith, George Scott, Rico Petrocelli, Jim Lonborg—but I liked Mike Andrews. Besides, those other players were so well known they probably got tons of mail. I thought Mike might have a little more time to focus on me, to write back really from the heart. He was probably quite lonely. Probably, in the locker room just before their games, while going through their mounds of mail, the other players made fun of his measly pile of bills and occasional copy of "The Second Baseman's Newsletter." Well, I would put an end to all that. About an hour or so after I sent Mike the letter that could turn his life around, I started checking the mailbox—nothing. I checked daily for months. I used to burst into tears if I ever even heard his name mentioned. For a period of time I hid our *Sound of Music* album because I was even angry with his sister Julie. I never got a reply from Mike Andrews.

My neighbor and closest friend was Jim Ross. We were in the same classes all our lives. Jim was brilliant. I was always much too far behind him for anyone to realize he was my rival, but I thought he was. He was always better than I was. In elementary school he wrote a poem about his toaster that was reprinted in a national magazine. I was tutored in handwriting and got a piece of candy stuck up my nose. In sophomore biology, I got in trouble for cutting the liver out of my fetal pig; Jim restored his to life, gave up bacon, and played the French horn with the Boston Pops.

For his celebrity, Jim wrote to Herb Alpert. Not a day went by that he didn't receive an envelope or a package from Herb. He got autographed Herb Alpert eight-by-tens, autographed Herb Alpert albums, autographed Herb Alpert concert tickets . . . If Herb got Kentucky Fried Chicken, he'd autograph the leftovers and send them to Jim. They grew close. "Tijuana Taxi" was dedicated to Jim. Originally Herb wrote it as a blues number, but Jim suggested a more upbeat tempo.

Anne Sullivan was only twenty when she presented herself to six-year-old Helen in front of her new student's home, on March 3, 1887. Despite her youth, Anne seemed to know very early on that her work with Helen would be history making. She wrote frequent updates on her progress, frustrations, self-doubts, and hopes for this remarkable child to her friend and mentor Michael Anagnos, the director of the Perkins Institution for the Blind. The world first came to know of the extraordinary duo of Helen Keller and Anne Sullivan through Anagnos's annual reports from the Perkins Institution. Soon the news of their miracle had spread through newspapers around the world.

Anne Sullivan took Helen to the Perkins Institution, the Wright-Humason School in New York City, and the Gilman School for young ladies in Cambridge to prepare her for Radcliffe. Helen graduated from Radcliffe in 1904. She felt that Anne Sullivan should also have received a degree, since "Teacher," as most people came to call her, spelled most of the lectures and books into Helen's hand, making her amazing success possible. I have often felt snubbed by my children's grade school in the same way. I've done the fourth grade four times without so much as an honorable mention. None of my children is deaf and blind, but Toshia has astigmatism and won't listen. I've worked harder at getting Toshia educated than at anything I've ever done in my whole life. I've been over her math book so many times I'll have the answers memorized by the time Alley uses it.

I can't tell you how many fresh-faced school counselors have looked at my exhausted frame and broken spirit and suggested I try a sticker chart. A sticker chart? I've tried stock options. Toshia would rather see the pulsating veins in my temples than receive a factory full of stickers. She's tough. The night we were up in the middle of the night working on the poster for her report on Anne Frank, I was ready to kill myself. I honestly started to think of Anne Frank as a slacker. It was then and there I decided never to do anything honorable or noble enough that some fourth grader had to write a report about it. So far, so good.

Helen's family went broke. Teacher solicited the many friends and philanthropists who took an interest in Helen to finance her costly education. Kleenex is on our school's wish list that they send home to parents. I don't want my kids to know how little their government cares about their education, so I don't tell them their overburdened teachers are forced to beg for Kleenex. When I donate Kleenex to the school, I tell them it's International Kleenex Day and that all around the world people are celebrating by sneezing more, doing crafts with Kleenex, wearing clothes made of Kleenex, and cooking traditional Kleenex dishes. Our school is so broke that someone from the school asked me if I would volunteer to teach some kids a dance for the spring show. Now *that's* needy. I'm not known for my contributions to the world of dance. I can't do the hustle. I don't even know all of the words to the song.

While at Radcliffe, Helen was approached to write a serialized autobiography for the *Ladies' Home Journal*. Despite Teacher's help, the project was difficult to organize. A friend introduced them to an editor named John Macy, who worked very well with Helen and eventually married Anne Sullivan. Macy helped Helen write and publish *The Story of My Life*. Everyone tells me that a computer would make writing so much easier for me. I write with pen on the back of used paper. It's not easy, but I know how. Anytime anyone has ever tried to show me how to use a computer, the exact same thing has happened. I get two chairs from the kitchen and put them in front of the Macintosh computer in Thomas E's room. The computer person sits down. I sit down. They punch in a few things on the keyboard. They pause. Nothing happens. They chuckle a little and say they're used to Windows. They punch in a few more things on the keyboard. They seem to settle in. They click on something. Nothing happens. They seem kind of embarrassed and mutter, "Okay, umm, it's down," and I put the chairs back in the kitchen. I've had that same computer lesson ten times. It has sped up my writing process immeasurably.

A teacher informed me that Toshia was eligible to receive some computer stuff through the school district. So, some guy from a place called the Computer Access Center called to set up an appointment for me to bring Toshia in and figure out what kind of assistive technology would be the most helpful to her. Right away I said to him, "I really appreciate your help, but I need you to know I do not do computers. I know nothing about computers. I don't even like computers. I'll bring Toshia in, but don't ask me anything about what she might need, because

I simply don't know." He said he understood. We went ahead and set up an appointment, then I asked directions to the place and he said, "It's on our website." I hate computers, and I mistrust those who use them.

Helen Keller and Anne Sullivan told their story on the lecture circuit, the Chautauqua circuit, and even the vaudeville circuit. Their audiences were moved by "the miracle" as much as they were moved by Helen's loving heart and buoyant attitude in the face of such deprivation. The two women became hardworking advocates and fundraisers for various causes. They were on the payroll of the American Foundation for the Blind. I once played for a charity on *Jeopardy!* I wasn't good at it. I lost a Disneyland dream vacation for several terminally ill children. My charity had to pay for my parting gifts. I'm not that smart, but at least I admit it. Alex Trebek acted as if he knew the answers the whole time. They were on the cards he read from, weren't they? He didn't like me. I had never seen *Jeopardy!* before, so I didn't know how to play, but I figured out early on that although I wasn't likely to know any answers, if I didn't push the buzzer before the smart contestants, with or without an answer, my charity didn't have a prayer. My plan worked to some degree. I proved myself a far better buzzer than either of my adversaries, but there were gaps in my abilities after that. Alex asked something (off a card) about a Pacific island, and I hit the buzzer while the other two contestants were wasting time thinking. I said, "Who is Tom Selleck?" That was when the genial host seemed to really begin to dislike me. It certainly kept me out of the winners' circle.

On October 20, 1936, Anne Sullivan Macy, Helen Keller's

beloved teacher, advocate, companion, and friend, died. Anne had always had problems with her eyes. She had had many eye surgeries, and was practically blind at the time of her death. Her health had been declining for a while. In the end she suffered a coronary thrombosis and died soon after. Teacher's poor health had kind of sucked her spirit from her a long while before she died. Helen and their assistant and friend Polly Thomson did what they could to cheer her up, but without much success. She probably hung on as long as she did for Helen. My cat Balou got so old we had a theory that she was actually dead for the last two years of her life, and just continued walking around to fit in. I spend much of my life trying to keep my vicious cat-eating dog away from my cats, but the night before she died Balou kept walking over to the dog. I think, since my cats are indoor cats and haven't the opportunity to go off into the woods to die, she was doing the closest thing, which was to drag herself over to the dog-shark and whisper, "For God's sake, just eat me."

It's hard to imagine Helen Keller without Anne Sullivan Macy. Critics suggested that Helen was controlled by her teacher and that her thoughts were not her own. Teachers, scientists, philosophers, and psychologists were prompted by her writings to argue the origins of ideas and the meaning of originality. They questioned Helen's frequent use of color in her descriptions. I sat beside Greg Louganis backstage at a show we were taping soon after he became a world-renowned Olympic diving star. He was such a great diver he actually hit his head on the board during a dive and still won a gold medal. He was quite nervous before appearing on this television show, and minutes before he was to go on, some production person flitted over to Greg, who was all made up, dressed, and ready to go, and moaned, "Oh, I told you not to wear white!" To which Greg innocently responded, "It's not white, it's eggshell." Some people see hues and gradations, and some people think blind people aren't supposed to say the sky is blue because that's copying.

Helen Keller traveled the world advocating for the blind. She enlightened lawmakers to the need to offer disabled people the opportunity to have productive lives. She met with presidents and heads of state. I met Senator Barbara Boxer on a flight to San Francisco the morning after an ACLU dinner we had both attended. She was in a window seat. Her husband was on the aisle. She had on dark glasses and didn't look as though she wanted to talk, so I introduced myself. She chatted nicely and then tried to turn back to the newspaper she was quite obviously reading, but I couldn't stop. It's obsessive-compulsive disorder. I often want to stop talking, I just can't. I'm like a balloon leaking air. I spin around the room and I don't stop until I'm flat and empty except for the spit inside. I just kept talking and talking. At one point her husband said to me, clearly intending to be sarcastic, "Why don't you just take my seat?" and I said, "Okay," and he got up and I sat down. I've always thought their marriage probably took quite a beating over that. So I talked and talked some more. At one point I think I actually pulled the paper away from her. Finally, I could tell she was giving up and coming over to my side by engaging and talking.

I love to hear what other people have to say, it's just that I often can't hear them over the sound of my own voice. The problem is that anytime someone tells me something about themselves, it reminds me of something that happened to me once, so I cut them off and I'm off and running again. I asked Barbara Boxer about a famous photograph of her and the other women in the House of Representatives just before Anita Hill was allowed to testify before the Senate Judiciary Committee during the Clarence Thomas hearings. She explained that on the Monday morning after the Senate Judiciary Committee had refused to hear Anita Hill's testimony, the women from the House of Representatives marched to the Senate. As she got to the part where she told me she marched up the stairs of the United States Senate flanked by determined female lawmakers, to my horror I heard myself say, "Oh, I went to the Senate once," and I began to tell the story of a public tour I once took. Believe me, in my head I was thinking, "Shut up, shut up, shut up." I just couldn't. Martin Luther King could come to my house tonight and say, "I have a dream . . ." and I'd cut him off and say, "I had a dream once, too, only in mine . . ."

Helen Keller made a gracious ambassador right from her first exposure to public life. She liked to be in the thick of things and people liked to meet her. She shook hands with thousands of people. In order to understand people better, she often ran her hands over their faces to read their lips and expressions. Most came away moved by simply having seen her.

She did have an unfortunate meeting with George Bernard Shaw, where, in a rather glib exchange, he suggested that all Americans were deaf, blind, and dumb. The story circulated in the papers. Shaw claimed to have been misinterpreted. I enjoyed *My Fair Lady* as much as the next guy, but we had to do a tedious research report on George Bernard Shaw in the eighth grade, so I have a certain bitterness toward the guy. Still, I felt for him on the subject of this social faux pas. I almost never say the right thing. Reba McEntire was seated across the table from me at a function one night. We had never met before. By way of introduction, I blurted out, "Reba, hi, I'm Paula. I was in Nashville last year and I saw a billboard for a cleaning product called Greased Lightning. It said it was the official cleaning product of country music. I didn't know country music had an official cleaning product. I can't really picture you down on your hands and knees scrubbing, even with an unofficial product." As soon as I said it, as with almost everything I say, I wished I hadn't. She might not have heard me because the centerpiece was in the way, but it seemed as though she didn't know what to make of me. She smiled, but she looked like her Christmas album cover—kind of frozen.

At the same function I heard Jane Fonda say she lived in Atlanta. I couldn't figure out why she lived in Atlanta. So, like an idiot, I asked. She told me she had been married to Ted Turner. "Oh, that's right," I said. "And you got Atlanta in the divorce?" Did Jane Fonda do a Christmas album? She certainly made the Christmas-album-cover face while she scooched slowly away. If social blundering ever becomes an Olympic event, I'm America's hope for the gold.

I said "fuck" to the First Lady once. I was at a fundraiser for Senator Boxer, and I got to have my picture taken in between the senator and the First Lady at the time, Hillary Clinton, who was there to help the senator. I had had a couple of glasses of wine. You know how, when you wake up on a morning after drinking, your memory of the night before, instead of being on a little video in your head, develops slowly, in single images, before your mind's eye like Polaroid photos? The next day I was lying in bed and I remembered standing between the senator and the First Lady, feeling a tug on my shoulder, and leaning down to hear the senator say, "You can't say 'fuck' to the First Lady." To which I heard myself respond, "I already said 'fuck' to the First Lady." Alone in my room, I was mortified just remembering it. I tried to think of what possible reason I had for saying that. I don't think there was one. I think I just threw my arm over the First Lady's shoulder and said, "Fuck."

Ms. Keller called her military hospital tour around the country during World War II "the crowning experience of my life." She embraced, comforted, and inspired the young servicemen who had suffered terrible losses at war and now also would belong to the world of the disabled. Deaf, blind Helen Keller greeted the world glowing with strength and life, and seeing her and learning about her somehow made other people feel they could bear their own burdens. Am I the only one that doesn't work for? I don't know. I liked her well enough when I was a kid. Of course, I only knew her when she was Patty Duke and she hit Anne Bancroft with a spoon, but I related to that. Now I find out she went to Radcliffe, she was a writer, she argued for peace during World War I, she was loved by people around the world. I start to feel very small. I'm not proud of this, but I start to think, "I guess Little Miss Blind and Deaf can do everything." I realize that this is not at all an attractive trait, but now that I'm a felon, I find I don't try that hard to impress anyone, so I'll tell you the truth: I am not inspired by someone who has nothing and makes something of herself. I find more lessons in the experience of someone who had everything and just pissed it all away.

Helen Keller died in 1968. Her burial urn with her ashes was placed beside her teacher's in the National Cathedral in Washington, D.C. Toshia told me once that they had a fire drill at school and they were told to go under their desks. I said, "Did they tell that to anyone else?" I hope they go back over that before the next dry season, or her ashes might be beside her teacher's as well. In the second grade, my teacher, Miss Green, dragged me out of the classroom by my hair because I didn't hear her say to put our painting on Joseph's desk. She thought I was talking and didn't hear. I don't think I was. I think I was painting and didn't hear. Anne Sullivan, a good teacher, would have spelled it into my hand. I feel fine, but this seems as good a time as any to say this: No matter how much she may beg, my ashes are to be nowhere near Miss Green's.

4

Charles Dickens: A Beloved Novelist and an Excellent Bookstore Employee

Charles Dickens may have been the most beloved author of all time. He wrote articles, edited magazines, and created brilliant novel after brilliant novel. I've churned out seven chapters in eight and a half years. Dickens must have had advantages, I just can't put my finger on what they were. He was born in England in Landport, Portsmouth, on February 7, 1812. They didn't have time-saving computer lessons back then. They didn't even have ballpoint pens.

His father, John Dickens, tended to spend more than he earned. When Charles was ten years old he was forced to go to work in a blacking factory, putting labels on black shoe polish. His father ended up in the Marshalsea debtors' prison. I'm a bit in arrears myself, and I tend to spend more frivolously when I have no money. When Alley turned eight, I went belly-up broke, so I rented a petting zoo for her birthday party. I picture her years from now, telling some shrink, "We could have kept the house if Mom hadn't rented that llama." The party was in the front yard, but right in our living room we had nine cats, a dog-shark, two tadpoles, a bunny, and a bearded dragon lizard. I could have saved a fortune if I had just let the guests come in the house.

When Thomas E turned three, I rented a fire truck for his birthday party. It was fantastic. This guy put all of the little party kids up on top of the fire truck and drove around the neighborhood with the siren blaring, and everyone they passed waved and yelled, "Happy Birthday, Thomas E!" It was great. So, naturally, when he turned four, my kids were all hammering me to rent the fire truck again. I told them I was sorry but I didn't make that kind of money anymore. I said, "What we could do is torch a neighbor's house. I'm fairly certain a fire truck will come." Kids being kids, that wasn't good enough, they wanted to know if they could still ride on it. I said, "They're not going to let you ride on the fire truck that comes to put out the neighbor's house fire. But I'm fairly certain I can get you a ride in a police car."

I haven't read anything about John Dickens's children taking ballet lessons, but that could have put him in debtors' prison. Most people in debtors' prison probably sent their kids to ballet lessons or jazz or even "character," which I have no idea what it is, but I can tell you my daughter took it and it requires fancy, high-priced shoes that are—can you believe the luck?—available at the ballet shop adjacent to the Westside Academy of Dance.

Charles Dickens himself couldn't have written enough to pay for all of the costume purchases kids' dance classes rope you into. That's gotta be the driving force in a thriving economy. Ballet costumes. Tights. The genius of it. What kid can keep a pair of tights intact? My daughter Allison toppled over, with no external forces involved, just toppled over, from out of nowhere on the kitchen floor, minutes before we left for her first ballet class, and tore a huge gaping hole in her brand-new tights. I'm not sure this recommends her to a career in dance. I don't know. I know nothing about ballet. I've never even seen *The Nutcracker*. I don't imagine, though, that there's a sugarplum fairy that's supposed to collapse a lot.

I fainted once at Fenway Park in Boston. It was a record hot day in Massachusetts, which means it was unbelievably sweaty and humid. The air was so thick it was like trying to breathe in a dry-cleaning bag. I know that because once, as a child, I played happily with a dry-cleaning bag for hours before I noticed print on it that said, NOT A TOY. I felt so foolish. Anyways, I was about twelve years old and I was at a Red Sox game with my family. I offered to go to the concession stand to get us snacks. I remember feeling it was a mature thing to do, despite the fact that, for myself, I would be ordering a package of Hostess cupcakes. I actually have long felt that Hostess snack foods are not top-of-the-line, but in a pinch I think you stick out your chin and say, "At least they're not Little Debbie's."

People don't line up at Fenway Park, they mob. I think this was my first experience where you couldn't tell on someone if they took cuts. In all of that heat, the mob got to me. By the time I got up to the counter, I was very weak. I could tell I didn't look good by the look on the concessionaire's face. Still, being a stoic New Englander, I clung to the counter, which, sticky with snack residue, may have clung back, and I said, "I'll have a package of Hostess chocolate cupcakes, a Coke, and a hot dog."

The last thing I remember seeing was my hot dog, sheathed in its bun, with my nickel in change resting on the end of the pink dog. When I realized I was too sick to eat, with my last bit of strength I said, "Cancel the cupcakes," and passed out on the counter. I came to while being shaken by a woman with a thick Boston accent and an urgent need for a snack, pleading, "Ya gotta get up, honey. Ya gotta get up." She wasn't trying to help me, she was trying to get me out of the way, so she could get a beer and a hot dog and quickly get back to watch the Red Sox lose. I ordered some ice and crawled with it to an opening on the floor to revive myself. The woman placed her order. I think that was when I realized there's no net.

There are those wonderful moments of clarity in life when one is reminded how irreparably flawed we humans are. Once, when I was nineteen, on the subway in Boston I lost my balance slightly and bumped into an elderly woman. I quickly apologized and she replied, "Well, hold on to something, stupid." There it is. That's it. That's it in a nutshell. I don't want to sound negative, but I think every fetus should be shown a film of that incident, maybe projected up on the uterine wall, and then asked if it wants to come out. I am a strong believer in a woman's right to choose, but I also think that in the last trimester, the kid should be given every opportunity to back out.

Fainting was the most excitement I ever had at Fenway Park. In fairness to the Red Sox, I've never attended a professional sports event when my team won. Once some nutcase sports fan who knows all of the game statistics begins to compile crowd stats, I won't be allowed into home games. No big loss. I've given it a try, but most professional sports bore the hell out of me. It's a whole bunch of people paid a whole ton of money to play for cities they're not even from. If they want to make professional sports exciting, they should recruit the players the way they recruit people for jury duty. So one day you could just go out to your mailbox and find, "You've gotta play." It's a near-brilliant plan that might well put a dent in the obesity epidemic as well.

Although I'm self-employed, my employer would never let me off to play football. It's just too damned stupid. Every now and then I'll be stuck in an airport bar or someplace where I'm bored and I actually watch a minute or two of football on TV. Two groups of men line up facing each other. Someone counts wrong. They run directly into each other. They end up in a big heap, like a big pile of dirty clothes that happen to have men in them. They lie there a minute, realizing what they've done, and slowly begin to get up, one layer at a time. At the bottom someone lies injured. I could have told you someone was going to get hurt, but the team of medics that run out always seem to react with surprise. Meanwhile, for the entertainment of the television audience, until the game can continue, two "color commentary" men exchange stories about the last time this guy got injured and interesting facts about his personal life, such as his favorite color and what pain reliever he prefers.

Sometimes they show shots of the fans, the mere sight of which should limit their membership. Paul Solomon, from *The NewsHour with Jim Lehrer*, once did a piece on Super Bowl fans. He talked to a behaviorist who explained that in competition among gorillas, the victorious male gorilla gets a testosterone increase and the defeated gorilla gets a testosterone decrease. Well, since everyone knows that, culturally, male gorillas view jewelry as effeminate and therefore won't wear Super Bowl rings, I can buy that a testosterone boost works as their incentive for a winning performance. I can also easily believe that we're close enough to gorillas for the same chemical rewards to apply to us. However, the gorillas get this boost or depletion from participating in the competition. There is no study using gorilla fans. There are no wimpy, fat, unathletic, loud, beer-drinking onlooker gorillas that can watch KoKo and Fluffy square off, claim the win as their own, and get a testosterone bonus as a result. Gorillas have it all over us.

In 1823 young Charles Dickens went to school in London. I was in London once. I heard that to adjust to a time-zone change, one should allow about a day per each one-hour difference. I was there for about three days, around ten years ago. I live in California, so there was an eight-hour time difference for me, and I'm still tired. I probably could have been a great writer if it hadn't been for the time difference. I told you Dickens had advantages.

Oddly, there was even a language barrier when I worked in London. I performed in two clubs and had two of the worst performing experiences of my life. At the first club I told my little jokes to almost dead silence until, toward the end of a bit about an argument my parents had repeatedly throughout the summer over zucchini, in which I frequently repeat the word "zucchini," I heard a teeny, tiny voice in the back (fortunately there were no distracting laughs to have to shout over) say, "What's zucchini?" After much prodding I was able to gather from the audience that in England they call a zucchini a "cour-gette." It's no wonder we broke away from England.

I foolishly concluded that Brits were reserved, since an entire audience of them heard me say "zucchini" a dozen times, had no idea what I was saying, and didn't make a peep. Then I went to another London club. I carefully avoided the word "zucchini." In fact, I steered clear of any mention of vegetables, but it didn't cause them to hold me any dearer. Within minutes of beginning to spin my yarns and share my clever observations with style, energy, and warmth, half the crowd was shouting, "Get off the stage!" To make matters more humiliating, a must in my life, the other half of the crowd began to shout, "Leave her alone." What amazed me most was that they did it with flawless British accents. It sounded like I was being heckled by the Beatles and an uncharacteristically angry Hayley Mills.

After a couple of years in school, Dickens worked as a clerk in an attorney's office and as a reporter in the House of Commons for *The True Sun*. He became increasingly popular, under the pen name "Boz," writing articles for the *Morning Chronicle* and the *Evening Chronicle*. By 1935 he covered events all over the country. I covered the political conventions for *The Tonight Show* in 1992. I was surprised how staged and fake it all was. Ted Koppel told me he was jealous that I got to say whatever I wanted to about it. I don't know why the news media covers politics. They might as well do animated coverage. The conventions, as well as most campaign stops, are really theater that the news media is tricked into airing. Now, when politicians make speeches, they put a banner with a slogan behind them to remind the listening audience and the speaker what they're supposed to be talking about.

They didn't yet use that technique in 1992, so, if the speeches had a point at all, the speaker often strayed from it. On one night of the Republican Convention, George Bush's grandchildren read postcards he had sent them and told the crowd what an excellent grandfather he was. Even the Republican delegates seemed lost and looked upward, hoping for a premature balloon drop. It may have been at that moment George W. Bush made a mental note to hang a mental note behind himself during his speeches should he ever run for president. I know the incident affected the whole family, because backstage that night I bumped into one of the little Bush grandchildren, and he was crying his eyes out.

I said, "Hey, what's the matter, little fellow?"

"I don't want Bill Clinton to be my grandpa," he replied.

"Well, of course you don't," I said, "but that's not what the voters are deciding."

"It's not?"

"No, we're having an election to decide who should be president of the United States."

And he said, "Oohh. Well, then, what was all that crap we were talking about onstage?"

Charles Dickens married Catherine Hogarth on April 2, 1836. Together they had ten kids. Dickens seemed to consider each new addition to their family a financial burden and became annoyed with his wife for "giving" him another child. Apparently he was out sick when they talked about sex in his "Health and Decisions" class, because he seemed to view the matter as out of his hands. Still, he was said to be a good father. His oldest daughter, Mamie, said he was a good father and then she went on to say that once when she was sick she was allowed to sit quietly in his room with him while he wrote. That made him a good dad? I haven't used the bathroom alone since I've been a parent, and I don't think one of my kids would speak well of me in a biography. I'm not saying that I could have written *A Tale of Two Cities,* as Dickens did in 1859. I didn't even read it when Mrs. Forbes assigned it in my eighth-grade English class in 1972. There is no question he was a talented man and that under any circumstances he would have been a better writer than me, but I haven't read one word anywhere about him helping with his kids' homework. The standard for being a good parent now is incredibly high. If you are not actually in their backpack, holding their fresh healthy snack and their bottled water in the ready position in school each day, you're considered neglectful and your name gets posted in the school newsletter along with the list of parents who didn't sell enough interdenominational holiday gift wrap and/or help write, publish, and distribute the school newsletter.

I hate homework. Sometimes I think it's worse for the family than drugs and alcohol could ever hope to be. I didn't do my own homework. If my kids aren't smart enough to get out of theirs, why should I do it? I get mad at them for not hiding it better. In 1836 Charles Dickens published *Sketches by Boz,* followed by *The Pickwick Papers,* which came to the public in serial form. By 1838 he had banged out *Oliver Twist,* and in 1839 he published my favorite, *Nicholas Nickleby,* but did he even once help his kid with integers, which I did a whole page of with my eleven-year-old once and I still don't know what they are or when one might necessitate their use? I'm in my forties and I've never knowingly used integers. Admittedly, my life is not over yet. Integers may well be a staple of life in one's fifties, but in that case I think the sixth grade is a little early to be teaching about them.

Toshia has some legitimate learning disabilities, and I have been counseled to break her work sessions up into ten-minute periods. Okay, but do we include the inevitable nine-minute pencil-drop-and-search, and the subsequent breakage and sharpening, which can vary in length depending on how amazed she is that the point broke right off, and the very real possibility of redroppage? She loves to erase. Most kids are eager to write in pen. Not Toshia. She'll happily pass on the more mature writing implement in order to gather a big eraser shaving mound. She'll even fake a mistake or twenty to have the chance to create eraser-shaving dunes along the side of her worksheet. Would that half hour be a part of the ten-minute work period? In a just world it would be applied to any time I might have to do in hell.

We spent hours one afternoon years ago reading a chapter in her science book about the parts of the cell in plants and animals, and answering the questions at the end of the chapter. That night in the bathroom she knocked the toilet-paper roll on the floor as she sat using the toilet. Hoping I would get up and get it for her, she pretended she couldn't find the toilet paper, which had landed behind the toilet, where it always does when you knock it off. I might have helped, despite my exhaustion from hours of:

" 'The nucleus is like the brains of the cell' . . . Okay, Tosh, what part is like the brains of the cell?"

"The cell wall?"

"No, but close . . . try again."

I might have walked over to pick up the toilet paper for her, but I had two of the little kids in the tub, and they'll drink the bathwater if I'm not looking. I've turned away for what seemed like seconds, only to look back and find that Thomas E must have whipped out a straw from a secret hiding place and sucked down everything but the tub toys. So I pointed to where the toilet paper lay on the floor. Toshia slowly scooched off the toilet seat and, obviously seeing where the roll of toilet paper had fallen, pretended not to. She does a pretend-looking that makes Ben Kingsley's Gandhi look like a bad Christmas pageant performance. My kid is terrific. She's a performer. She's funny. She's strong. She's beautiful. But there was a moment, as I watched her, naked butt crouched by the toilet, deliberately averting her eyes from the toilet-paper roll, moaning "I don't see it," that I realized she was not likely to become a scientist. We could have skipped the anatomy-of-a-plant-cell homework. A few hours of towel-drying the beach would have been a more effective use of my time.

One night years ago on *The NewsHour with Jim Lehrer*, Judy Woodruff was moderating a discussion about the Super Collider project. She was joined by a scientist who thought there was nothing to be gained by the expensive Super Collider project and by the scientist who was the head of the project and was, obviously, pushing heavily for continued funding of the project. Judy turned to Mr. Pro Super Collider and asked quite simply,

"Why do we need the Super Collider?" Clearly he was expecting this question because, without missing a beat, he answered, "Well, Judy, everyone knows the importance of the nucleus."

I felt so ashamed. I've never known the importance of the nucleus. Sure, I've faked it at parties, but . . .

I take my children's education quite seriously because I know the pain and shame of ignorance. I stepped into Toshia's room one evening years ago and found her engaging a naked Barbie doll and a similarly clad Michael Jackson posable action figure in unprotected sex. I have always answered my children's questions about reproduction fully and honestly, because I really don't want them to feel as stupid as I am. I find they sometimes forget some of the facts, though, so I occasionally review them, and this seemed a good opportunity to re-explain sex, so I did. Toshia was riveted. I then turned to the Barbie and Michael Jackson dolls and said, "What I want to say to you is that I can see neither one of you is wearing protection."

I then explained about sexually transmitted diseases and also that you don't have unprotected sex unless you fully intend to raise and provide for the child that may come of it. I finished by encouraging my daughter always to feel free to ask me anything and be assured that I would answer her honestly and when I didn't know something I would find someone who did. Right away, Toshia asked a very good question about STDs, which I think I fielded handily. Then something strange happened. Her head began to shift from side to side and she said she had another question.

"Okay," I said, bracing slightly.

"What if," she said, continuing this little head-and-neck

dance, "what if you were just fooling around and you got pregnant?"

I thought my head would come off my shoulders, but I stopped right there and did perhaps the wisest parenting I've ever done. I said, calmly, "What do you mean by 'fooling around'?"

To which she replied, "Running in the backyard. Could you just fall on one and get pregnant?"

I thought I had done such a good job. Apparently, though, I had forgotten to explain the human aspect, like "The penis is attached to a man and doesn't just come up in the yard like an automatic lawn sprinkler that you might fall on if you weren't fully expecting it." On the other hand, she might be right. It would certainly explain the Dickenses' situation. It may be one of those handful of unfortunate marriages where the man was unforgivably careless with the placement of his erect penis in the backyard and his wife, to make matters worse, was unbelievably clumsy, ten times.

I read *Oliver Twist* when I was in the sixth grade. I had seen the movie and the Ephraim Curtis Junior High version of the musical, so I could follow the book. I don't remember much academically from the sixth grade. We were part of a special program in which, instead of studying history, we learned about caribou. It has really made all the difference in my life. We were told it was an experimental program, but in retrospect I think it may just have been a bet between two tenured teachers. No matter. There's really only one thing I remember with clarity from the sixth grade, and that's Keith Stoodley's head.

I was in the sixth grade in 1970–71. It was the first year

girls could wear pants in our public school. We were specifically told it had to be a "pantsuit." My lavender pants, vest, and paisley shirt with the hot-dog collar were pointed out as an example of the correct kind of "pantsuit." No one could know then that twenty-four years later I'd be on Mr. Blackwell's worst-dressed list. Anyway, by 1972, mixing and matching was a tide that the Sudbury school system could no longer hold back, and they were forced to teach us about caribou in pretty much any "threads" we showed up in.

Linc, from *The Mod Squad,* was the only person who could ever use the word *threads* to mean anything other than "more than one string" and get away with it. Contractions are the closest thing to hip talk I can use without just sounding silly. I met Linc once. Clarence Williams III used to hang out at the Improv in Hollywood in the mid to late eighties, when I did. One night I was sitting across a big, crowded table from him out in the dining room area of the club. The show room was through some doors in the other room. Some particularly popular comic went on in the show room while Clarence and I were sitting there, and everybody else at the table fled to watch the comic onstage, leaving just Clarence and me across the table from each other. I felt a bit awkward, but I did know his name from the credits on *The Mod Squad,* so, to break the ice, I said, "Clarence, we've never met officially. I'm Paula Poundstone."

He said, "I know who you are," in that monotone voice, without moving his head or his eyes. He sounded just like Linc. It sounded like he had gone undercover, had infiltrated my gang, and was this close to cracking my drug-smuggling ring and putting me behind bars for a long, long time. My threads must have given me away.

Keith Stoodley was in Mr. Walker's class. I was in Mrs. McKenna's class, but they had teaching teams in the sixth grade in Sudbury, so we were all part of the Walker-McKenna team. The boys had long hair back then, but one day Keith Stoodley came to school with his head shaved. The Walker-McKenna team totally lost their focus. We were old enough that most of us tried to be polite, but it was a sight, an elephant in the room. No one could concentrate on the lessons about the caribou, not their feeding habits or their social groups. Now that I think of it, maybe they did teach us history that day and I just didn't hear it. It was a frustrating day for Mr. Walker and Mrs. McKenna. No progress was made in any subject.

"When you are dividing fractions, you do what simple steps with the equation? Katie McCabe?"

"Invert Keith Stoodley's head and multiply? . . . Ooops."

No matter what the topic, our minds were prisoners of the lure of Keith Stoodley's head. Finally, during a team meeting, which was when both teachers talked to both classrooms as a group about how we were "young adults" and would therefore, next year, have lockers, Mr. Walker lost all patience with our inability to focus and yelled, "Would everyone just stop right now and stare at Keith Stoodley's head."

The more savvy of us within the Walker-McKenna team knew that this was the end of the Keith Stoodley we had known. I never found out why his head was shaved. Sudbury had only about three black families, and I think there was an Eskimo family on Barton Drive. Hardly enough to justify a robust Aryan youth movement. We had hate groups, of course, but they were mostly about architecture. Sudbury was a colonial town in Massachusetts, and it was going to stay that way, even if a group of concerned citizens had to go around the law to protect their dearly held values. Once or twice, some outsiders tried to remodel their kitchens with high ceilings and bright colors and someone broke in, stained their furniture dark, installed rustic beams, and hung a decoupaged plaque of the guy with the drum from the Revolutionary War band. We didn't need those kinds of people in Sudbury, where the zip code is 01776.

I read *Nicholas Nickleby* as an adult. It is so great. I named my first cat Smike, after one of the characters in *Nicholas Nickleby*. My sister Peggy was named after a dog my dad had when he was a little boy. She could so easily have been called Spot. Like most of Dickens's novels, *Nicholas Nickleby* is long, with lots of characters whose lives intersect and influence one another, surprising the reader with twists and turns throughout. I'm bitterly jealous. I do think it makes me special that my feelings of jealousy transcend my historical time. For example, lots of people learn about and admire Benjamin Franklin. I'm one of the few, though, who look at a one-hundred-dollar bill and think, "I could have thought of 'a penny saved is a penny earned,' if I'd had the chance." I can't even imagine how Mr. Dickens kept it all straight even in his own head, let alone the complication of all of the papers and the inkwell. I would have constantly spilled ink. I've seen pictures of his writing in books. There are little cross-outs here and there, but no big ink spills or smudges. I hate cross-outs. If I'm writing and I accidentally begin a word with the wrong letter, I actually use a word that does begin with that letter so I don't have to cross out. Hence the famous closing, "Dye-dye for now." A lot of my letters make no sense, but they are often very neat.

Long, rigorous walks were a notable part of Dickens's daily life. He walked far and fast, and even when he got older, his younger friends could barely keep up with him. I'm sure it's where he organized his thoughts. It's no wonder I can't write. I walk my kids to school every day. It's four blocks. Dickens couldn't have organized a postcard in that short distance, let alone his novels *The Old Curiosity Shop* and *Barnaby Rudge,* which he wrote and published in serial form during 1840 and 1841 in his new weekly magazine, *Master Humphrey's Clock.* That, of course, is where the story comes out a bit at a time, like how they televised *Lost in Space.* They had some of the worst set and costume design in the history of television, and I still loved every minute of it. In one episode, Penny went into a cave and talked to just a voice that she called "Mr. Nobody." I realize now that they had probably gone over budget the week before, and the clever writing staff worked around the lack of funds for the weekly alien costume. Brilliant. Many an enlightened viewer has speculated that, now that they think of it, Dr. Smith might have been gay, but no one seems to have noticed that Don could have been a speed freak and, at the very least, was not a good navigator.

Some guy was using his cell phone during takeoff on a Saudi Arabian Airlines flight a while back. He got in big trouble because cell phones can mess up the navigation equipment on the plane. His punishment was fifty lashes. Man. You only get that here if you're black and you're suspected of a crime. Clearly the guy screwed up and endangered the people on the plane, but still you've got to wonder about a pilot who needs the navigation system for takeoff. I could steer us out of Los Angeles International if I had to, and I can't even tell left from right.

There are arrows on the runway. Gee, I hope it was at least a satisfying phone call for the guy. Perhaps he closed a deal or got notification of his receipt of the Nobel Peace Prize. I hope it wasn't just a call from the National Organization for Women thanking him for his contribution and confirming his address. I could so easily see myself forgetting and making a stupid mistake like using my cell phone to check my machine during takeoff. I'd probably just be picking up a message from American Airlines telling me that my connecting flight was canceled as the plane crashed.

Dickens became a ringleader of London's literary society. His best friend was a writer named John Forester. Dickens would sometimes gather groups of friends together to read his new works to. His comings and goings were events to his friends. When his family spent summers in Boulogne or settled in Genoa for a while, there were big send-off dinners, and friends continued to visit him wherever he went. I travel a lot, but I never stay that long anywhere I go. I was just in Billings, Montana, for one night. Not a soul stopped by. If I'd been there the whole weekend, my hotel room would have been the social hot spot of the Wild West. All of Hollywood would have followed me. I travel alone. Sometimes my cab pulls up outside of Departures at the airport and I'll see people locked in tearful embraces before one departs separately, and I wonder, "What cab company is that?" My guy didn't even get out of the car.

Dickens and the missus visited the United States in 1842. His book *American Notes* describes his trip. I just finished the book. It took me months. It's not that it wasn't good. It's just that I'm tired, and reading puts me to sleep. I can fall asleep reading an Exit sign. Anyways, in a nutshell, he didn't like us. Although in 1868 he stopped by again and took it back. I know I shouldn't take it personally. It's not like I was around in 1842, or for our vindication in 1868, but really, if he didn't like America prior to the successful airing of the hit show *Three's Company,* I don't imagine he would in the years subsequent. Mr. Dickens thought Americans spit too much. He described many carpets in public places practically covered in expectorated chewing tobacco. I would say that writing a whole book about it was a bit extreme, except, in the fifth grade, Steve Michaels spit in my hair at recess, and twenty-seven years later in a drunken twenty-year high school reunion incident, I extracted an apology from him. Steve Johnson fell behind me on the stairs in the sixth grade and bit me in the ass and I let it slide all these years, but spitting—I agree with Dickens—can ruin a nice visit.

Although a widely celebrated artist in his own country, Charles Dickens was quite put out by the intrusive style of his American fans. I became quite defensive as I read *American Notes.* Of course, it wasn't me personally that he disliked, but I know I'm an obnoxious fan. One night a few years ago, while I was dining with Mary Tyler Moore and her husband Robert Levine in a fancy Italian restaurant in New York City, we discovered Billy Joel dining with some friends at a table beside ours. Discreet hellos were said and how-are-yous were exchanged when a very recognizable actor entered the restaurant among a group of people. Well, given that this wasn't an awards show, it was beginning to be quite a coincidence. This actor was a tall, somber-looking white guy dressed in a rather dashing black suit with a black shirt. I relatively quickly pegged him as one of the stars of *Sense and Sensibility.* I couldn't think of his name, though, and I hate that. I'm sure it's a sign of near idiocy, but I've stayed up all night trying to think of a name I've forgotten. One night in Seattle I went through the alphabet, thinking of every name I could think of, beginning with each letter in order, to come up with Strother Martin's name at 9:00 a.m. the following morning. The following night I thought, "Who was that guy whose name I couldn't remember?" Everyone should just have the same name. It'd be so much easier. I don't think we'd get confused, either. Tons of us are called "Mom," yet I've never left the mall with the wrong kid.

Billy Joel, his friends, Mary, and Robert all knew this guy from different movies that I hadn't seen, but none of us knew his name. The others, better people than I, could have dropped it, but I was facing a whole night of "Aaron, Abba, Abraham, Acacia, Adam . . ." So I said I'd go ask him his name. My companions tried to dissuade me, but I boldly stood and headed for the actor's table. This was the point at which an asterisk was carefully marked beside my name in the Big Book of Losers. Hip people called an emergency meeting the following day to resolve unanimously that I should never be among their ranks.

I stood beside the actor's table, as he was engaged in conversation. I waited and waited. It soon became clear, even to me, that he was blowing me off. I was trapped. I was now standing in the middle of the restaurant, facing severe humiliation in either direction I turned. This guy was great in *Sense and Sensibility,* by the way, but I was seriously considering using his steak knife to sever my limbs and other protuberances one at a time and place them on his bread plate. Saving that as Plan B, I tapped him on the shoulder. When he looked up I said, "I loved you in *Sense and Sensibility,* but I can't think of your name and neither can my friends." I have a fantasy that Strother Martin would have been far more forgiving, but it seemed to really piss off Mr. X. Sensing a misstep on my part, I tried to explain, "I have a lot of kids, so I, uh, don't go out a lot. The last movie I got to see was *The English Patient,* which I saw on my birthday, by myself, three years ago." Mr. X glazed over and his female companion, her English accent dripping with impatience with me and people as stupid as me in general, protested, "He wasn't in *The English Patient.*"

Well, I didn't think he was in *The English Patient,* I was only pointing out, by sharing a little about my own life, that I'm a busy person who doesn't go out to see just any trash and that, if he considered the source, he could appreciate that it was a compliment to be recognized by me at all, given that I've only time to see highly recommended films. He didn't see it that way. I tossed a fake smile over to my table to pretend we were really hitting it off and I might just table-hop all night. The actor closed his eyes, heaved a big sigh, and said slowly, in a distinguished manner, "Alan Rickman." I knew even then that it was too late for this fake, but I snapped my fingers, slapped my forehead, and declared, "Yes!"

I stepped away and feigned an interest in the pretend angel frescoes on the wall as I eased my way back to a table I no longer belonged at. It was only about 8:00 p.m., but Mary and Robert started yawning with recently acquired exhaustion. I walked them a few blocks home. They were careful not to disturb the neighbors by talking to me. I had to walk past said Italian restaurant to get back to my hotel. I felt I had to try to fix my little indiscretion. I furtively stepped back into the restaurant and begged to speak to the fawning maître d'. Totally ashamed, I called him aside and confessed that I had offended his famous patron, Alan Rickman.

"Oh, no," he said, as his eyebrows shot up.

I quickly handed him my credit card and asked to pay for the Alan Rickman party's charges to possibly make up for my clumsy Clampett approach. Behind his hand the simpering maître d' whispered, "Who is Alan Rickman?"

"Look, don't say that to him," I said, "but it's that tall white guy in the black suit at the middle table." I watched him convey to Alan Rickman that his tab was covered. I felt a bit stronger until he staggered back, horrified, to report, "Alan Rickman is so embarrassed." Dickens would have hated me. I have no class.

When Dickens was thirty-one, in 1843, he wrote *A Christmas Carol*. When I was four, I happened to learn about the body part called the forehead, so I quite naturally believed that when I turned five I would have a fivehead, which, in turn, means that I now sport a forty-something head. In 1844 Dickens wrote *Martin Chuzzlewit* with a thirty-two-head, then he stayed a number of months with his family in Genoa, where he wrote *The Chimes*. He found it hard to write there.

Finally, something I can relate to. I can't figure out how he gets to take his whole family someplace so he can write. When I got my kids to school late a couple of times, we got a letter from the school district threatening to throw them out. I don't think I'd get any leniency at all if I took them to Italy in the hope that I could write better there. Actually, I did get them to school late several times. It's not my fault. My daughter Toshia is the thief of time. She is a sleight-of-hand artist with time. She comes into the bathroom in the morning and looks like she's getting ready, but it's a trick, she's getting unready. I have a rule that if it's the kids' fault that we're running late, I won't help, but if I've slowed us down, I'll help them catch up. Many mornings when I'm really tired and the alarm goes off, I tell myself, *Fuck it, I'll help Toshia put on a sock,* and I reset the alarm for twenty more minutes of sleep.

So I got this letter from the school district saying that if they were late again I would have to go before a board of late-parent punishers and argue why my kids should be allowed back in school. The school district listed the members of the board, and one of them was a police officer. The next day the kids were going especially slowly. Toshia came near breaking the twenty-five-minute sock. I had asked them to hurry in every way I knew how. By the time we were getting in the van, I was ready to crack. I was trying to explain that the stakes were high for me in getting them to school, and in a burst of bad parenting, I exaggerated a bit.

I said, "You guys, I got a letter from the school saying that if I get you to school late one more time I have to go to jail."

Without missing a beat, Alley said, "We will miss you, Mommy," and Toshia echoed, "Ya, we will miss you, Mommy." Neither kid shaved so much as a second off their time. They're very attached to me.

In December of 1965 I won high praise for my portrayal of one of three nameless elves in the Fairbanks Elementary School

Christmas play, brought stunningly to life by Ms. Shons's first-grade class. I gave a surprisingly blithe, devil-may-care performance, notable for the completion of my two lines of dialogue despite the dropping of my cone-shaped construction-paper elf hat. That's the only way to really measure the talent of an actress. I've always thought Meryl Streep was good, for example, but as I watched her in *Sophie's Choice* years ago I wondered, "Yes, an exceptional performance, but could she continue it if she dropped her cone-shaped construction-paper elf hat?" In 1845, Dickens and his best buddy John Forester performed in their first play for charity. They really enjoyed it and were quite good. Could they have measured up under the cone-shaped construction-paper-elf-hat standard? No telling, but Dickens's friends and family mounted a number of highly acclaimed productions after that. The queen even came to one.

When I was bombing in London, I went to the queen's house. I went as a tourist—she didn't invite me so that she could pick my brain: "What do you think of my face on the pound? Too serious?" I went to see the changing of the guard. How did that become a tourist attraction? It's as dull as it sounds. The shift change at the IHOP has more pageantry. I stood in a crowd at a fence in front of the palace, waiting for something to happen. Occasionally the crowd, hearing a rumor of some sort of activity on the other side, would shuffle over. Nothing would happen. Soon there'd be another rumor and another shuffle. An older British gentleman behind me began telling people that he was a former member of the queen's guard. To prove it, for free, without being asked, he narrated the virtual inactivity before us. A visiting North Carolina family, convinced of the authenticity of the little fellow's claims, began asking him questions, the answers to which only a true insider would have known.

"What's the queen doing right now?" they twanged, riveted.

"Right now," he said, after a bit of consideration, "she's having a bit of tea and a biscuit." Talk about knowing your subject. Tweedle Dum wasn't that familiar with Tweedle Dee's routine. This guy was unbelievable. I have a feeling you could wake him from a dead sleep and ask him what the queen was doing, and without so much as a second to rub his eyes, he'd fire back, "Right now Her Majesty the Queen is deep in a royal slumber on her royal bed on her left side, drooling just a teensy weensy bit." Before Dickens met his wife, he had been head-over-heels obsessed with Maria Beadnell, who blew him off eventually. I was never in love with anyone. I was once going to marry a gay Iranian soup cook to keep him in the country, but he came on to me, so I dumped him. Love is tricky, I guess.

I have obsessive-compulsive disorder, so I have been hopelessly obsessed with many unlucky individuals. I was so attached to a shrink I was seeing at one point that, when I went to my Tuesday noon appointment and discovered that an earlier patient had hung himself in her office, my first thought was "Great, she'll have an opening Tuesdays at 11:00 a.m."

In 1855 Dickens welcomed an opportunity to hook up once again with Maria Beadnell. She had gained some weight and lost the fascination she once held for him. Dickens kind of liked that, which isn't very nice, but, on the other hand, if Denzel Washington ever puts on a pound or two and hosts a funny home video show, I'm sure I'll relate. In 1852, publication of

Bleak House began; in 1854, *Hard Times*; in 1855, *Little Dorrit*; in 1859, *A Tale of Two Cities*; in 1860, *Great Expectations*. I've been thinking of opening a laundromat. On the side of the individual serving package of laundry detergent that I used to get from the vending machine at the laundromat in Boston, it said, CAUTION: EYE IRRITANT. I would think so. I imagine you could reliably post that warning on anything—wood, baby shrimp— even water, if you blast it in there hard enough. Generally I'm not one to lecture, but don't put stuff in your eyes.

Dickens began giving public readings of his works in 1857. The readings were spectacular; they were performances, full of energy and emotion. I wasn't there, of course, but I have a feeling he sweated a lot. Often when I perform, the production crew leaves a towel onstage for me. It's so much pressure. I'm a stand-up comic. I just talk on stage; it's not that physical. I could do it with ankle weights. I feel like I should sweat if they went to the trouble of putting a towel out. Clearly they think performers do. Someone must have. I've considered faking it.

I have never figured out guest-towel protocol. Years ago, Mary Tyler Moore mistakenly invited my children and me to her country home in New York. Her house was perfect. Her bathroom had fancy hand towels. I seriously considered not washing my hands after I used the bathroom so I wouldn't mess up the towels. On the other hand, I thought, if there's a smudge in the house somewhere, they'll know it came from me because the people at Mary's house are way too clean to leave any residue. Finally I decided to just ask her, point blank, "What's your hand-towel policy?"

I should have asked when she first invited us: "How would

you and the girls like to come visit at our country house in New York? They can ride the horses and swim in the pool."

"Well . . . that sounds nice, Mary. Thanks, but do you have decorative hand towels in your bathroom, and, if so, are they for use?"

Anyways, as soon as I worked out the hand-towel protocol, I felt instant social ease all the way until I stepped into the bathroom to discover my kids had poured water into the dish with the little angel-head-shaped soaps and liquidated their facial features. In my house, when we break something, it's an inconvenience, but we replace it at the Rite-Aid or the Disney Store. The most fragile material in our house is hard plastic. My kids are not in the habit of being careful. Mary's house is festooned with precious antiques, little pieces of history that have survived such things as the Crimean War, the Inquisition, the Gold Rush, and Sotheby's—survived everything, that is, until they reached the unsteady grasp of my children. Our hosts remained gracious and kind even as we reduced their home to rubble.

In 1858 Dickens fell in love with Ellen Ternan and separated from his wife. He had been unhappy with Catherine for a while. He never got over being upset with her for "giving" him so many children and, as a result of all of this "giving," having lost her shape and her place in his heart. He wasn't very nice about it, either, just dumped her. My cat Scout won't come near me. Our only contact in the last couple of years has been me grabbing her to shove pills down her throat, so she associates me with that ordeal. Come to think of it, I've lost my shape a bit, too. So that may be a factor.

In 1859, *A Tale of Two Cities* was published. I was born in 1959. Boy, every hundred years, look out, huh?

In June of 1865, Dickens was in the Staplehurst railway accident. His health began to decline after that. He escaped himself, and helped other people out of the wreckage. I was on a plane that crashed. It hadn't taken off yet. Still, the front wheel fell off, the nose crashed and disassembled, and the propellers shaved themselves into pinwheels on the pavement. The pilot declared it a "catastrophic failure of equipment" and put the stairs out for us to "deplane." Why do we "deplane"? We don't "debus," we don't "decab." It's such a phony word. It seems to me an emergency is the wrong time to try to impress people with fancy vocabulary. A simple "The nose has unexpectedly fallen off this plane. Let's not use it. Get off" would have done the trick. Surely my health has declined since then.

I went to the doctor in 2002 for the third time in my adult life. The nurse walked me into the examining room, handed me a gown, and said, "Strip down to your bra, put this on, and the doctor will be in in a few minutes."

Then she quickly shut the door. I stood there frozen with fear. I don't wear a bra. I didn't want the doctor to come in and think I couldn't follow directions, or that I was faking severe abdominal pain so that I could flash medical professionals, so I quickly fashioned a bra out of the crinkly paper on the table. I don't wear a bra because I don't want to talk to auto mechanics. The only way for me to avoid auto mechanics is to buy new cars and get rid of them when they break. Bras are expensive. I can't afford both. I'd rather buy a new car than support my breasts.

In 1867, Dickens returned to the United States for a very successful tour of his public readings. Either we were spitting less by 1867 or he happened to arrive the day after we cleaned the rugs. He liked America this time, and Americans were able to forgive him for his earlier rude comments about our rudeness. When Thomas E was in preschool, talk about rude. You'll never convince me that humans are inherently kind. God, those kids were mean to each other. They didn't have "show and tell"; they had "Look what I have that you can't have." They fought so much. I don't know what they had to fight about, either. It's not like they could disagree on a subject. When two preschoolers talk to each other, they very rarely speak on the same topic.

PRESCHOOLER A: The butterfly came out of the cocoon.

PRESCHOOLER B: Firefighters are going to come chop the door down.

Where's the disagreement there? And yet an exchange this benign typically boils over into the classic "You're not my friend." A preschooler's friendship inventory is fluid. If one kid happens to stumble onto the same subject matter as that of the guy he's in conversation with, he immediately issues a piercing, dog-rousing cry of "Don't copy me," as his reply. Thomas E had a kid he played with every day at school, and they did nothing but fight. I was with Thomas E at school one day when his fighting friend sat down beside me, pointed to Thomas E, and said, "I don't like him," as though this was to be our secret bond and I had at long last found my ally. "Him, yeah, isn't he awful? I wish he'd stop following me home. I like you better. You're not as much of a poopy-head. Will you be my son?"

At the end of Dickens's life he did public readings of his works, despite his doctor's warnings about the physical strain it was causing him. He'd be helped off to rest afterwards. I've often fallen asleep while reading to my kids. I usually keep saying words for a while before they realize I've dozed off and am no longer reading, just talking in my sleep. It takes them a few minutes to realize that "Go ahead, you slimy son of a bitch" isn't part of the text of *Ramona the Pest.* I love to read to my kids; I give a full performance as if there were a casting agent in the house each time. I do *Green Eggs and Ham* as an angry Frenchman, *Where the Wild Things Are* as if I were actually raised by wolves, and *The Grouchy Ladybug* in a homicidal rage. It's kind of pathetic. I think I've seen my kids exchange glances that seem to say, "Mom's career never really quite took off." There's something very *What Ever Happened to Baby Jane?* about my career. Certainly in my makeup style.

On June 8, 1870, Dickens collapsed from a stroke at his home and died the following day. Now that he's gone, I can tell you that I liked *The Old Curiosity Shop,* but, for me, Little Nell could have died chapters earlier.

5

The Wright Brothers: Flying Planes and Bussing Tables

Wilbur and Orville Wright designed, constructed, and flew the world's first airplane. I am in love with Wilbur Wright. He's dead, of course, so I won't go out with him no matter how many times he asks. There probably is someone for everyone, just not necessarily alive in the same century. Posthumous love. It's just one more crack in the "nature is perfect" philosophy, eyelashes being another. Sharp, pokey things that fall out fairly frequently and painfully into the sensitive eye. What are they doing there? Hardly perfection.

Milton and Susan Wright had five children: Reuchlin, Lorin, Wilbur, Orville, and Katherine. Wilbur was born on April 16, 1867, in Millville, Indiana. The family moved twelve times before settling in Dayton, Ohio, where Orville was born on August 19, 1871. Milton was a bishop in the Brethren Church. His work required him to travel a lot. Once he returned with a toy for the kids that lifted itself into the air with a rubber spring. Though they were only eleven and seven at the time, Wilbur and Orville later pointed to this gift as the origin of their interest in flight. I think maybe too much emphasis gets placed on a child's external influences. Though my father once brought me a kilt from a business trip to Scotland, I didn't take up the bagpipes, but I do keep Scotch tape in my carry-on bag, and I don't feel at ease without having several rolls about the house. My son loves to tape things together. He has two or three rolls of tape in his room right now, and Santa Claus always puts a few rolls in his Christmas stocking. The reason for this was unclear to me until now.

I didn't buy duct tape when Tom Ridge told us to. Don't tell. I gather that we were supposed to buy duct tape so that when there's chemical warfare we can use the tape to seal off a window in a room in our homes where we're supposed to gather our families and live for a few extra minutes. Gee, I don't want to be messing with tape for the last few minutes of my life. I get frustrated putting up a poster. Sealing a window sounds like a tall order, and I'd die with adhesive on my teeth. I may as well use Saran Wrap and really piss myself off, maybe bleed to death from the serrated edge. That's not what I want to do with the last few minutes of my life either. For the last few minutes of my life I want to do something I've always wanted to do, which is clean out the junk drawer in the kitchen. I think if I knew I was going to die in a few minutes, I could finally throw some stuff away. I could say to myself with certainty, "I'm not going to twist-tie in the next few minutes. Certainly not one hundred times."

Susan Wright was a descendant of German carriage builders, and was good at building stuff herself. She built a sled and a shed for her kids. I just learned "righty tighty and lefty loosey," but I can't tell left from right without pretending to eat, which slows my manufacturing rate to a creep. As for blood-lines, my grandmother and great-aunt chewed snuff and carried around "spit cans" that they occasionally dribbled into. Our family crest is a nasty splat.

I learned about genetics in biology in the tenth grade. We studied the dominant genetic traits of fruit flies and then mapped out on paper which kind of fruit fly to mate with which kind of fruit fly to produce a particular fruit fly. For ex-ample, a long-winged, red-eyed fruit fly instead of a short-winged, black-eyed fruit fly. We had to etherize test tubes full of fruit flies and quickly sort them before they came to and mated indiscriminately. They were knocked out during the selection process, so a personality profile wasn't possible.

When the desirable male and female were chosen, they were put into a separate test tube and came to in each other's company. I put some teeny, tiny, inviting throw pillows in mine, with a little Marvin Gaye playing softly so the fruit flies didn't vibrate. The way they hover, it's amazing they have the accuracy to procreate.

Even the most dedicated students couldn't necessarily com-plete the assignment, because the test tubes had some sort of gloppy stuff in the bottom for the fruit flies to eat, and many fell into it and drowned before they recovered from the ether. Once, while waitressing on the graveyard shift at the IHOP, I rescued a drunk guy from drowning in his over-easy eggs. I rec-ognized the symptoms because of my biology experience and leaped into action, finally bringing meaning to the scores of senseless fruit-fly deaths I had witnessed. It was a long unit. Our biology teacher, Mr. Ruopp, had to take the test tubes home at night to grade them and make sure that no one was genetically engineering a fruit fly that could take over the world. Mr. Ruopp was young and extremely good looking. He remained single for longer than you'd expect because of the swarm of misplaced fruit flies that puffed out of his shirt and worried about his head in an atomic-energy-symbol flight pattern whenever he moved, until we got to the fetal pig unit. Except for the bugs, he looked like Derek Sanderson from the Boston Bruins.

Wilbur Wright got smacked in the face with a stick during an ice-hockey-type game called "shinney" when he was eighteen. There's no record of the final score of that game. Thomas E takes hockey lessons. On the first day of class he skated out onto the ice in his bulky uniform and I was so disappointed that after taking him to all those figure-skating lessons and all the expense, I now couldn't tell him apart from all the other hockey students wearing helmets, pads, and face masks. Then I heard the coach say, very clearly, "Nobody shoot the puck," and right then one kid shot the puck across the ice. Found him. In the fifth grade I sat too near the high-jump bar in gym class, and when an overweight classmate missed clearing the bar, they both came down on my head. A full recovery is still expected.

Schools in Arkansas are combating the obesity epidemic by weighing students and keeping "health report cards." However, to avoid the possible ridiculing of students with unhealthy weight reports, schools are cleverly mailing the cards home instead of sending them home with the students. The education experts who came up with this plan must have been homeschooled in a closet. If a kid is fat, the other kids can see that. If they make the sad mistake of making fun of an overweight student, they don't require school data to back them up. Even sadder is the suggestion that there's an overweight child whose parents don't know about it until they get the figures from the school.

"Son, come in here a minute. Wedge yourself through that door and come on in here. I just got your health report from the school, and according to this, you're huge. How long has this been going on? Have you been hiding something from your mother and me?"

When Wilbur was twenty-two and Orville seventeen, their mother died. Wilbur cared for her in the last couple of ailing years of her life. Orville had quit school and talked his brother into joining him in the printing business after they built a press out of odds and ends that shouldn't have worked but did. As a teenager I lived for a while with the Masiero family. Renie Masiero could make delicious soup out of anything. When I helped to clean up after dinner, she was always catching me just before I discarded something that I thought for certain was inedible:

"Don't throw out those coffee grounds. I can make soup with that."

Or:

"What did you do with those eggshells?"

There were toilet-paper rolls in her daughter's wedding cake. She never threw anything out, and she was the best cook I've ever known. My kids think I cook. They think "Remove from carton and cook at 350 degrees for thirty-five minutes before removing plastic cover" is an old family recipe. They've never seen an ingredient, and they have no idea that vegetables don't grow frozen. They figure when there's an early frost it's good for the crops.

In 1892 the brothers opened the Wright Cycle Company on West Third Street in Dayton, Ohio. I used to work at Wiley's Comedy Club in Dayton, Ohio. The backdrop on the stage was a painting of the Dayton skyline. Dayton can pretty much rest easy about being on the al-Qaeda target list. There aren't a lot of memorable landmarks. No Twin Towers or Transamerica building. Mostly just the Mead building stands out. The architect of the al-Qaeda attack on the company that makes the spiral notebooks would not work his way very far up the ladder.

"The American children will not be able to write down their homework assignments. It will be beautiful. There will be no more spitballs."

I hate spiral notebooks. I hate spiral notebooks because I'm a recycler. When you pull the paper out, it leaves that confetti everywhere and I don't know what to do with the metal spiral. Renie Masiero used to make a casserole out of those, but I don't have the recipe.

Wiley's was right beside a bait shop that surely cut into my ticket sales. It was Dayton's entertainment complex, and the competition among venues was tough. I got my cat Balou when I was working there eighteen years ago. Thomas E and I buried her last spring. Thomas E is a wild child who has a problem with impulse control, but for some reason he managed to be gentle with old Balou. They were good for each other. She brought out his peaceful side, and he brought out her pulse. I took him out of school on the day she died, so he could help me bury her. He was only six, but muscle-bound, like a literate Bam-Bam. Our yard is the eyesore of the neighborhood. I keep it that way on purpose, to match the house. The dirt in the yard is like cement. We had to use a pickax to dig the hole. My poor boy swung and swung, sweating bullets, and after about fifteen minutes he had dug down about two inches and he stepped back and said, "Okay, I think that's good enough."

I said, "I think we gotta go a little deeper. We're not planting her, we're burying her."

I think he had visions of leaving her paws sticking up, hoping she'd bloom in the spring.

In 1896 the German engineer Otto Lilienthal fell out of the sky and was killed while testing one of his gliders, and the news of this reminded the brothers of the flying toy their dad had bought them. This set their wheels in motion to explore the science of flight. If Mr. Wright had brought them a deck of cards or a hoop and a stick instead, I'd still be collecting frequent choo-choo points every time I use my credit card.

Wilbur wrote to the Smithsonian Institution in 1899 requesting whatever information they had on the science of flying. I've been to the Smithsonian a couple of times to see Dorothy's ruby slippers from *The Wizard of Oz*. I'm uncomfortable in museums. I look too quickly at things, and I'm always afraid I appear shallow to the intellectuals. I have a feeling I'm going to step away from a painting and one museum member will turn to another and whisper with a mixture of pity and amusement, "She didn't get it. That painting doesn't even kick in for another five minutes."

Many times I've looked at empty exhibits, and that can be

humiliating. It's happened frequently at the zoo. I'll be staring into a tank for a while when a zookeeper happens by and tells me there's no animal in there. I try to pretend that I was well aware of that and happened to be deeply interested in the stick in the enclosure that had been raised in captivity.

The ruby slippers are actually kind of disappointing up close. They're not made of ruby. They're just shoes with sequins. It's going to turn out the winged monkeys didn't have wings. We went to see Debbie Reynolds at the Hollywood Bowl once. She did a tribute to Judy Garland and, I guess by way of justifying to the crowd why she, Debbie Reynolds, should be allowed to tread on the sacred ground of Judy Garland songs, she told about their close friendship. She said that she used to go to Judy Garland's house to visit her and Judy would put on a Judy Garland album and sing along with it. Seen in the light of the golden days of Hollywood legend, it sounded charming, but I got thinking about it later and it seemed like it was colossally bad manners. Judy had a guest and she was listening to her own albums and singing along? What if I whip out a tape of "Paula Poundstone Live at Wiley's in Dayton, Ohio" when my neighbor Doris comes over with her fat Chihuahua, Taco, to bring me eggs she got on sale at Ralph's? I'd be buying my own eggs soon, that's what. I'm not one to judge Judy Garland, but that seems rude.

It was probably good for me to see a little glitch in the Judy Garland story. I used to worship her. I wanted to be like her. You know, the frail personality who existed to perform. I used to want to lock myself in my trailer on a movie set and hold up production while the producer and director begged me to come out, never getting mad or firing me, just waiting, knowing I'd give the performance of a lifetime when I emerged, making all of my little personality quirks seem a small price to pay.

I've only had one movie role, and it was in a 3-D science fiction film made by Earl Owensby Studios in Shelby, North Carolina. Earl made lots of money in farm equipment and used it to build a movie studio. Mine was one of the few movies made there that Earl didn't star in. They made the Elvis story. I had to share a trailer with the rest of the cast, so I couldn't really lock myself in. I was never in the trailer alone, plus it was really smelly and there were lots of flies. I once tried to stay in the little bathroom longer than my turn, but the fumes from the blue chemical in the toilet almost killed me. No one seemed to notice I'd been missing. Still, I thought I gave a strong performance once I came out.

Wilbur and Orville read the printed material available on the science of flight and watched a lot of birds. They decided that Lilienthal's mistake was in piloting his flying machine by shifting his legs to control the center of gravity. It was determined later that he had not returned his seat to its original upright position for takeoff and landing. The Wright Brothers believed the key was in the center of air pressure, which they observed birds controlling by a motion of the wing. It was while absentmindedly twisting an empty bicycle inner-tube box that Wilbur discovered a method of duplicating birds' wing adjustment. I bite my nails. It's holding me back in the area of scientific discovery, and it's unattractive. They called his technique "wing warping."

They built a kind of a glider that featured their wing-warping invention and flew it like a kite. Wilbur sought a test site with sand hills and the right wind conditions. He wrote to a couple of weather stations to get more information on their environs, and heard welcoming details from a place called Kitty Hawk, on the outer banks of North Carolina. I watched the Weather Channel a bit during the first of the four hurricanes to hit poor Florida in those couple of months. I never understand the Doppler thing. News stations like to advertise that their weather person can show that Doppler thing, but I don't even know what it is. Someone needs to tell them that they don't need to report the hurricane while standing out in it, either. They can point the camera out the window and tell us it's raining and we'll believe them. It's not necessary for us to see channel 7's Biff Chang in a bright yellow slicker clinging to a lamppost yelling, "It's really coming down out here! Back to you, Cheyenne." I'd feel better getting the news from someone who has the sense to come in out of the rain.

The dirty little secret about Florida is that it is miserably uncomfortable for all but two months out of the year, and during those months Floridians continue to jack the air-conditioning up so high that the buildings there are all but uninhabitable. There have been no definitive studies as to why this is so. I have a theory, having worked clubs, colleges, and theaters in cities throughout Florida numerous times, that many of those who have migrated to Florida from other states have committed crimes for which they have not been caught and, racked with guilt, they've said to themselves, "I'll just never allow myself to be comfortable again." The more unbearably hot the temperature outside, the more unbearably cold they make it inside. If it were as cold outside in the winter as they make it inside in the summer, they'd put the heat on. It makes no sense.

This is not known outside of the state because many of the senior citizens who retire to Florida are told it's just them when they ask, "Is it cold in here, or is it just me?" The few who figure it out often slip into dementia before they're able to escape and warn the rest of us. Anybody who was born and raised in Florida and hasn't left clearly can't, and therefore may never know a better way of life.

Tourists come and go, of course. They experience the bad weather, but leave convinced they just came at a bad time. During the summer in most of Florida it rains every day at about 5:00 p.m. Not a little shower to cheer up the flowers, but a huge, torrential downpour that stops traffic and floats alligators to a change of roadside stagnant-water-filled ditches. It pours for about an hour and evaporates so quickly in the staggering heat that by 7:00 p.m. the residents are able to seamlessly pretend to the tourists that no such rainstorm ever took place. One or two might break ranks and acknowledge the storm with a smooth comment like, "Oh, you came on a rainy day," as if every day weren't equally harrowing in the Sunshine State.

Four hurricanes in a row sounds like a mysterious feat of nature until you realize that the temperature increase when you step out of a building in Florida is a quick one hundred degrees. I don't know anything about all that high-pressure and low-pressure stuff, but I wouldn't be at all surprised if it turned out many hurricanes start out in the lobby of the T.G.I. Fridays in Florida.

I have heard some people, mistakenly in my view, try to explain the phenomenon of the Florida hurricanes as some sort of natural comeuppance due for the voting debacle in 2000. I discourage this kind of thinking. The idea that natural disasters are an extension of man's penal code is a double-edged sword. Strom Thurmond used to say that about the earthquakes in San Francisco. He used to say they were God's way of punishing gays. Apparently Strom never noticed how many tornadoes whipped through his holier-than-thou section of the country. If there's a God, tornadoes must have been Him just looking for Strom Thurmond. That's why they flipped houses and tore off the roofs. It was God saying, "Oops. Sorry to bother you, but have you seen Strom Thurmond?"

In September 1900, Wilbur packed up the brothers' glider and headed for North Carolina. He had an adventurous journey, including a boat ride to the little place called Kitty Hawk. The trip was lengthier and more rigorous than expected, and all he had to eat was some jelly that his sister Katherine had made and packed for him. I've read a few books that recount the history of flight, and not one left out the story of the jelly. Jelly holds an important place in the history of flight. It's no wonder Welch's grape jelly has its own website.

Kitty Hawk was a very small town. When I lived in in Manchester, Massachusetts, with the Masiero family as a teenager, many a night I enjoyed a delicious hot bowl of used-tea-bag-and-uncooked-popcorn-kernel soup at Renie Masiero's table. I now live in Santa Monica, California, but I still take the *Manchester Cricket* newspaper, filled with all of the Manchester news that's fit to print. It's eight pages packed full of who became an Eagle Scout, who got engaged, who retired, and who made a rousing speech about potholes at the last town meeting, and it's delivered to my house every week. Last week's headlines screamed, "Another Paperboy Dies from Exhaustion on Long

Delivery." Farther down it carried detailed coverage of the "Fall Hydrant Flush." "Fifteen Years Ago in Manchester" is a popular feature on the lower quarter of the front page that tells what happened in Manchester fifteen years ago. Guess what. Someone became an Eagle Scout, someone got engaged, someone retired, and someone made a rousing speech about potholes at the town meeting.

Wilbur stayed with Kitty Hawk residents Bill and Addie Tate, and his brother Orville showed up some days later. I stayed with Tim Leary and his wife in Hollywood part of one summer. He was a very kind man. I needed a place to stay and I had almost no money and his wife had said to me offhandedly at a party that I could stay with them sometime. I think she meant it more like when someone asks, "How are you?" but they have no intention of listening to how you are, and they are, in fact, a little put out if you say anything more than "fine." I took it another way. I asked for a confirmation number and changed my mailing address. I pulled up at their house with my 1965 Mustang and a couple of suitcases, feeling a bit ashamed to have to rely on their generosity, but Tim came out to the driveway, stretched his arms wide, and said, "Welcome to one of your homes on the planet." It was so . . . Tim Leary, and I appreciated it so much. A few weeks later, however, I had overstayed my welcome and his wife asked me to leave. I think they were hoping when they made the offer that I had lots of homes on the planet. Nope. Just the one. They were about thirty years older than I was, so I'd creep in quietly from working a nightclub at night, trying not to wake them, only to hear their car pull into the driveway an hour or so later.

It took wood, wires, white French sateen fabric, and two

weeks of being a spectacle in the Tates' yard for Will to build the flying machine for its first trials at Kitty Hawk. It was a glider with double wings, a rudder, and an eighteen-inch slot on the lower wing for a pilot. The button that you push to lean the back of your seat four degrees farther back came later. The inventor of the adjustable seatback is lesser known and perhaps didn't apply himself as well as the obsessive Wright brothers.

I don't know why they have the adjustable seatback feature. They make such a fuss about putting it up for takeoff and landing, as though a seat not restored to its original upright position is such a safety hazard that it could cause an otherwise fully functional aircraft to plummet from the sky. They police the aisles looking for the tilted chair. If they can't eyeball it, they'll use a level. Why do they have adjustable seats if it's that dangerous, anyway? It doesn't make it a bit more comfortable. It's hardly worth the risk.

A few days after Orville arrived, the brothers carted the glider out to the beach with the help of Bill Tate. They put strings on it and flew it like a kite. They found that the glider responded to their controls, and Will felt confident enough to try boarding it. He must have had a boarding pass and a government-issued ID, because in a few minutes he was in the eighteen-inch slot in the lower wing.

I was the only passenger on a flight once. It wasn't a jumbo jet; it was a thirty-seat puddle jumper. Still, I was the only passenger. It was embarrassing. There was a pilot and a co-pilot. They seemed embarrassed, too. You could tell they took it personally, as if their flight didn't have a good enough draw. They tried to pretend it was full. They kept talking into the PA. This was a few years back, before all of the tight security, so I parted the little curtain to the cockpit and stepped in.

I said, "Look, I'm the only one here. You can just talk to me. You don't have to talk on the PA."

I just stood there, and the copilot continued to stare straight in front of himself and keep up his charade.

"Ma'am, if you could just take your seat. The . . . uh . . . captain has requested that you take your seat and fasten your seatbelt."

"What are you talking about?" I said. "I'm standing right here. The captain's lips didn't even move. Those are your thoughts, little buddy. You don't have to say, 'The captain said.' If you want the passengers to put their seatbelts on, you can say it yourself. Be a man."

He stole a quick glance back at me and, finding me still there, quickly resumed staring out the front of the plane, talking into the PA.

"Ma'am, if you could just take your seat."

I turned to take a seat. I don't know why, but I looked at my boarding pass and took my assigned seat. I try so hard to do the right thing. It said 5A, so I sat in 5A. This is embarrassing to admit, but the copilot got back on the PA and asked me to move for ballast. It could have been worse; he could have said, "If you could just throw one thigh over the aisle, I believe this puppy will straighten right out."

They said I could sit anywhere behind row six. Totally humiliated, I dragged my bag back to row seven and I flopped down, only to hear the copilot get back on the PA.

"We see you've chosen the emergency exit row . . ."

He proceeded to explain how I had to be willing to get others off.

A few days before they went home, Wilbur flew in the glider. It went about four hundred feet, so there wasn't enough time for beverage service. They flew a last unmanned glider flight before they left. The glider crashed in the sand, and the brothers went home to Dayton. Bill Tate retrieved it after they left, and his wife clipped the fabric off the wings and made dresses from it for their daughters, Irene and Pauline. On windy days thereafter, the young Tate girls were often blown into trees on their way to school.

In photos, their camp and workplaces are immaculate. The cans in their kitchen are lined up with the labels all facing the same way. Both Orville and Wilbur must have had raging obsessive-compulsive disorder. I think it was the key to their success, although it wasn't just that; they had engineering skills as well. I've alphabetized the cereals in my cabinet before, but I frequently push on the hinged side of a door instinctively. The Wright Brothers built meticulously, tested, tested, and retested, and they did it all while fighting sand, bugs, sun, wind, and rain—in suits. I can't get over anybody who can camp on the beach without getting all hung up in the tent with the whisk broom.

The Wright Brothers didn't become known to many until their friend, the aeronautical engineering enthusiast Octave Chanute, asked Wilbur to give a speech to the Western Society of Engineers. After following the Wrights to Kitty Hawk in 1901 to watch them work, he talked Wilbur into addressing their gathering in Chicago. I performed at the IBM booth at

Comdex, the annual Computer Convention in Las Vegas, in 1994. I think the guy at IBM who hired me has long since been fired for doing so. He told me, with a straight face, that booking me was part of an overall effort to shed IBM's straitlaced, conservative, button-down image. He said the company had changed, and when I pushed him to tell me how it had changed, he said the employees now wore blue sweater vests. They did, too. They wore them there on the floor at the convention, but they didn't look that comfortable in them, as though they didn't know how to wear them. It seems cruel to just throw IBM salesmen out onto the computer convention floor in sweater vests without some sort of training or seminar on how to wear them. Some of them had both arms through one armhole, and others had them on over their suit jackets. I can't tell which thing people associate me with more closely—computers or the introduction of a "now" look.

Wilbur was so nervous, he regretted agreeing to speak at the Western Society of Engineers as soon as he agreed to speak. I'm not a good speaker myself. I can do my act, but outside of that I always say the wrong thing. In court, the judge kept asking me if I had anything to say. I had lots to say, but nothing that was going to help me get back to my children, so I said, "Thank you. No." He asked me repeatedly. I believe *Webster's* defines this as "goading." I swear I could hear Yosemite Sam's saw coming through the floor under my chair, cutting the hole I would have fallen through into jail if I had said a word. Each time I declined to speak, I thought appreciatively of my eighth-grade independent-study teacher, Mrs. Doughan, who once backed me up against a wall and demanded, "You're argumentative, aren't you?" There are questions in this world that can't be answered.

Why do some heterosexuals believe that same-sex marriages could destroy the sanctity of their marriage? I'd be insulted if my husband suggested that two other people getting hitched could somehow make what we had go to seed. I haven't seen that idea in a Valentine—"My love, in order to hold fast our commitment, I will go to the ends of the earth to keep gay couples from marrying."

"That's nice, honey, but we haven't slept together in weeks, your work bores me, and the bathtub needs caulking. Are you sure it's Mrs. and Mrs. Jones who are driving our love asunder?"

I was so proud of my home state of Massachusetts for advancing the civil rights of all citizens by allowing same-sex marriage. I was surprised that my state was the pioneer state. I actually think of Massachusetts as quite conservative in the main. I mean, I would have been more surprised if it was Mississippi, but nonetheless I was surprised. I kept waiting for the other shoe to drop. Maybe they would allow, for example, same-sex marriage, but forbid same-sex divorce, thereby making it a moot point. Honestly, I don't know why anybody wants to get married. I can understand doing it for tax purposes and hospital visitation, but why waste all that money on a wedding with the photos and the videographers and the hoo and the ha when most marriages split up? I think they should print those expensive wedding photos on perforated paper so that when the couple separates they can tear the pictures neatly down the center so as not to waste a lovely photo of the family dressed up so nicely. Maybe if enough time passes, you can forget what the occasion was and just have a nice photo of your side of the family. "Mom and Dad look wonderful in this . . . Why was I wearing that big, puffy white dress? Beats me."

I met a woman who was about to get married for the fifth time. None of the husbands kicked, either, she divorced them all. She was about to have another wedding, too, not just make a quiet legal commitment. I asked her, "Do people even come anymore?" She kind of chuckled and said, "Not as many." I didn't say it, because I didn't want to rain on her parade, but I was dying to ask how the couple planned to get through the vows without laughing. I assume they create their own at this point: "I promise to have and to hold . . . to love, honor, and cherish . . . just a whole lot . . . certainly for a while."

On the plus side of weddings, there are the appliances. The timer has been out on my toaster oven for months. It has the whole family on edge. It's cost me hundreds of dollars in bread just to get a few slices of unburned toast, and the house is always full of smoke. I have a million things to do every morning; I couldn't possibly stand around watching the toast toast. If I had that kind of leisure time, I could go buy a toaster. I don't. If we ever suffer fire damage, I might get married to get a new toaster, for the sake of the children's safety, but I still don't think I'd have sex.

The Wright Brothers never got married. They didn't need to, they were engineering geniuses. They could fix a toaster timer, I'm sure. Their sister Katherine ran their house back in Dayton while they experimented in Kitty Hawk, and Charlie Taylor ran their bicycle shop.

They returned to Kitty Hawk in 1901 with a new glider.

Some other aeronautical engineers came as well, with their own flying machines to test, but the Wrights did not welcome collaboration. Their 1901 glider had balance problems. It didn't have enough lift, tended to buck, and was difficult to control. They flew it, measured, recorded results, and tried again and again.

A circus clown I met in Sarasota, Florida, showed me a boomerang he had made out of the Styrofoam from a meat package. He told me the key was flattening the sides of the pieces so that it had lift. It soared out and shot right back to him each time he tossed it. He showed me how to make one. It couldn't have been easier, so I told him I had a funny feeling I couldn't do it. He kindly said he would give me his Styrofoam meat package boomerang if I came to his show the next day. I said, "Thanks very much, but if I had time to go to the circus, my smoke alarm wouldn't go off every day, would it?" I was right, of course. One night at home after I made tacos, I used the Styrofoam meat tray to craft my own boomerang, which plummeted to the ground repeatedly until my cat Brittle attacked it because it smelled like meat and my son had a huge tantrum from disappointment. I held him tight, patted his wild dreadlocks, and quietly whispered, "I'm sorry, honey. Mommy is not a very good builder and I did get the directions from a clown."

Things could have gone so differently. If either of the Wrights had had children, they couldn't have done what they did. Children blast the single-mindedness of one's purpose like a big pile of Acme dynamite. I didn't have a moment's peace to squish the sides of my Styrofoam meat tray pieces properly. The

Wright Brothers could barely have repaired bikes, let alone invented the first airplane, if little Orville Jr. or little Wilbur Jr. needed Daddy to sit with him while he pooped in the toilet. Someone else would eventually have made a successful plane, but it would have been much later because their rivals weren't that close. The whole world would have turned out differently. We'd still be about twenty years away from the discovery of the Cinnabon, and might have avoided the obesity epidemic altogether.

How come the jet fuel at an airport doesn't smell as much as the Cinnabons do? I think they pump the smell in on purpose, as a form of subliminal advertising. It has to be some sort of gas spray. If the actual baked good were that pungent, you'd pass out from the fumes before you could get it to your mouth. Some airports are almost a mile long, but you can follow the Cinnabon smell to the four-by-four concession booth from anywhere in the building. In the midst of a snowstorm, with zero visibility, the pilot can pop open the cockpit window, pick up the Cinnabon scent, and sniff his way to the runway.

The brothers took turns piloting their 1901 glider. They were cautious with their manned flights. Wilbur had promised their dad they'd be careful. I wish I could extract those kind of promises from my children. My son bit a rope that was fastened to the side of the house, threw himself off the porch and pulled his front teeth out, and he still doesn't seem remorseful about any part of it except having lost one of the teeth in the grass so he can't put it under his pillow. I told him the tooth fairy doesn't come when kids rip their teeth out with a rope. Mr. Wright must have made it clear to his sons that if they broke every bone in their bodies there'd be no get-well-soon cards and he wouldn't sign the cast.

So their flights were focused on controlling their craft as it skimmed close to the sand. Besides, each crash that damaged the plane required days of repair, which means the flight delay was invented at Kitty Hawk in 1901. I wonder if they took turns lying to each other about what was wrong with the aircraft or when and/or whether it would actually take off.

"I'm very sorry for the delay, Mr. Wright. We're not sure, we're waiting to hear, but we should be ready for boarding in about . . . very soon."

"Thank you. Can I speak to whoever is in charge?"

"I'm in charge, sir."

"I see, and your name is . . . ?"

"I'm Mr. Wright."

"And, Mr. Wright, you don't know when the flight will be leaving?"

"Very soon, sir. We're just loading on the peanuts and the little liquor bottles for the teeny, tiny alcoholics, sir."

"So I don't need to bother getting another flight?"

"Of course, you can if you want, Mr. Wright, but we should be departing soon . . . sir."

"Isn't that the wing lying on the ground beside the plane, Mr. Wright?"

"I don't know anything about that, sir, but I wouldn't go too far from the gate area if I were you, sir. The voucher hasn't been invented yet."

The poor control of their 1901 glider shed doubt on their previous calculations. Back home in Dayton, they built a wind tunnel in their workshop and tested their theories of flight and recalculated many times. I can't figure out how they learned what to calculate. Neither brother had gone to college.

I make my kids do math problems every day (because we're using a textbook called *Everyday Mathematics,* so I feel I have no choice), and we couldn't figure out how to keep the Styrofoam boomerang airborne.

Toshia was once supposed to solve a "math problem of the week" and write out what steps she took to figure it out for homework in Ms. Bon's class. The problem was to price various-sized pieces of a square with the total cost of $8.00. We sat, as we often have, in a gym doing homework during Alley or Thomas E's gymnastics class. I thought I just got her started on the problem. She appeared to work studiously for a while, but when I noticed her pencil had remained motionless for so long it was gathering dust, I checked her work. For Step One she had written, "My Mom told me the prices of the pieces." Okay, I might have "helped" more than I should have, but that wasn't the first step she took, it was step fifteen.

Step One was: Removed notebook from backpack at slowest pace possible.

Step Two: Sought pencil at half speed of Step One.

Step Three: Rubbed skin above lip.

Step Four: Stared lifelessly at problem for ten minutes.

Step Five: Pushed eraser into cheek.

Step Six: Waited for Mom's head to turn away.

Step Seven: Looked everywhere but at paper.

Step Eight: Fantasized about different hairstyle.

Step Nine: Whined that I couldn't do problem.

Step Ten: Claimed that two equal parts of one whole are thirds.

Step Eleven: Poked pencil up nose while Mom tried to show relationship between parts of square.

Step Twelve: Watched veins stick out in Mom's neck.

Step Thirteen: Watched Mom desperately try to explain relationship between parts of square.

Step Fourteen: Stared with alien expression.

Step Fifteen: My mom told me the prices of the pieces.

In his book *The Flyers,* Noah Adams says, "The Wrights had been using the Smeaton air density coefficient as part of the equation for predicting lift," although what that is I couldn't tell you, despite hundreds of days of *Everyday Mathematics.* Otto Lilienthal had used the Smeaton air density coefficient as well. He, of course, fell out of the sky. I'm not sure how much wind-tunnel testing anyone needed to do to figure he had something wrong.

Many modern pilots have made the point that, although it's easy to forget, the Wrights not only invented the first successful flying machine, they invented the skill of flight. So, when a flight didn't go well, they could never be quite sure whether the design of the plane was at fault or their piloting was off. I have that problem with driving. My new van kept making a beeping noise just before I backed into stuff. The last thing I said before every crash was, "What the hell is that noise?" I called the manufacturer to complain. It turns out it's supposed to be a warning signal. Whose bright idea was that? I don't need that kind of distraction while I'm trying to back up. It's hard enough rewinding the cassette tape, keeping my soda from spilling, and talking on the phone.

I was pulling into a parking lot one day when a young girl pulled out of a space and hit me. She jumped from her car and said, "I don't know what the rule is, but I don't think it was my fault."

I said, "Oh, I know the rule: red cars go first."

Surely she's a judge by now.

Orville and Wilbur built and tested their last glider at Kitty Hawk in 1902. They made about a thousand flights. Well, not flights, glides. They were two hundred, three hundred, four, five, or six hundred feet each, and not above the height of a man. They weren't just scooches, but technically they were not yet flights. This time the Wright Brothers left Kitty Hawk ready to build a new machine with an engine and a propeller, one that would fly.

The French were big into flight. They were advanced and experienced in balloon travel. You're not supposed to let helium balloons go, you know, because when they bust they often land in oceans and rivers, and sea turtles mistake them for jellyfish and eat them. The balloons can get stuck in the sea turtle's intestines and kill them. So, although jellyfish would argue otherwise, you're not supposed to release helium balloons outside. Anytime a jellyfish can get to a phone, it orders a balloon bouquet for someone. I remember fondly the front-page picture of the guy who flew in his lawn chair by tying helium balloons to it. I think he even got arrested for being unauthorized in FAA airspace. I think he shot at the balloons to descend. Probably some sea turtle with a lawn chair stuck in his intestines called the cops on the guy. Sea turtles are way too slow to cough up a lawn chair, even when it becomes clear it's not a jellyfish.

In the fall of 1903 the Wright Brothers brought their

"flyer" to Kitty Hawk. They assembled and tested it in their shed in the cold on the outer banks of North Carolina. By the beginning of November, Orville felt certain they would make their first engine-powered flight in about a week, but in a test on November 5, they lost the propeller shafts and had to wait for repairs. The flight delay was really coming along; it's less celebrated than the first flights, but no less a part of our lives.

On Wednesday, December 17, 1903, after weeks of delay and with the help of some men from the lifesaving station on the beach, Orville Wright climbed into the cradle of the flyer, which ran down its launching track and flew 120 feet in twelve seconds. It was man's first successful engine-powered flight.

Is *ass* considered a curse word? I have read aloud to my daughter Alley's class for years. Once, when I picked up *Emil and the Detectives,* the book I had been reading, from Ms. Gibson's desk to begin to read, I saw she had attached a Post-it asking if I had read "silly asses." At first I thought it was the name of a book she wanted me to read to the class. I looked up at her and said, "No, is it good?" Below the question about silly asses, it said, "choose a 'different' word." Helen Keller understood that that wet stuff coming out of the pump was water faster than I understood what the hell Ms. Gibson meant. She could see that I didn't understand her note, so she explained that she thought she had heard me read aloud the words "silly asses" to the fifth graders. I said I had no idea, and I started flipping through the book, stammering, "I . . . I . . . I . . . might have. I didn't notice. It's not what the story is about. It's about a little German boy who gets pickpocketed on a train trip and catches the thief with the help of a neighborhood full of boys he meets." By now, of course, Ms. Gibson and I had said "silly asses" several times, just trying to clarify what I couldn't say. Later I looked up "ass." It's in the dictionary. It means "donkey." It's in the Bible, too, though it's not what the story is about. Certain, therefore, that "asses" wasn't the problem, and wanting to comply with Ms. Gibson's wishes, I resolved to change the next mention of "silly asses" to "ignorant asses," but I think it's silly.

At the beginning of each school year, our district invents more forms for the parents to fill out about the rules. They have to be read, understood, agreed to, and signed by the parents and the students by the following day. I usually have to pull an all-nighter. Before Thomas E could attend kindergarten, he had to sign the "illicit drug policy" form stating that he would not deal in the drug-free zone surrounding the school. I showed him where he could deal. I explained to him that his territory was the block east of there, but for safety he was not to sell to anyone he didn't know. If they keep cutting school budgets, they'll be begging the kindergartners to sell drugs as a fundraiser, just like they beg them now to sell cookie dough, raffle tickets, and inter-denominational wrapping paper.

One of the rules that we had to sign this year was that our children would not use "offensive language." I wrote a note back to the teacher, asking her for the offensive-language list. I'm happy to go over it with my children and make sure they know what not to say, but if I don't know, it'll be difficult to commit to.

The press coverage was mostly inaccurate about the Wrights' historic flight, and in fact a lot of newspapers didn't think it was a big enough deal to cover. If they'd been accused of child molesting, they'd have been a household name within the duration of their twelve-second flight: HIGH FLYING WRIGHTS CAN'T GET ANY LOWER, and JUST EXACTLY WHAT KIND OF FLY BOYS? The success of my career was greatly exaggerated in articles that publicized the charges against me in order to make a more dramatic falling-from-grace story. I was a little jealous of myself when I read how big I was, but it was certainly the first I had heard of it. I'm hoping to become beloved when I die.

I'm going to nap a lot before I die, to cut down on the tragedy of my passing. So that no one has to say stuff like, "She seemed so alive." It's an idea I got from my dead cat Scout, may she rest by the side of the house. We're atheists, so I believe any peace she was gonna have had to come before she died, perhaps during the many years she spent vomiting from the rocking chair. I swear she took pride in how many surfaces she could hit. She used to get the chair rocking for distance. Still, I don't want to foist my beliefs on you.

Thomas E and I were reading his new RIF (Reading Is Fundamental) book *All About the Sun* in the library with his first-grade class when one of his classmates came over and started telling us that the sun was going to explode during the Rapture. I said, "I guess it's not important to decide if Thomas E should brown-bag or have hot lunch next week, then."

Orville and Wilbur decided they needed to continue developing their flyer closer to home, to have access to their machine shop. They found a patch of prairie, less than an hour away by train, owned by Torrence Huffman. For the first couple of months they didn't get much further along. Things kept breaking. They didn't have the wind they needed. They invited the press once or twice, but the flights didn't go well. I often choke when there's press at my performances. Even when I do well, they tend to devote a paragraph to what I was wearing, and it has never been the right thing, of course. Fashion is an entire industry of people who have taken their eye off the ball, or perhaps never even laid eyes on the ball to begin with. It makes sense, though, because there's money in it. It's not just catty criticism; it's a gold mine. The very designer who convinces us of what we "must have" this year and that it's worth the extra money because it will last, admonishes us at the same time next year that that old stuff will never do, and we fall for it every time. I understand fashion people caring about what people wear, but why a journalist? Even one as low on the totem pole as an entertainment reviewer. It hasn't always been that way. No one ever wrote, " 'Let my people go,' Moses demanded in a simple wash-and-wear knee-length tunic and kicky, devil-may-care high-laced sandals."

Mr. Huffman, the owner of Huffman's prairie, thought the Wright Brothers were "fools," according to Noah Adams's biography.

A lot of people thought they were just dweeby guys in suits who were working on something silly. The guy who invented the pogo stick must have really faced some derision. People started feeling sorry for the Wright brothers.

The French, anxious to franchise Au Bon Pain in airports throughout the world, considered themselves the rightful inventors of flight, and rejoiced at any stories they heard of the Wright Brothers' failures. Hell-bent on their balloony travel ideas, the Aero-Club de France guys started claiming that the Wrights exaggerated tales of their successes. The French called them *les bluffeurs,* which is French, but I'm happy to translate it for you. It means "the bluffers." Thank goodness I've kept my year of high school French fresh. This lack of trust must be a French trait. The one paper that I wrote for my French class was pretty good, I guess, because Ms. Fritche accused me of plagiarizing it. Plagiarism requires a lot more motivation than I ever had in high school. You'd have to carry a book to copy from it.

When there was news of the Wright Brothers' machine taking to the sky for longer and longer periods, an American member of the Aero-Club de France sent his brother-in-law, Henry J. Weaver, to verify it. According to Fred Howard, in his book *Wilbur and Orville,* Weaver talked to Amos Stauffer, "who farmed the fields adjoining Huffman's pasture. 'Well the boys are at it again,' Stauffer remembered remarking to the helper with whom he had been cutting corn on October 5, the day Wilbur made his thirty-eight-minute flight. 'I just kept on shucking corn until I got down to the fence,' he told Weaver, 'and the durned thing was still going round. I thought it would never stop.' "

Orville and Wilbur applied for a patent for their flyer and purposely avoided publicity while they waited for their innovation to be provided legal protection. I was surprised to learn that, from the start, the Wright Brothers thought that the airplane's most important use would be in war. Shortening the trip to Grandma's doesn't seem to have ever been the goal.

The U.S. government was the first customer they approached to sell their airplanes to. However, the government had already funded Charles Langley's very public failure with a flying machine, and was unwilling to make a deal without seeing demonstration flights, and the Wrights refused to demonstrate their machine without a contract. Eventually they came to terms with both the United States and France. Both customers wanted airplanes demonstrated with abilities somewhat beyond what the Wrights had yet achieved. The inventors headed back to Kitty Hawk to rebuild their camp and perfect their new plane. This time they were followed by members of the press, most of whom hid in the woods to spy on the Wrights' remarkable work.

The American soldiers hid behind rocks during the Revolutionary War, but they brought a band with them. Remember the two guys with fifes and the guy with the drum and the head injury. The British redcoats still stood up in a straight line to fight, but our guys hid behind rocks. The British probably had no idea where their adversaries were, until they heard the musical rocks. The revolutionary soldiers were probably pissed when they realized the music had given them away: "Fellas, could we party later?" It's no wonder they were wounded. It was probably friendly fire.

The Wrights coped with the press more than they courted it. I came to admire Martha Stewart's poise during her legal ordeal, despite the shameful exploitation by the press. Early one morning, as I lovingly prepared my daughter's lunch bag and my lizard's entrée salad, I listened to an NPR reporter's description of Martha Stewart's arrival at her first day in court. The reporter said she stepped from the car with dignity, carrying a beige umbrella with which she obscured her face from the crowd. I thought, "I've gotta get an umbrella. Maybe even a rain hat and a yellow slicker like the fisherman on the Gorton's Fish Sticks box."

I make Toshia's lunch every day because our school lunches are contracted through companies like Taco Bell and Domino's—and that's healthy food compared to the absolute crap they sell our kids from vending machines during their "nutrition break." It really is a disgrace, and there's junk-food trash all over the schoolyard as well, because the nutritionally bereft middle schoolers don't have the strength to put their trash away. They have a terrible seagull problem as a result. Sometimes it looks like the set of *The Birds*. Children have to shield their heads and scurry in a zigzag pattern from class to the vending machines. I could swear I saw Suzanne Pleshette's dead body lying akimbo on the stairs.

The pilot sat upright in the Wright Brothers' new plane, and there was a passenger seat. The center seat hadn't yet been invented. I selected my seat on the self-service ticket machine at the airport the other day. The screen showed the seating chart and said, "Touch where you would like to sit." Looking around for surveillance cameras, I sheepishly touched my butt. What an odd command. Is that part of the PATRIOT Act?

Wilbur was to demonstrate an airplane in France, and Orville would show off their new airplane in Washington, D.C. Orville and their assistant, Charlie Taylor, had packed the machine Will was to use and shipped it a year before. When Wilbur opened the crates in France he found broken and missing parts, which meant days of added work for himself. Sometimes my shampoo and conditioner explode in my suitcase, and it can be an annoying cleanup job, but the first time I leave it at home I end up in a hotel that doesn't provide it. I've stayed in some bad hotels, places that proudly boast "phones" in their advertising.

When I covered Clinton's inauguration for *The Tonight Show,* NBC put me up at a place that no cabdriver had ever heard of. The rooms were furnished with porch furniture. The elevator operator doubled as the cook, which meant that when the top floors were booked, they took the over-easy eggs off the menu. The hotel had vacancies on Inaugural weekend, and it was located right in Washington, D.C. Not only that, but I was working in my room on Inauguration Day, heard a noise outside my window, and looked out and saw the parade. This hotel was so bad it was on the Inaugural parade route and it wasn't sold out. Even snipers wouldn't stay there. It didn't have shampoo and conditioner. Even the most heinous assassin likes to avoid hair breakage, and of course they can't risk hair-care products exploding in their luggage. A dripping suitcase can attract unwanted security attention.

One time when an airport security guy rubbed that little bomb-detecting cloth on my bag, he said there was evidence of nitroglycerin in my bag. I said I didn't have any. He said it's also an ingredient in lotion. So I was either a terrorist or under suspicion of being very dry.

By the time Wilbur was ready to demonstrate their plane in France, the French people thought he was as full of hot air as their favorite form of flight, and the Americans accused the brothers of greed for not flying for two years while waiting for their patents. An audience member at a show I once did worked for the U.S. Patent Office. He said he had taken the day off to come to my show. I don't see how he could enjoy a show with all those patents pending.

It took several weeks to repair the parts and assemble the flyer. Finally, on the afternoon of August 8, 1908, before a small crowd at the Hunaudieres racetrack in Le Mans, France, Wilbur Wright meticulously made ready his airplane on his launching ramp and took off to soar over the heads of the naysayers. It was an aerial "I told you so." He did turns that demonstrated control of an aircraft such as no one had ever seen before. It was unparalleled and spectacular, and the spectators were amazed. It was over in less than two minutes. Then he waited thirty minutes for his luggage. In twenty-five years of flying, I've had the first bag off the conveyor belt at the baggage claim just one time; they bring you a lei and a glass of champagne.

The airlines once lost my bag, and I waited in a long line at the baggage-claim office to circle the picture of the bag that looked most like mine on the laminated "Which of these bags looks most like yours?" chart that they give you. I filled out forms, turned in my claim checks, and waited some more before I got my turn to talk to the clerk. I handed her the forms and verbally described the bag and she asked, "Do you need it?"

I was temporarily stunned by the sheer genius of the question. I mean, most people probably just answer yes, but for the one in a million who doesn't, she just saved herself minutes of work. For that one traveler who has some sort of epiphany right then, perhaps just becomes a Buddhist and renounces all material things right there . . .

"Do you need it?"

"Why, no, I don't need it. Material things are wrong. Thank you for helping me grow."

For that one saved soul, it's well worth answering such a painfully stupid question.

I once lost my tickets on a return trip from Boston with my daughters. I was told I had to get to the ticket counter quite early in order to pay a fine and get new tickets. Once there, I asked the ticket agent what costs the fine is applied to, since the tickets themselves have no value; they just represent the seat on the plane, and their value had not changed whether I had the original ticket or not. She said that the fine was to discourage people from losing their tickets. Isn't that nice of American Airlines to build character on the side? Once you're a member of their frequent-flyer program, you can earn a free flight to Hawaii or a free personal hygiene training with every twenty thousand miles you fly. Maybe she misunderstood. I don't need discouragement from losing airline tickets. No one encouraged me to begin with. I lost them. I didn't deliberately throw them out the car window. Besides, I don't need to pay a fine to be discouraged from losing my tickets. Having to stand in line to talk to this woman would be more than enough of a deterrent.

I kept that to myself so that it didn't lead to another American Airlines Passenger Character Development Moment. So I got our three tickets. She asked if I needed to check any bags and, even though I had flown from Los Angeles to Boston only a couple of days ago with the same bags, which fit handily in the overhead compartment and beneath our seats, I double-checked. I said, "I have four bags, but we have three tickets and each passenger is allowed to carry on two, right?" She said, "You're fine."

Toshia was five years old, and due to cerebral palsy, she walked with a walker back then. At one point everything appeared to be fine.

I had rented a baggage cart for the bags. I could carry them all myself, but it drove my feet through the floor tile. Because we had gotten to the airport early, we were making our way to the gate, but we were in no hurry. I was pushing the baggage cart and pulling the stroller. Alley was toddling, because she's a toddler. I never understood that Frank Sinatra song about Chicago where he calls it a "toddling town." I can see how a two-year-old toddles, but a whole town? Does he mean the buildings? It's no wonder I always get lost in Chicago; you can stop in somewhere for a bite to eat and the neighborhood toddles away.

Anyway, the next thing I know, we were about twenty-five yards from the gate and Alley was on the floor screaming and banging her head. I stared at her with my mouth open for a couple of minutes before I realized she was mine. I recognized her uvula. I grabbed her, put her in the stroller, bent her in the middle with my knee, and, using most of my strength, clasped the seatbelt buckle. The stroller was a little bit padded, but Alley was still banging her head in it anywhere she could, as much as she could. If you saw an animal doing this in the woods, you'd think it humane to shoot it to put it out of its misery and avoid contaminating the rest of the species. I was in a pinch, so I asked Toshia to push the luggage cart. We waited in line at the gate and gave the ticket agent our tickets. I shouldered the bags, took Toshia's hand, and pushed the stroller with the monster in it. We just started down the ramp when the gate agent stopped me and said I needed to check my bags. "No, I don't," I said, although I was seriously considering checking Alley. "Yes, you do," she answered, giving no indication that she noticed the little problem we were having. I said, "I flew here with these same bags and never had to check them." She stepped away and came back with her supervisor, with whom I had the same basic exchange, only now my teeth were clenched.

The worst part of it was knowing that in fifteen minutes or so I'd be in a seat on the plane, listening to this same Good Samaritan over the PA saying, "Thank you for choosing to travel with us today."

Every airplane has a flight attendant who makes that same silly speech into the PA. I always want to say, "Look, Betsy, this airplane is going about where I need to go, around the time I need to get there, for about the amount I can afford to pay. Betsy, I didn't even know you were going to be on this flight."

Just when I thought I was as pissed as I could be, the supervisor said, "Ma'am, we're just trying to help you." They still hadn't acknowledged the record-breaking tantrum that continued at full steam in the stroller. I lost it. I said, "You want to help? You want to help? Then you pick these bags up and haul your ass down that ramp." To my surprise, she did.

I don't generally talk to people like that. Especially people who are going to be serving me drinks. Spit blends right into a soda.

A couple of days later, Wilbur flew for a crowd of one thousand, and the next day he proved to three thousand that they were wrong and he was right. I drool just thinking about it. There's no record of it, but if he didn't yell, "See!" then he wasn't entirely human. To a lesser degree the pogo-stick inventor must have had the same experience.

The Wrights couldn't in good conscience give the military advantage of airplanes to just one country, so they made a deal to sell planes to the United States as well as to France. I don't know why. If everyone is going to use planes, in the interest of fairness, why not just continue to kick the shit out of each other on the ground? It's like cats puffing up. Cats puff up so they can look bigger to an enemy, but they all do it. If two cats puff up in a fight, the ratio is the same. They may as well not puff up. Besides, don't all cats know about puffing up? Can a puffed-up cat really fool another cat?

"Oh my God, that other cat is huge. Retreat. Retreat . . . Hey, wait a minute. Where does his actual skin start?"

While his brother continued to fly in France, including winning a contest for the longest flight of the year, Orville prepared for the official trials of their airplane before the military at Fort Myer, Virginia. Orville blew away crowds of skeptical onlookers as well. There were other engineers with other flyers, but the Wright Brothers' crafts had greater dexterity. When Orville made a half-circle, some reporters even cried. It's a good thing they're dead now. They'd come apart at the sight of a holding pattern.

Wilbur and Orville were now international sensations. The Earl Owensby Studios 3-D sci-fi film that I starred in is a cult classic in England. I was scantily clad in one scene, which they have replicated on the DVD cover with an attractive model in my place. They didn't even do me the courtesy of using my head and her body. You have to have thick skin in this business, and I do, but apparently it's not attractive enough thick skin to be scantily clad on the cover of an Earl Owensby Studios 3-D sci-fi film DVD cover and snag a sale to more than immediate family.

The brothers broke each other's records for flight endurance almost daily. I challenged Thomas E to see if he could go longer without a tantrum than I could without a soda. I never realized how addicted I am to soda. After a day I provoked him. Somebody told me once, as though it was highly significant, that they used soda to clean rust off car bumpers. I said, "Don't worry, I always open a fresh can."

Orville crashed during the official military trials of his plane on September 17, 1908. His passenger died, the plane was ruined, and he was hospitalized with critical injuries, and the military still bought their planes. They must have offered one hell of a rebate. Do car dealers ever really accidentally buy wa-a-ay too many cars? Does advertising their sad lack of business acumen or poor mental health ("insanely" low prices) really attract customers? It seems cruel.

Not long after Wilbur flew an awe-inspiring exhibition flight at the 1909 Hudson-Fulton exhibition in New York, far outperforming the brothers' chief aviation rival, he stopped flying. Orville continued to train pilots. They were stuck dealing with patent infringements and claim jumpers in the end, which isn't what they had hoped for. I've been throwing coins in fountains for years, and I never wished for a cat to pee in our hall corner, myself. I guess we don't entirely chart our own course.

Wilbur Wright died of typhoid fever on May 30, 1912, and Orville died of heart failure on January 30, 1948. I'm glad they died before having to see the day when the airlines began to charge money for the food that nobody wanted when they gave it out for free. Surely that plan will put them back in the black.

We're all in the debt of the Wright Brothers, perhaps Grace Slick more than most, but their work must have left no lives untouched by now. The clergy in airport chapels, for example, that's got to be the lowest possible rung of opportunity in that field. There's nothing but pretzels at their potluck dinners. Were it not for Wilbur and Orville Wright, airport clergy would simply not be in the business.

6

Beethoven: A Brilliant Composer and in Debt to the Tune of a Million

Jim Ross was my best friend when I was growing up. His family lived sideways down the grass hill and across the street from us from when I was two until the end of my fourth-grade year. Jim, his wonderful siblings, and I spent hours upon hours spinning around their living room while pumping the Yellow Pages or a Sears catalog back and forth in front of us to increase the speed of the spin, while accompanied by John Phillip Sousa music on the record player. That is the width and breadth of my knowledge of classical music, and I still get dizzy when I think about it. The study of Beethoven has not come easily to me.

Born in Bonn, Germany, on December 16, 1770, to Maria Magdalena and Johann van Beethoven, Ludwig van Beethoven was one of the greatest composers of all time. Jim Ross was a musical prodigy. He played the French horn in the Boston Symphony and the Boston Pops as a teenager, and went on to become a conductor. I memorized a Burl Ives album when I was young, and proudly sang his song about a goat that ate a guy's shirt off the clothesline whenever my mother asked. When Burl Ives died, the *Enquirer* had an unflattering photograph of him, in the upper corner of the cover, captioned, BURL IVES'S COURAGEOUS LAST WORDS. I think they claimed he muttered something like "I don't care." That's not courage, by the way, it's from "Jimmy Crack Corn." He was out of his head. I was around classical music at the Rosses' house a lot as a kid, but it never quite took. Playing classical music or even talking about it around me is like spelling in front of a toddler. I only know that Ludwig van Beethoven was one of the greatest composers of all time because Schroeder, from the *Peanuts* comic strip, had a plaster bust of him on his toy piano.

Toshia takes piano lessons. She says she likes to play the piano, but she hates to practice. I'm musically illiterate, but that sounds like a hairline distinction to me. That girl can slice and dice a word like a Ronco product. So I tell her, "Then you don't have to practice, honey. Just play. Play for about thirty minutes. And, by the way, play this music the teacher gave you."

At the time of Beethoven's birth, Germany was a part of the Holy Roman Empire. I'm sorry, but I have to kind of gloss over that little detail because I know nothing of it. The word *holy* makes me kind of nervous, being an atheist and all. I'm a friendly atheist. I respect and admire those of different beliefs. I met Sister Helen Prejean at a fundraiser for a terrific group called Death Penalty Focus. She wrote *Dead Man Walking,* and is a wonderful fireball of an activist. She spoke to the crowd at this event just after I did, and for some reason I had mentioned that I was an atheist. When Sister Prejean got to the podium, she said, "Paula, we have to talk." I knew she was kidding and it was funny, but it's not the first time someone has said that to me upon hearing my beliefs, and I think it's notable that you never hear that the other way around. I've never gone up to a member of the clergy and said, "Hey, listen, what the hell have you been thinking?" as though their beliefs had somehow just not been carefully thought out and a little chat with me could set them to rights. We eat Roman Meal bread and then I use the plastic bread bag to pick up my dog's poop, so that word isn't foreign to me. I once saw an older woman walking her dog in Beverly Hills. She was carrying a wad of tissue, which I assumed she was going to use to clean up after her dog, but after the dog pooped, I saw her wipe its butt with the tissue and drop it on the ground. Maybe I'm not really an animal lover. I tried not to judge. Perhaps she lived alone with a working toaster oven, so it took her weeks to free up a bread bag.

Ludwig van Beethoven was the oldest of Maria Magdalena and Johann van Beethoven's three surviving boys of the seven children they had. History has not been kind to Maria and Johann. Maria is remembered as having been rather miserable. One biographer claimed that she didn't often smile. I've only seen one picture of her. I don't imagine there are a lot more in existence, since cell phones didn't yet have cameras on them back then. Although it's true she wasn't smiling in the portrait I saw of her, it's a bit much to conclude that she looked like that all the time. In my seventh-grade school photograph I have a goofy look on my face and big, bulging, uncontrollable hair, but . . . okay, bad example. Still, I haven't come across any evidence that she was unhappy all the time. She did lose four children, of course, but author Nancy Loewen assures young readers, in *Beethoven Profiles in Music,* that "this happened quite often in the eighteenth century, since people didn't know the best ways to feed and care for their infant children." So I still don't see why she'd be remarkably more unhappy than other mothers of the time.

Maybe Mrs. Beethoven looked serious when she first sat down to be painted, and every time she started to smile the portrait painter said, "Hey, go back to how you were."

I don't know how anybody with three kids could sit for a portrait. If my kids weren't hanging off my frock, poking at my snood, pestering me for a junky snack, surely they'd be constantly bonking into the easel and playing in the paint, leaving my portrait with an even more unstable look. Centuries later biographers would write, "Poundstone couldn't maintain a snood on her head and rarely smiled due to her shame over the tic-tac-toe pattern on her cheek."

Biographers such as Brendan January (*Ludwig van Beethoven, Musical Genius*) have made much of Mrs. Beethoven telling their landlord's daughter to remain single. "For what is marriage? A little joy, but then a chain of sorrows." I used to think there was something wrong with me because I never partnered. Now, after hearing so many friends talk about their failed relationships, I realize that both Frau van Beethoven and I are geniuses.

My kids once asked me if some recently divorced friends of ours would be coming to a party we were giving. I explained that whichever parent had their kids that weekend would likely bring them. After they sat quietly taking that in for a minute, Toshia ventured, with great concern, "I hope that never happens to us." I said, "Toshia, I think we're in the clear there. I'm single. It's one of the few perks of having me for a mom. I'm not likely to break up with me." Through it all, my love endures.

Johann van Beethoven is said to have started his son on the piano at the age of four. He also instructed young Beethoven in the clavier and the violin. The clavier, by the way, is a stringed keyboard instrument that I don't think there's a lot of call for at this time. I've never heard of anyone scalping tickets to a kick-ass clavier concert. I think Lurch was the last guy who really made any money at the clavier. Johann Beethoven was a court musician, as was his father before him. I don't think we have court musicians anymore. I didn't hear any when I was there. I think there may be a talent show on Fridays. Anyway, Johann was a court tenor and also a respected music teacher. A number of interviews with Beethoven's contemporaries tell of his father beating him to get him to play the piano. Still, I'd like to know how the interviewer asked the question. Of course, I'm not advocating child-beating. I don't even like classical music that much. However, I do think this tale gets told out of context. People beat their kids for all sorts of reasons back then. They beat them for being improper, impertinent, impudent, and a whole series of other vague transgressions beginning with the troublesome *imp-*. They beat them because God told them to and because the devil himself told them not to. I'm not suggesting that it was a good idea. I'm just stating that this guy, whom history has trounced as cruel, gave the world Beethoven. There's a whole bin of CDs over at Tower Records that would suggest this was a good thing. I'd bet my *Very Brady Christmas* album that there's not one artist on today's Top Ten list who will still be selling over two hundred years from now. Sometimes I hear what's popular now and I think, *Gee, a whack or two might have helped.*

I did think it was cruel of them to play loud Christina Aguilera music to prisoners at Guantanamo Bay to get them to talk. Cruel to the prisoners, and cruel to Christina Aguilera to print it in *Time* magazine. They played Nancy Sinatra really loud at the Branch Davidians to get them to come out in Waco. Who comes up with these ideas? It seems so cruel to the artist. Imagine having your song picked. At least they didn't ask her to perform it live, that would have been really cruel. They should have asked me. People have walked out of my shows before. I tend to go on a long time because of my obsessive-compulsive disorder. It's hard for me to stop talking, so my shows sometimes have a *They Shoot Horses, Don't They?* quality about them. I wouldn't mind if it was for peaceful disarmament. I'm not sure how the Waco plan would have worked, if it did work. A bunch of people illegally stockpiled arms, barricaded themselves in, and refused to come out because they believed their leader was God or Jesus or some sort of heavenly employee of the month, and suddenly they hear, "These boots were made for walkin' . . ." and they come to their senses? I think it's time to cross "play music really loud" off the government interrogation tactic list. If it were an effective technique, Hard Rock Café employees would spill their guts every time they clocked in.

Maybe Beethoven would have gravitated to the piano naturally, but how many of us have wished our parents had made us stick with the piano? I quit just after I mastered "Hot Cross Buns" because I wanted to stay home and watch cartoons. The cartoon series *Wacky Races* came out on DVD last year. If it weren't for the pause button, I wouldn't be able to go pick up the kids at school. I used to see it on TV when I was little, and I have often referred to the lessons I learned from the weekly animated slice-of-life car-race story. No one ever seemed to know what I was talking about.

Beethoven's dad got him a piano teacher early on who also happened to be a drinking buddy of his, and sometimes they came home late at night, awakened young Ludwig, and made him play. If Beethoven had been a rock-and-roll prodigy, it would have been just the thing. Okay, so his father didn't organize his time so well, but I would still point out he got Beethoven out of it, and remember, this was before they had day planners. Santa Claus worked all night and everyone thinks he's great, but a guy has a couple of drinks and trains one of the world's greatest composers in the wee hours, and he's a bad father.

I've never found a job harder than parenting, partly because there are so many self-appointed experts. Even when something goes right, I'm sure I did it wrong. One day seven-year-old Thomas E had a huge tantrum while we walked to school, and eleven-year-old Alley looked at me and said, "He didn't get that way by himself."

I don't think I've ever met someone who didn't know how to raise my kids. My daughter once happened to have a stomping tantrum as we walked by a guy passed out on the sidewalk, who stirred enough to mumble, "Try a positive-reinforcement sticker chart." Interestingly, to be an expert on raising someone else's children, one needn't have had any of one's own. I was required to sit through a foster-parent training with a social worker who informed us that she didn't think parents should turn off the television for their children, but rather she liked to see a home with a small-screen television surrounded by stimulating toys, so that the children might choose something else. Really? My children would crane their necks around Cirque du Soleil to see the stock report on television.

Perhaps it's even worse when someone has a kid or two and uses their example as a template to guide you. There are no other children like my daughter Toshia. There just aren't. She once told Allison that I said I was going to introduce them to Frenchie from the movie *Grease*. Most children, I'm sure, tell tales here and there, but there's not another child on the planet who would even think to fabricate a story surrounding Frenchie from *Grease*. Since it's not true anyway, wouldn't you go with John Travolta or Olivia Newton John? I don't know why I even let my kids watch *Grease*. It's the story of a young girl who loses her virginity on graduation day, turns up in leather with mercilessly teased hair, and goes up in a Ferris wheel while the whole school celebrates. I guess I'm hoping it works as a deterrent. Toshia's afraid of heights, Alley loves animals, and Thomas E has tantrums when his hair sticks up.

I once bought a book of "creative summer activity ideas for children." These included, "Melt an ice cube."

We've done that accidentally before, as in, "Who the fuck left the ice cubes out? Now they're melted," never as a planned activity, though. Gee, where I grew up we used to skate on a frozen pond in the winter. If my parents had been more creative, there'd never have been a dull moment during spring break.

Johann Beethoven is said to have been an alcoholic, though I've seen no record of his having had a bunny. On occasion young Ludwig and his brothers would retrieve their father from a drunken outing, and once Ludwig even intervened between his father and the police to prevent his arrest. Of course, I can't defend the father on this point, but I can't condemn him, either, knowing as I do the devil drink. It's not like there were a lot of places to get help back then. Malibu hadn't been discovered yet. I was lucky. Although I didn't have many friends who knew I had a drinking problem, I was, at that time, able to afford a paid intervention. Several hired and talented actors surprised me with a confrontation in my living room one afternoon while I was cleaning the dusty slats of my venetian blinds. One lady must have forgotten her lines, because she said the only way to really do venetian blinds was a little bit high. There was a really good guy who actually cried. He said he couldn't stand to see me keep hurting myself. It was very moving until he called me Pamela. I recognized him later on *Days of Our Lives*. I'd better not screw up again. I couldn't afford working actors. I'd have to see if any grown child actors might want to drop by and implore me not drink, as a kind of springboard back into the business. Andrea McArdle could pop out of my cleaning closet reprising "Tomorrow," although I'm not sure that would be enough when I've got a taste for a white wine. Or someone from *Eight Is Enough* could caution me that even one is too many.

Beethoven's father would get angry when he caught his son improvising on the piano. He told him he wasn't ready and needed to stick with the music assigned by the teacher. This may have been the elder Beethoven's greatest act of genius. Later in Ludwig van Beethoven's life, friends and socialites would beg him to improvise on the piano privately or for their party guests. Those lucky enough to hear Beethoven improvise bragged about it in the way people today say they once heard Springsteen before anyone knew who he was. How can any parent not give Mr. Beethoven credit for his son becoming brilliant at something he repeatedly told him not to do. I've inadvertently done the same thing with my son and arm farts at the kitchen table, and I insist on full credit for it, no matter where it takes him.

In about 1780, Christian Gottlob Neefe became Beethoven's teacher. I assume his terrible father paid for it. I studied with Mrs. Kopp from pre-piano until about halfway through my mastery of the *Step-by-Step* piano book. A composer, organist, and conductor, Herr Neefe began Beethoven's serious study of composition and became his mentor, helping him get a job with the court orchestra when he was just twelve. I took care of the Bleakneys' turtle while they were out of town when I was very young. They lived down the street from us. They had five kids. Rob was my age, and he used to eat paste when we did art. I don't think he would have gone out looking for it, I don't think he had a problem, but if it was there in the big plastic gallon jug, waiting to adhere two parts of a colorful project, he'd have a fingerful. The Bleakneys had a dog named Happy, and I think they were. Mrs. Kopp didn't hook me up. I was headhunted. It was well known what a good job I did taking care of our dog, Somewhat Depressed.

My older sisters and I went to Mrs. Kopp's home on Saturday mornings. We took our piano lessons one at a time while the other two sat on the couch awaiting theirs. Mrs. Kopp sometimes gave us a hard candy from a glass jar on her coffee table. Once, at the beginning of my lesson, Mrs. Kopp said to me, "Just a moment, I have something special for you," and she stepped out of the room. I looked at my two older sisters sitting oafishly on the couch, having completed their turns, and I felt sorry for them. Clearly Mrs. Kopp recognized my talent, whereas she had to mine for and make the best of what she could unearth of theirs. Where had all of the bullying and teasing gotten them? Vacuous and dull. I'll bet they wished now that they hadn't scratched my face with the jagged seam of the button nose of my Tatters doll. Perhaps, I thought, they even regret laughing so hard when I got a broken-off piece of candy necklace stuck up my nose. These things can happen to great musicians. We're deep. We live life to the fullest. We use all five senses even when eating a candy necklace. I did, I felt sorry for them. My sister Peggy had never said as much, but she threw herself into a rendition of "My Favorite Things," in a way that made it clear she thought she was the forgotten Trapp child. She had a modicum of talent. Might eventually work her way up to page-turner for the church organist, if I put in a word, but it was me who Mrs. Kopp had something special for. Just as I had begun to think I should try to reach out to them, Mrs. Kopp returned with a piece of math paper for me to spit my Root Beer Barrel candy into to save until my lesson was over. That was the "something special" she had for me. That was it. A piece of paper to spit my candy into.

Beethoven was so lucky to have Neefe, who not only taught him, but also helped him produce his first compositions and lobbied to get him funding to go study and make a big splash in Vienna. I have not read of Neefe giving Beethoven anything as special as a piece of math paper to spit his Root Beer Barrel into. If he did, I believe Beethoven would have left it behind, as I did. I would hope Beethoven didn't eat used candy even if he was the one who used it. I know I never have.

It doesn't sound as if Beethoven had the immeasurable benefit of pre-piano class either. That was a series of classes at Mrs. Kopp's where the students marched around the coffee table, jingling bells, clanging triangles, and drumming on Quaker Oats containers, hoping against hope that someday they'd be permitted to touch the piano. Beethoven's dad has never been properly credited with the idea, but clearly pre-piano borrows from his technique for teaching improvisation.

In Bonn, where Beethoven was raised, one had to go to elementary school, although no paperwork remains to say that he did. So much for the permanent record they used to threaten us with. When Alley finished elementary school, one would have thought her reserve unit had been called up. They had a fifth-grade dance and a fifth-grade field trip to the beach, where it actually said on the permission slip that the purpose of the trip was "fifth grade bonding," which seemed a little late, since the trip was two days before the end of the fifth grade. They had a "culmination" ceremony, where they . . . culminated, I guess. They sang a song about how they might never see each other again. I think it was from just before the battle scene in *Les Misérables*. Maybe with the potentially lethal effects of the obesity epidemic, they didn't want to leave any loose ends over the summer. They sold balloons that said CLASS OF 2005, which just made me sad because I had been hoping that Alley and many of her classmates would go on to the sixth grade.

Beethoven wasn't any good at math, which kind of blows a hole in the theory that music helps with mathematical reasoning. I don't know who is in charge of keeping track of educational theories, but they've been out sick a lot. Every year our school principal makes a speech about how children whose parents are involved in the school are the more successful students. However, I read an article in *Time* magazine that disputes this. I don't know who's right, but if it turns out I've been supervising pumpkin bingo unnecessarily, I'm going to be pissed. For a while they said you should play Mozart to your baby for brain development. Some people still believe you can further the baby's brain development in the womb with Mozart music. They don't even start the fifth-grade bonding until the second-to-last day of fifth grade at our school. Can't we wait to enroll the baby in music appreciation until it's finished gestating? I have heard somewhere that the Mozart-music-baby-brain-development theory has been debunked. I'm glad. I listened to my mother's Johnny Cash albums in my developmental years. If Mozart develops the human brain, there's no telling what havoc *Johnny Cash, Mean As Hell* has wrought on it.

I recently saw an article by a doctor who said you're not supposed to clean the wax out of your ears. What happened to the world I used to know? Surely Johnson & Johnson has been desperately trying to keep this under wraps for years. It must have devastated the flexible-swab department. Cotton balls probably absorbed some people, but still there must have been layoffs. They're probably in meetings every day trying to think of other uses for Q-tips. Handi Wipes were so lucky to have 1,001 uses. If it turns out one use wasn't such a good idea, you've still got a thousand good reasons to buy them. Q-tips, though—if you've got a box of Q-tips, you're cleaning your ears. You might be doing one or two other jobs on the side, maybe a creative summer activity for kids, like absorbing a melted ice cube, but there are only so many of those.

In 1787, Maximilian Franz, the elector of Cologne, allowed Beethoven to go to Vienna. Mozart was a huge deal there already, and the hope was that Beethoven would study with him and gain recognition in that musically rich city. When Beethoven played for him, Mozart was impressed. He turned to someone there and said, "Keep your eyes on him; someday he will give the world something to talk about."

When I first went to Los Angeles to "showcase" at the Improv comedy club in Hollywood, many big Hollywood agents and producers said stuff to me like "I love you," and "You're really special." I kept hoping they knew something I didn't. If I had listened more closely, I would have realized that they said that to everyone.

I walked out of the room after performing one night, and Ted Bessell was right in front of me. He didn't realize I was behind him, and I overheard him say to someone, "I liked that girl." Talk about your full circles.

I stopped watching prime-time television when Radar left *M*A*S*H,* but believe me, before that I put in more than my share of the phenomenal number of hours Americans waste watching TV. I don't watch anymore, not because I think it's so bad. It's just that I get so obsessed. *The Dick Van Dyke Show* has almost religious significance for me. In times of sorrow, I draw strength by reading from the book of Mel. Sometimes I'm a bit out of touch without watching television. I once got really drunk at a fundraiser at Larry Hagman's house. I told him I had never seen that show he was on until one night when I was trying to order a drink at a bar and all of the customers as well as the bartender were glued to the television. I looked. It was a scene of a whole group of people writhing on the floor, having been shot. "Oh, Rob!" I exclaimed, and tried again to order a white wine. The bartender shushed me, pointed to the screen, and said, "It's *Dynasty.*" Larry Hagman stared at me as though he was hoping that, given time, I'd make the story relevant to something. Then he said, "I was on *Dallas.*" Why, I've asked myself a thousand times, didn't I quit drinking right that minute? I think, sometimes, that I am addicted to saying the wrong thing.

Beethoven's trip was cut short by the news of his mother's failing health. She contracted tuberculosis, so he had to rush home. If someone gets seriously ill or dies on an airplane, legally the crew must land the plane at the nearest airport. That makes sense if the passenger gets sick, but once they're dead, there's no sense screwing up everyone else's plans and ruining the dead guy's legacy. There's always the overhead compartment.

I've had a cough for couple of years now. I know it's allergies because I haven't deteriorated, and if it were TB, surely I'd be dead by now. My cough is loud and annoying, I'll grant you, but I'm amazed by how many people have turned to me with the rudest voices and said, "Are you sick?" At our school holiday program, a mother sitting beside me heard me cough and said, "Oh no, I'm giving a very important party this weekend. I can't afford to get sick." Well, merry fucking interdenominational holiday season. Whatever happened to "Are you okay?" I hope people didn't scooch down the bleachers from Mrs. Beethoven in her final days. Anyways, she died.

At sixteen, Beethoven took charge of his family. His father's drinking had left him not so useful. Johann lost his job as the court tenor, and young Ludwig arranged with the elector to have his father banished and to provide him a severance, with a portion sent directly to Ludwig to care for his brothers. Since I first read about this, I have carefully locked up the Beethoven biographies I'm studying when I'm not using them. If my kids find out they could have me exiled and get part of my severance, I'll be coughing in a shack near the San Bernardino Greyhound station. It may already be too late. Alley asked me just the other night if we had the elector's phone number. Johann Beethoven talked his son out of following through on the plan. If I could talk my kids out of stuff, I wouldn't have seen two Mary-Kate and Ashley movies.

In the late 1780s, Beethoven's productivity in composition slowed to a creep and he didn't get up a good head of steam again until the early 1790s. Sadly, modern biographers insist on employing armchair psychology to interpret the whys and wherefores of any period of creativity or dry spells. It may well be that his inability to mourn to the satisfaction of some modern-day shrink temporarily stymied his musical voice. It could just as easily be that he didn't have any lined paper during that period. When I thought I could save our living room rug, my lack of productivity was easily measured by how frequently my cats threw up. Cats just don't self-diagnose well.

"That Barbie shoe came right back up again. Maybe I need to go to the vet."

The very day I have the carpets cleaned, the cats vomit all over them. I've long suspected that the carpet-cleaning guy had a hand in it. He's probably got pockets bulging with Barbie shoes that he slips to people's cats after he cleans their carpets. Now I write toward the hope of buying a new rug. Someday my body of work will be interpreted by the Hoover Institute. Beethoven banged out a bunch of stuff between 1789 and 1792. He wrote pieces with names like "Wo064," which explains why classical music fans don't shout out requests. Apparently Beethoven used to save his creativity for the actual tunes and didn't waste it on titles. Most of what he wrote at that time was consistent with the popular styles of the time. Most observers found nothing extraordinary in these early compositions, with the exception of Wo087, which contained elements of Beethoven's original musical voice.

Perhaps he couldn't do much out of the mainstream because of the system of patronage. Like many musicians of the time, Beethoven was supported in part by rich people, so he was obliged to create what they liked. The upper classes could have their own musicians. It was the precursor to the iPod. I'd love to be a patron. Alley wanted an iPod. Even if I could have afforded to get her one, I'm not good with anything computery. I could never program the thing. It'd be easier for me to book the bands.

"Aretha, it's wonderful to have you. I'm such a big fan. You can just set up here on the map rug. Be careful of the Sit n' Spin. If you could just start with *'R-E-S-P-E-C-T,'* I'll be right in here sifting the litter boxes and then I'm gonna jump in the shower and could you do 'The moment I wake up before I put on my makeup . . .'?"

"Van, thanks for coming. I'm just going to do some sit-ups.

Could you jam out 'Domino' for me, man? You can sit in that chair if you want, just push the cat off, or you can sit behind it if you want."

Jackson Browne played "The Wedding March" at Toshia's wedding when she was about nine. She didn't get married, she just had a wedding. One day she told me she wanted to get married. I asked her what it was about marriage she thought she'd enjoy, and she said, "The dress." I explained to her that marriage is a life partnership often including sex and joint decision-making and that, although I share Frau Beethoven's view on the likelihood of that being very much fun at any time, perhaps Toshia wasn't quite ready for marriage. Keep in mind, we had only recently laid to rest the idea that penises popped up in the backyard. A wedding, however, which is what it sounded like she was referring to, we needn't have put off.

We planned a beautiful wedding. Kathy Najimi officiated brilliantly. Jackson Browne played "The Wedding March." We had about fifty guests, a balloon arch, wedding cupcakes, a honeymoon at Baskin-Robbins with a bicycle escort, and we played Ping-Pong for hours afterwards. Thomas E was two. He was the ring bearer, in a little tuxedo and black slipper socks. He wouldn't get out of my arms to walk up the aisle and do his job at first, so I made a path of Chee-tos and he ate his way to the brides. It was the best wedding I've ever been to. There were two brides, so that Toshia could share the fun, excitement, and attention of all of the activities with a friend. Our neighbor friend Katie filled in at the last minute because Toshia's school friend, whom she originally asked, was forbidden to participate by her father. Her mother had previously approved. The father left a really mean message on my machine. Toshia was jilted at nine years old. This father was so stupid, I think he thought it was an actual wedding ceremony. I've never spoken to the guy again because I'm afraid I'll say the wrong thing.

"I wanted them to just live together, too, but they insisted on getting married. She doesn't have to take our last name, you know? She could hyphenate."

"I have something to tell you. Julie Andrews and Christopher Plummer aren't really married. Do you need to sit down?"

I'm not good with the parents at our school. When my son was in preschool he offered a classmate a cookie to show him her private parts. The teacher spoke with him about it. I spoke with him about it. The mother then spoke to me about it in a bit of a twitter. Of course I apologized and told her that I had talked to him. She didn't drop it, though. She said, "You should get him a book about body parts." I couldn't help feeling that, even though such charges against me had been dropped, she was assuming I was training my children to be sex offenders. I think I just nodded my head, but I had to practically hold my lips closed not to say, "Well, I guess that's why Boy Scouts don't sell cookies. Look, you idiot, he's a perfectly healthy, curious little boy who is still in the process of learning manners. We have body books, thank you, but they're not likely to be the solution. We have a book about the Grand Canyon, but I'd still like to go there."

Beethoven was never too good with women. He was a bit of an unkempt slob, and didn't seem to put much stock in the importance of his appearance. When they found Saddam Hussein in that hole, I'll bet there wasn't one leader in the world, whether heinous dictator or democratically elected man of the people, who didn't immediately think, "I've got to put a mirror in my hole." I guess Beethoven was not a classically attractive man either, and keep in mind, this was before those shows where a team of hair, makeup, and wardrobe people could grab someone on the street and tell them they're ugly. They sometimes do give the person a nice suit and a lovely hairdo, but we all know that the day after the TV show, after they shower and put the new clothes in the laundry, they look the same, only now people have told them they were ugly on television. Why is that good television? If you want to hear people being rude to each other, volunteer in a sixth-grade classroom. You don't have to put up with commercials. My friends in the sixth grade used to tell me I looked like Eddie from *The Courtship of Eddie's Father*.

Beethoven had a history of falling in love with women who were already in relationships. I had a brief crush on John Kerry. I didn't have Beethoven's problem; it was before he was with Teresa Heinz. Have you ever noticed that, I assume as a cost-cutting measure, they don't give you ketchup with your fries at McDonald's, but when you ask for some, they give you a truck-load? I auditioned for a Burger King commercial once. It was just a voice-over, and all I had to say was, "Get your burger's worth." I didn't get the job. It's a failure that has haunted me for years. What could I have done wrong? I must have put the emphasis in the wrong place. *Get* your burger's worth? Get *your* burger's worth? Get your *burger's* worth? What could they have wanted?

Beethoven believed himself to have been quite virtuous throughout his life. The judge said I was the best probationer he ever had. Talk about proud. I don't talk about it much, but

Beethoven seemed to find lots of occasions to tell people about the lofty heights of ethical standards to which he had always held himself. Yet many of his contemporaries described him as dark and brooding, and there's a story about him throwing a plate of food at a waiter. I guess he didn't get his burger's *worth*.

I was as good a table busser as I was a probationer, but never a very good waitress. I couldn't stop cleaning and I tended, therefore, to resent the customers because, in my mind, I made the tables all nice and they came in and messed them up. Early one morning at the IHOP, a day-shift waitress grabbed me by my uniform and jacked me up against the wall in the hallway by the ladies' room.

"Have you been rinsing off the syrups?" she hissed, like a Dead End Kid.

"Yeah," I stammered. I thought it was a good thing.

"If you rinse off the syrups, the manager is going to want us all to rinse off the syrups," she said before releasing my crinkled uniform front.

From that day forth I rinsed the syrups on the sly at great personal risk—partly, I now know, because I had raging OCD and couldn't help it, but partly because I knew it was the right thing to do. Beethoven is not the only one who ever strove for the uppermost rung of morality. I couldn't get over Turkey turning down $26 billion to let our planes fly out of there at the beginning of the war with Iraq. I'm antiwar, but for $26 billion they can fly out of my living room. I never knew this before, but apparently my morals cut off at $25 billion.

In the late spring of 1792, composer Franz Joseph Haydn stopped by Bonn, and Beethoven was able to show him a cantata he had written. Haydn had a positive reaction to the piece, and Beethoven had lots of people, including his teacher and the elector, speaking highly of him, so Haydn said he'd take him on as a student in Vienna where he lived.

Beethoven headed for Vienna in early November. It must have been hard to be away at Thanksgiving. I used to get Thanksgiving invitations from people who said, "We're having people who have nowhere to go. Won't you join us?"

Well, that does sound like a group of fascinating conversationalists. Can I come early? I'd like to be the first loser there. Beethoven never went back to Bonn. I don't think one German student from my high school left able to speak one sentence of German. We had a good language department, but German was a bit weak. Years later I saw one of the German teachers working at a tollbooth. He might still be there. He's the one who yells *"Dummkopf!"* if you miss the basket.

Less than two months after Beethoven left Bonn, his father died. Beethoven didn't go back for a funeral or anything. Maybe he didn't feel he got his *burger's* worth from the guy, or maybe, like me, he felt that a funeral would be no help to a dead guy, and just went on about his business. My kids are fascinated by the topic of death. I may, on the other hand, be too dispassionate about it. Alley trotted down the stairs once while I was vacuuming and, happy as a clam, asked me, "Mom, who would you rather die, me or Thomas E?"

"You, why?" I said, and went back to vacuuming. She has seemed so distant since then.

Thomas E once asked me, "Mom, is it true when you die you don't eat anymore?"

He is a boy who enjoys a snack.

"Yes," I explained. "You're dead. Your body doesn't need any more fuel. You rot, the worms eat you. Why?"

He left looking a bit freaked out, reappeared a few minutes later, and asked, "Mom, when I die will you put an apple in my mouth?"

I was so proud of him for choosing a healthy snack in the end. I haven't set much of an example in the healthy diet department. I know that McDonald's is killing our country, but, truth be known, even when I'm eating an orange, I'm hungry for a Sausage McMuffin. Certainly, anytime I've ever eaten an apple, I've been living a lie. The hardest thing about trying to avoid junk food is that there are no real viable substitutes for those foods.

One night after work I had a distinct and specific craving for a McDonald's apple pie, so I stopped by the Golden Arches before heading to my hotel. When the server asked, "May I help you?" I blurted out, "Yes, may I please have an apple pie?"

I was so happy to be so near something my body needed so badly that I was crushed when she said, "I'm sorry, we're all out of apple pies tonight."

I had to rethink everything—my dreams, my desires, my purpose in life, right and wrong, nature versus nurture, paper or plastic. I closed my eyes. My breath came in short, painful gasps. I swayed slightly, and when I could speak I said, "Okay, I'll have a Big Mac."

"Would you like to have an apple pie with that?" she responded.

There must be statistical evidence that shows that suggestive selling rakes in the cash from the handful of people who totally forgot they wanted a large order of fries and a shake with their cheeseburger, enough to offset the remarkable number of customers it pisses off. I am subjected relentlessly to a form of suggestive selling by my son every day.

"Honey, would you like an ice cream?"

"Yeah, can I have a double scoop?"

"I guess."

"Can we get it at Cold Stone?"

"Well, uh, sure. I could get a second job."

"Can I get a Gameboy with it?"

I could take him to an all-you-can-eat buffet and he'd ask if he could have all I can eat. He could teach Ronald McDonald himself a thing or two about suggestive selling. When he was seven years old I told him that I had heard on the news that the workers making the Happy Meal toys in some oppressed country had gone on strike and won an increase to seventeen cents an hour pay for a workweek reduced to ten hours a day for six days a week and the privilege of getting a drink of water without being yelled at. Alarmed, he asked if he could write a letter about this to the president. I was so proud. My son the activist. At seven years old he could not only see the big picture, he could color it without going out of the lines and tape it to the wall. He sat at the kitchen table laboring over that letter, pulling and pushing the pencil up and down the page, with his tongue held tight out the side of his mouth. When he'd completed it, I asked if I could read it. His letter implored President Bush to intervene in this situation, not in the interest of the suffering workers, but because of his very deep concern that if we didn't get this thing straightened out, we could end up without the Happy Meal toys.

The girls and I wrote letters to President Bush about the genocide in Darfur (against). The White House responded with a picture of Bush's dog. I like dogs.

I often wonder if Haydn drew happy faces on Beethoven's work when it was good, then I go back to wiping smudge marks with a damp cloth. Beethoven studied with Haydn for fourteen months. Haydn was supposed to teach him something called counterpoint, which is the music above or below the melody line, only I don't think there is any in "Billy, Don't Be a Hero," which has been stuck in my head since the mid-seventies, when it played a major role in bringing an end to the Vietnam War. A teacher named Johann Schenk looked at some work on counterpoint that Beethoven had submitted to Haydn, and found that it was not marked with the teacher's corrections. It's possible that Haydn had given verbal corrections to Beethoven, or that Beethoven was making intentional counterpoint mistakes to get attention and Haydn was ignoring them to modify his behavior, but even so, it appears Schenk convinced Beethoven that Haydn was skimping on the counterpoint instruction, and, unbeknownst to Haydn, Beethoven began additional instruction with Schenk. I guess this counterpoint concept is not easily transferred.

"And as he started to go, I said, 'Billy, keep your head low-ow-ow.'"

The Beethoven-Haydn relationship was strange, and it's difficult to ascribe motives to their not being honest and straightforward with each other. Haydn wanted Beethoven to give him credit for being his teacher on the title pages of his published music. Although I find that an odd request on

Haydn's part, I can't help feeling a twinge that no one ever asked it of me. My father asked me to change my name. I think it was right after I told him I got the necklace candy stuck up my nose, so he may have had good reason. Still, no one has ever wanted to receive any kind of credit for my work. My high school basketball coach issued me an unmarked jersey.

Beethoven gave Haydn compositions that he had written in Bonn and claimed to have created during this time in Vienna, hit him up for loans, and led him to believe he was getting a smaller stipend from Elector Maximilian Franz than he actually was. Poor Haydn submitted these "new" compositions to the elector with a plea on Beethoven's behalf for him to receive more financial assistance. The elector was pissed. I can't help wondering upon which shelf Beethoven tucked away his high ethical standards while he conned his mentor. It was the kind of thing Eddie Haskell would have advised the Beaver to do. I love *Leave It to Beaver.* I think it's more important to me than it should be. My cat Deacon is named after Richard Deacon, the actor who played Lumpy Rutherford's dad, Fred, and my cat Rutherford is named after said Fred Rutherford, although they're nothing alike. I love old television.

I'm not proud of this, but part of what I loved about night feedings was cradling my soft warm babies while they drank, against the glorious, flickering backdrop of a *Perry Mason* video. One night while one of the babies was sleeping, I looked up to see my cat Annabelle bathing his head. The sound of her little sandpaper tongue scraping through his hair was what alerted me. She was making it all go in the same direction. Naturally, my first instinct was to push the cat away, but then I thought about it. The baby was lying snug and undisturbed, and who knew more about hair, Annabelle with her thick, shiny, Siamese coat, or me with my brittle, faded, dye-job strands that look like unbent paper clips? I left her to it and she did a beautiful job, without the use of smelly creams or sprays.

Later in my exciting life, I happened to be watching the credits roll on *Perry Mason* and discovered, with a thrill, that the hairdresser was Annabelle. Just like that, no last name, just Annabelle, like Cher. I can lose my house, my dignity— everything—but you know what? My cat once did Raymond Burr's hair.

Why did Cher have a fragrance? I have never understood the connection. I'm sure Cher didn't go into the lab and make it.

"What do you think? More musk?"

Did they squeeze her to get it? No wonder they don't sell it anymore. There must have been a limited supply. She was never a heavy woman. Not to single Sonny's widow out for this, because she's certainly not the only spouse of a deceased official who has ever done this, but why did she take his place in Congress? What recommended her to this office? She wouldn't have filled in for him if he died before a Sonny and Cher concert. If your surgeon dies the night before you go under the knife, does his spouse just sub in automatically? I would sooner have had Cher ascend to Congressman Bono's seat of power. At least we know, because of the "Half Breed" song, that she would have brought experience and sensitivity to minority issues.

Haydn took a trip to London and left Beethoven set up to study with Johann Georg Albrechtsberger in 1794. Given that Albrechtsberger was a substitute, I can't help wondering if

Beethoven told him that Haydn always let him read comic books during class and never gave him homework. There is something about having a substitute. Heroin doesn't alter the consciousness of a human being to the degree that having a substitute does. Mother Teresa probably changed her seat when the substitute called the roll:

"Teresa, Mother."

"Hee, hee, hee."

Anyways, Beethoven got his Albrechtsberger's worth and continued study with Antonio Salieri, who was the Imperial Kapellmeister and the director of Vienna's opera house. All of Beethoven's teachers found him stubborn and difficult at times, which may have been the result of his forging his own musical path. I was in complete compliance with Mrs. Kopp, and not one of my pieces has made it to publication.

Mrs. Kopp's son Barry was my high school geometry teacher. Well, not actual geometry, but pre-geometry, where you don't use lines or angles, but you march around the coffee table with a protractor and a straight edge, longing to study geometry. My kids had a cardboard book called *The Book of Shapes*. I looked at it while I cleaned up one night. It was about six pages long. On one page there'd be a picture of a square, and it would say "square," then a page with a circle followed by the word "circle." It got about as sophisticated as "oval." I think that was the climax. I closed the cover and noticed it was co-authored. They just needed each other to bounce ideas off of, I guess. I've often thought that if Harmony Books sues me for taking too long to write this opus, I'd use *The Book of Shapes* in my defense:

"Your Honor, you see here *The Book of Shapes,* Exhibit A. And may I draw Your Honor's attention to the fact that it has two authors? Well, sir, I am only one person. I rest my case."

Beethoven's music divided people in Vienna's musical circles. Some felt that he was moving too far away from the traditions of their beloved Mozart and Haydn, but others with more vision saw Beethoven's greatness and encouraged his creativity. Or perhaps that's only the obvious conclusion, and it wasn't that way at all. Perhaps the people who encouraged Beethoven had the more limited vision, and those who feared his departure from tradition saw into the future all the way to Madonna. Madonna came to a show I did in Chicago a long time ago when they were making *A League of Their Own.* I had been told that she and Penny Marshall would be there, and I was flattered and excited, but when I got offstage and headed for my dressing room, a security guy threw himself in front of me and yelled up the stairs, "Madonna! You want anyone else up there?"

After a moment or two of explaining that I just needed to grab my notebook, my blush, and my bright red lipstick, which I use to organize my thoughts and fool people into believing my cheeks and lips are redder than they actually are, and that I had left them in there because it was my dressing room, because I was telling my little jokes on stage that night and that I would never hurt Madonna, I was allowed in. The theater owner had kindly provided some pizza and beer in honor of Madonna's presence. I'm usually lucky if I can get a soda or two from any place I work, and if there are really devoted fans in the house, they sometimes have cat toys delivered to me backstage. So on this night I knew the pizza and beer were for Madonna, Penny

Marshall, and their entourage, and I was happy to be there and thrilled to be able to tell the woman who played Myrna Turner what a hilarious job she had done. However, I had barely picked up a slice before Madonna and Penny Marshall started honking, birdlike, "I'm bored," to anyone who would listen. Thinking back, I realize I should have offered them a cat toy, but I had no manners.

Prince Karl Lichnowsky and his wife, Princess Christiane, liked Beethoven so much that in 1793 they asked him to live with them. Prince Lichnowsky became Beethoven's patron. The prince and princess were pianists, too, and on Friday nights they had chamber-music jam sessions. These performances before the Lichnowskys' guests gave Beethoven a good deal of exposure as a piano virtuoso among the Viennese. Exposure is very important in the show business. My first television appearance was on *Evening at the Improv.* I did it for the exposure. Surely you remember it. Each show had several stand-up comics, and some celebrities were strategically placed among the live audience at the Hollywood Improv where the show was taped. Jim Backus sat stiffly, with his arms folded at a table a few feet in front of me, the entire time I was on. I made a solemn vow then and there that I would never laugh at a Mr. Magoo cartoon and would never be any part of getting the Howells off the island.

In 1795, Beethoven started churning out the hits, and Prince Lichnowsky helped him publish his Opus 1. I told you exposure was important. Soon after my *Evening at the Improv* appearance, I created my "What if you followed someone around singing a song from *The Sound of Music*?" routine, which will surely be remembered for generations to come.

On March 29, 1795, Beethoven played his first public concert at the Burgtheater in Vienna. He played the B-flat Major Piano Concerto, which was later titled "No. 2." He must have been up all night thinking up that name, but that B-flat Major Piano Concerto moniker had to go. It was wrecking the whole thing. I have always wished I had been at the meeting where they came up with the name of the margarine spread called "I Can't Believe It's Not Butter." Someone at the end of a boardroom table yelled, "I got it! I got it!" and that's what he had. Apparently, "Ew, What Is This Stuff?" got voted down by a narrow margin.

I used to eat tons of margarine. I thought it was the healthy alternative to butter. That's what the margarine people said. Then one night Alley and I were watching *The NewsHour with Jim Lehrer* and the secretary of Health and Human Services said that he was calling on food companies to label their foods with the kinds of fat they contained, so that consumers would have a fighting chance to avoid a man-made fat molecule called a trans fat, which had been identified as one of the villains in the obesity epidemic. I had, until then, never heard of a man-made fat molecule. If I had heard it on Fox News, I would have been sure it was untrue. It sounds ridiculous. Who would invent a fat molecule? Why not create our own learning disability, or an exploding pacifier, and slip that to our children? The news piece next showed shelves in a grocery store and pointed out food products containing the offending molecules. The camera stopped on Oreos. Alley and I looked at each other and screamed, "Fuck, not the Oreos!" Soon they came to the margarine. I practically spit out my margarine-soaked raisin toast. I had honestly believed that margarine was good for you. You know those huge containers of it that you see at the grocery store and say, "Who could ever eat that?" I did. About one a week. It turns out it's heart disease in a tub. I can't get over how a whole industry could be so dishonest. Not one whistle-blower in all of margarine?

Don't you remember the ad where the Native American woman says, "You call it corn. We call it maize"? Wasn't that a margarine ad? She lied to us. They probably didn't even call it maize. She probably just said that so we'd embarrass ourselves at Native American parties.

"Say, fellas, can you pass the maize? . . . The maize."

Beethoven billed himself as Ludwig von Beethoven at the Burgtheater because *von* meant you were royalty and *van* meant you were a maker of overpriced sneakers that weighed heavily on one's feet. I took my kids to the Vans shoe store, having been lured in by an ad that said, "Buy one pair, get half off a second pair." They didn't mention that it wouldn't be half off any shoes that the children chose, or that the prices started from such dizzying heights that even at half off they could devastate a family's finances.

We never seem to get the deal that gets us through the door. We paid more at Payless. The Hour Glass glasses store told us to come back the next day to pick up Toshia's glasses. The optometrist there also wore glasses. They didn't seem to help her. She called my son a girl and then bumped into the desk and the door on the way into the eye examination room. If her glasses were made there, they didn't spend the full hour. She sure didn't go blind reading the customer service manual. When she walked out of the little room she looked at me, pointed to Toshia, and said, "What's wrong with her?"

I almost fell over. I did an involuntary take worthy of Lou Costello, and said, "I'm sorry?"

And she said it again. "What's wrong with her legs?"

I said, "Gee, I've never quite heard it put that way by an adult. She has cerebral palsy, but it doesn't have anything to do with her vision, does it?

"I just like to know," she kind of barked.

Sure, no sense being totally in the dark, I thought. I didn't say it. I didn't even have to hold my lips closed. I just lost heart.

Beethoven had no use for the common people. Had he lived in our time, he might have been a Bush. Barbara von Bush would likely have been in harmony with Ludwig when she explained in an interview that the Houston Astrodome's newest residents, the displaced flood victims from Louisiana, were underprivileged to begin with and were therefore better off. Not being that big a baseball fan, it seemed callous to me. In an effort to restore the family's good name, George W. Bush immediately made a generous donation of his favorite inflatable pool chair, complete with beverage caddy, to yet another lucky family in the flood-ravaged area.

Beethoven really liked the idea of ascending to higher class status, so he kept the *von* deception for as long as he could. I let a kid at basketball camp think my name was Janet. I wasn't trying to change my class, I was just too shy to correct her, and then, once I answered to "Janet," I couldn't say it wasn't my name. I didn't care. I've never been all that attached to Paula. I wasn't used to Janet, though, so my response was often a little delayed. It really frustrated that basketball camp kid. She yelled at me a lot.

"Janet! Janet! . . . Janet! Are you deaf?"

Beethoven began going deaf in 1796. Experts now postulate a variety of diagnoses based on the autopsy report, but there's no agreement on what caused his hearing loss. I think it's worth noting that 1796 was a full 209 years before the dangers of Q-tips became public. Although Beethoven was said to have been a slob and perhaps didn't clean his ears, wouldn't it just have been his dumb luck if it was the one part of personal hygiene he focused on and it made him go deaf? It was a gradual loss. It started out with just a buzzing or ringing off and on in his ears. I couldn't stand that. I was once on a plane a few seats over from a little kid who yelled, "I wanna go bye-bye," over and over again throughout the entire flight from L.A. to New York. I cracked. I heard her mother say the little darling's name was Rio, so I leaned forward somewhere over Ohio and said, "Rio, you're on a big airplane going from L.A. to New York. It doesn't get any more 'bye-bye' than that."

In 1796, Beethoven toured Prague and Berlin. He was away for five months. That sounds insane to me. I go on the road for about eight nights a month, never for more than about four in a row, and that's only partly because I have kids. I once flew home to California from Florida for two hours and then right back to Florida, and that was when I only lived with cats. In the 1980s when I was on the road, the club owners put the comics up in an apartment, and you were often stuck there every day until it was time for the show. It was a bit like working for Stromboli from Pinocchio, except that the apartment had a couch that the comics from the week before had had sex on with the waitresses. I don't remember that in Pinocchio's cage.

Beethoven went over great in Prague and Berlin.

The young composer was often described as unattractive, with a pockmarked face and ungraceful, stocky form. He had no luck with women and never obtained the Kapelmeister job that his grandfather had had and Beethoven had always coveted, but at this relatively early time in his career, his letters and diary entries show that he recognized the greatness of his gift. He called his work his "divine art" and believed that it was what he was here for. I feel the same about vacuuming.

Beethoven once wrote to a music journal that had reviewed him negatively, that they should tell their reviewers "to be more circumspect and intelligent, particularly in regard to the productions of younger composers." He also expressed concern that bad reviews might scare them off. When a composition of his was criticized, he said that someday people would appreciate it. Many biographers have suggested that these comments lacked humility. Easy to say if you're not a genius. I can be brimming with virtuous humility about the "maize" joke. He was right, and he was bucking a tide. Poor Beethoven, just like his dad, who cruelly introduced his son to what became his "divine art," is as damned by modern interpretation if he did, as he would have been if he didn't. I haven't seen Bugs Bunny cartoons set to any of the hits of Beethoven's biographers. Ludwig van Beethoven, on the other hand, has been credited with bringing out the star quality of the violin.

Toshia took violin in the school music program in the fourth grade. I don't think she practiced even once, which has got to be some kind of a record. She carried the violin back and forth to the car at first, but eventually she even lost interest in transporting the instrument. Even my roadie aspirations for her swirled sadly down the drain. Eventually I made her return the violin to the school so that it wouldn't be stolen from my car. It'd be just my luck to be carjacked by a crack addict with a passion for the string section. Then one day when I went to pick her up at school she flew out of the classroom with a huge smile on her face and yelled, "Our concert is tonight!"

I said, "Tosh, you can't play in a concert. You've never even practiced."

"I did today," she responded.

Maybe she used the Suzuki method or something. One practice and the student is an accomplished professional. I was only sorry it was too late to get the relatives in from back East.

Beethoven churned out fugues, variations, symphonies, concertos, and sonatas. Not one song apparently. I may as well confess that I'm a little lost with all of the technical music jargon, although my dog sings when I blow randomly into my harmonica. Beethoven carried a notebook everywhere he went, and jotted down notes, and notes about notes that he developed, sometimes over years. Toshia had to have a three-inch, three-ring binder for the eighth grade. It was on her back-to-school supply list. A three-inch three-ring binder? I assume they were working on a NASA project. Foam tiles were on the list as well. I carry a notebook, too. Beethoven may have dashed off the first combination of notes of the Ninth Symphony as he walked along the Rhine. My notebook has some of my first reflections on Viagra commercials. I think Viagra is a wonderful medical breakthrough. I think it's great that there's something someone can take to restore a part of life that gives them so much pleasure. However, now that we know it's available, could we take the ads off television? They've degenerated. It used to at least be a kind of virile-looking guy talking proudly into the camera. Now they don't even have that. I saw one ad that was just kind of a tired-looking woman in a terry-cloth robe whining, "It works for my husband."

Then there's that funky voice that rattles off, "If you have an erection for more than four hours, call your doctor."

That's gotta be a tough call to make. I'll bet nobody calls at three hours and fifty-nine minutes. I would imagine you'd put that call off until the last possible minute. If we learned anything from the Terry Schiavo case, it's to be prepared. In fact, I heard that even having a living will is inadequate because you can't include every possible scenario that might occur. You're supposed to legally appoint someone to make those decisions if you are unable. And it should be someone who likes you. So, to apply this lesson to the medical miracle Viagra, I think when it's prescribed the user should hide a note in the doctor's office saying something along the lines of, "Help, I've had an erection for more than four hours," so that in that unfortunate event, they don't have the added burden of having to say the words. They can call their doctor and simply say, "Quick, look behind your diploma."

The Ninth Symphony was good, too.

In 1804, Beethoven completed his Third Symphony. He was going to name it after Napoleon because at first he thought he liked Napoleon. Then Napoleon got carried away, crowned himself emperor, and occupied Vienna, so Beethoven named the symphony *Eroica* instead, narrowly escaping naming it after a complex. This symphony marked the beginning of his "heroic" period, which included music that was said to invoke noble emotions on a grand scale. Who knows? I say it's hard to know what was in the mind of the composer without words or pictures. A piece could represent a soldier's quest through fear, tragedy and triumph during warfare, or it could just as easily depict a real estate deal. Here, during the rich melody of the strings, a man drives along and sees a bus bench ad for a real estate agent, here the trill of the flutes tells of his fantasy of finding a little two-bed, two-bath fixer-upper with a detached garage and a sunny kitchen. In come the horns telling him to pull over while he writes the numbers down and wonders why real estate agents put pictures of themselves in their ads. The crescendo could be the climax of a battle, or it could be the clash of the counteroffer, and the sustained, mournful oboe note could be the ebbing of life on the battlefield or it could be the reading of an unfavorable mold report. I heard Don McLean perform "American Pie" once, and he said, "People often ask me what this song means. It means I never have to work again."

Part of the reason I've never been a big classical music fan is that the disc jockeys on the classical music stations whisper. I have to turn the radio up so loud to hear them that when the music comes on it startles me. I did just buy a Beethoven CD, though. I played it at home by myself, and I must say I really enjoyed it. I don't know which pieces were on this particular CD. One started out slow and then went bada bump, bada bump, too doo doo, and then deedle deedle. It was kind of like the beginning of "Boogie Nights." I wonder how full that lyricist's notebook was.

Later I put the Beethoven CD on while I made breakfast for the kids. They each got out of bed and said, "What is this?" More, it sounded like, for clarification, than to put the CD in their wish-list letter to Santa Claus.

I want them to be more cultured than I am, so I told them what people used to tell me: "This is Beethoven. It's classical music. They say the Beatles studied classical music and were influenced by it."

"Nuh-uh," they chorused, which, come to think of it, was my reaction when I was told that. It'd be like telling them there are elements of Shakespeare in *Captain Underpants.*

Beethoven was arrested once when the police mistakenly thought the grubby, unkempt composer wandering around lost in thought was a grubby, unkempt Peeping Tom walking around looking in windows. They let him go after he convinced them that he was Beethoven, which he might have done by humming a fugue and not hearing part of what they said.

When they figured out that he was Beethoven and wasn't a Peeping Tom (or if he was, he was just looking for inspiration), and they could find no anti-grubby-and-unkempt statute in their books, they let him go. The cats ate some of the strings on our venetian blinds, so only one side pulls up. If I forget to lower the shades at night and need to run across the room naked, I just throw a pizza slice over myself, and the rest of my tantalizing form is obscured from view by the lopsided shade and can no longer inspire Beethoven.

Voyeurs used to be a shameful subgroup. Now reality TV has made them advertisers' largest and most sought-after demographic target.

I was once asked to be on *Oprah* to talk about women who

drink at home alone. The producer who called to ask me seemed genuinely surprised that I wasn't flattered. I told her that although I've made quite a name for myself as a drinker and a loser, I'm really a stand-up comic first. She said Oprah might be able to squeeze in a reference to that. What happened to television? It used to feature hugely talented stars behind whom there may have lurked a private problem. Now it features huge problems and the people who tell about them. They'd ask Beethoven to do Oprah's "Unclean Men Who Can't Get Women" show, and they might touch on his connection to the "Boogie Nights" song if there's time after the break.

Opera was important in Vienna's music scene, but Beethoven's first crack at one, *Fidelio,* didn't go over well, which disappointed him. Still, his popularity and productivity in other genres of music continued to grow. He had deals with a few different publishers, and his work was played more and more frequently in public. Beethoven complained that he had become socially isolated at this time because of his hearing loss, but he was also consumed in a legal battle with Artaria & Co., over the publishing rights to his String Quintet in C, Opus 29, and was writing three or four pieces at a time. Three or four pieces at a time? Unless the pieces are all in whole notes, that's a lot of little black dots to fill in. I'm not sure when Beethoven thought he would have had time for parties if he hadn't been going deaf. I'm writing one book, and my three-year-old Rollerblades still have the tags on them.

I can't read more than one book at a time. I don't know how people do that. I'll bet it's a characteristic of people who cheat on their partners. If you're feeling that your mate is distant, you might want to check out how many books are beside their bed. Actually, I take that back, I read aloud to each of my kids individually. So, in fact, I read at least three books at a time. I finally figured out, after years of talking to my kids on the phone when I travel, that I should bring the books I'm reading to them to read over the phone. Phone conversations are hard with little kids, even with my kids, who are quite experienced at it. We miss each other painfully, but you can only say that so many times without making it worse. The conversations would often get quite dull long before we wanted to hang up. From my hotel room there wasn't really that much of interest to bring to the chat.

"I didn't use a bellman today. I'm trying to save money so I don't have to leave you as often to go to work, but of course, then I feel guilty that I didn't use the bellman, who might have a family, too. He said, 'Welcome to the hotel,' really nicely, but I don't think he meant it. Of course, when I do let them take my bags, they put them on a cart, wheel it inside, and another guy takes it up, and now who am I supposed to tip? Do I give a buck to every employee who runs over and touches my bag? I had to run serpentine through the lobby just to get my bags to the room for free. Honey . . . Honey? Are you still on the phone?"

Sometimes they didn't say much about their day to me, because their lives must have seemed dull after I told them about how many little free soaps I got. So I finally figured out that I should read to them. To ease the pain of separation, I have tried to create the illusion for my son that I am available by phone anytime he needs me. I have taught myself never to answer the phone groggily, so that at three in the morning when he can't sleep and he calls to ask me to read, he has no idea that I wasn't waiting right there with the Hardy Boys open to the right page. He puts me on speakerphone. I'm not sure he's always listening. I'm not really sure he's always in the room with the phone. I think he just likes the sound of my voice. He's comforted. I'm flattered. I suspect he's not always listening, because he interrupts to speak on unrelated topics. At 3:00 a.m., during a chase scene with monsters in *The Tiger's Apprentice,* which I really felt I was nailing emotionally, he said, "Mom?"

I said, "What, honey?"

"I bought you a cupcake."

"Well, wasn't that sweet of you. Thank you, my little man."

Then I was back into the book, roaring like a tiger, panting as I read of the young boy's narrow escape. He interrupted again.

"Mom?"

"Yeah, hon."

"Can I eat your cupcake?"

"If you want to you can, sweetie."

"Thanks, Mom, I'll make you a nice healthy salad."

Biographers have made much of a very personal letter Beethoven wrote to his buddy Franz Wegeler, back in Bonn, on June 29, 1801, while he was living in the tiny country town of Heiligenstadt for a brief period, to restore his health. The letter began by saying that he was getting the price he was asking from his several publishers. It sounded as though composing was coming easily to him, and he specifically wrote to Wegeler, "You want to know something about my present situation. Well, on the whole it's not at all bad." He then went on to describe at length his recurring bouts with diarrhea, continued loss of hearing, and general malaise with frequent despair.

I think people have found this letter interesting because it tells us his state of mind during what was a very creative period. I think it tells us how remarkably human he was. I don't know if it's good news or bad news for the rest of us, but, with the exception of his creating 138 opuses, a couple of bushels of WoOs, and more than his share of Hesses, whatever the hell those are, he's the spitting image of us. Later in his life he suffered from liver disease, which doctors say was at least made worse by drinking. I hate to be one of those drinkers who think everyone is in the same boat, but it sure does read like he may have tippled a bit of wine during the crafting of this letter.

I can just see him perched on a stool at a table with a quill and a bottle of wine, cheerily reporting his proud musical successes to his friend and then, by half a bottle down, realizing that, on second thought, life sucks, he doesn't know where to turn, he'll likely poop himself to death, but the good news is he won't hear a bit of it. The letter is in a museum in Germany. I wonder if it's too late to check it for drool and forehead prints. I love the guy for being like me, and I will listen to my CD of his music whenever the kids are out of the house.

I found Alley's fourth-grade journal while fulfilling my need to move a stack of books from one shelf to another. I guess they had to write a bit about their weekend every Monday. Each entry began with a declaration of how boring and uneventful the weekend was, followed by details of going to her friend's house, to the beach, out to dinner, hiking, playing baseball, welcoming friends into our home, visiting Disneyland, and any number of other activities that she clearly enjoyed. She doesn't drink, so she has the process backwards, but like you and me and Beethoven, she is descended from apes that could focus on the dull grind of tomorrow's grooming instead of swinging from the trees.

By October 1802, Beethoven had not exactly yet pulled himself up by his bootstraps—which, again, I appreciate. When I was thirty-two, Beethoven's age at the time, although I occasionally tugged at my elastic waistband—which only caused it to tear farther away from the thick cotton of my cottony briefs, making them wearable for only another six years—I had not yet found my way to taking my bootstraps firmly in hand, either. While still in Heiligenstadt he wrote a letter to his brothers that said he welcomed death, and he included his will. It's now called the Heiligenstadt Testament. In it he asks his brothers to explain to the world that the reason for his unhappy and antisocial demeanor was his deafness, a malady that he had, at that time, kept from public knowledge. Clearly he was aware that he had sometimes been a jerk, and was hoping to be excused. However, Beethoven was known for being moody and intolerant long before he began to lose his hearing. Apparently he was just as pissed off by what he could hear as by what he could not.

On the other hand, in the midst of the tragedy of his failing hearing, he may have forgotten his earlier transgressions. Beethoven lived for creating music, and he hadn't been able to get a foothold in any other part of life. The fear of being unable to pursue his "divine art" must have nearly stopped him in his tracks. When I was being skewered on "fair and balanced" news programs and run ragged from shrink to shrink to shrink to lawyer to court to "higher power" meetings, I used to play the

Cassie song from *A Chorus Line* where she sings, "God, I'm a dancer. A dancer dances," really loud over and over again in my car. Poor Beethoven didn't even have that.

He continued various flirtations with various women, and expressed to friends his desire to marry, but it never happened. When Beethoven died, among his things were love letters that he had written to someone he referred to as "my Immortal Beloved." It was clear that the intended recipient was also in love with him, which seemed to be the key missing element in his prior amorous pursuits. The letters bore no date, and there's no record of anyone named "Immortal Beloved" around there at that time, which has created a mystery that has bedeviled researchers since the discovery of the letters. Anton Felix Schindler, Beethoven's first biographer, who had served as his scribe and right-hand man during his last ten years, decided what year the letters were written and to whom, but a shadow of doubt was later cast on that information when it was discovered that Schindler had fraudulently written stuff into some of Beethoven's "conversation books," in which people wrote to him when he could no longer hear them, and altered facts about his subject. I think it was the comments written in balloon lettering with red ink that said stuff like, "Boy, that Schindler's been doing some excellent scribing today, huh?" and "What's that you say, Herr Beethoven? You get most of your ideas from Anton Felix Schindler?" that gave them a clue that the books had been messed with after Beethoven's death, but it may have been the happy-face stickers on the pages.

Schindler said the "Immortal Beloved" was Giulietta Guicciardi, and a number of biographers share that view, but experts have a variety of theories as to who was the likeliest candidate to have been the mysterious "Immortal Beloved." Some say it was Dorothea von Ertman, some think it might have been Amalie Sebald, or perhaps Josephine Brunsvik. I was in rehab with an elderly drug addict who was certain she herself was the "Immortal Beloved," but I don't think she had thoroughly detoxed yet. When the younger drug addicts played their rap music a bit too loud, shouts of "Is that you, Ludwig?" could be heard coming from her room.

In Lewis Lockwood's book *Beethoven: The Music and the Life*, he carefully lays out research and reason that knock many comers off the list. I read on anxiously, my heart pounding like my dog's when he's after a squirrel, feeling confident that if anybody had finally and definitely solved the mystery of the identity of the "Immortal Beloved," it would be Paul Drake or this Lewis Lockwood guy. His reasoning was sound, his book was thick and way over my head. I knew when I reached page 199 of Mr. Lockwood's book, I would know for certain who "Immortal Beloved" was. I read on, and there it was! Antoine Brentano! And I realized, yeah, probably, and I don't know her, either. Unless it was someone I did know, like Josephine the Plumber or something, it really doesn't enhance the story much for me. I can't believe so many people have spent so much time trying to figure it out. I guess there's stuff we just have to know for no good reason sometimes. How many times have my kids done something they weren't supposed to do and I have made it far worse by insisting that they tell me "why" they did such a thing, only to hear, "Because I wanted to"? It's like Lucy and Charlie Brown with the football, as are so many things. Why do I ask "Why?" I know better. Every bit of my experience and that of my parents and of generations before them tells my brain that the answer to that question will toss me into a boiling pit of deep, empty dissatisfaction, but I cannot stop myself from asking it. I think the next time I hear "I just felt like it," or "because I wanted to," or the devil's own "I don't know, I just did," I'm going to say, "Oh, yeah, well, Antoine Brentano was most likely the 'Immortal Beloved'!"

I like it that no one can say for sure who she was. Whether he intended to do so or not, Beethoven had at least one thing that was not public knowledge. Privacy is a precious and endangered commodity. I saw a piece on the news that said in ten or so years you won't have to tolerate the security lines at the airport because they will already know everything about you when you step into the building. That is a creepy idea. That is a dangerous idea. I'd rather risk being blown up. I don't want to be walking to my gate and have some TSA guy sidle up to me and whisper, "You know, you can have that removed."

In 1813, British troops knocked off Napoleon's troops in Spain, and this was really good news to the Viennese. Not satisfied to just celebrate with the little sausages that come in a can, Beethoven's very good friend, Johann Maelzel, an inventor who crafted the master's ear horns, talked him into writing a little ditty to commemorate the British general's victory. The *Battle Symphony* had one movement called "Wellington's Victory." Maelzel and Beethoven arranged some concerts to present the new symphony and the Seventh Symphony. They were a smashing success. However, during the concert on January 2, 1814, Beethoven tried to conduct and, since he couldn't hear, fell out of sync with the orchestra until Kapellmeister Umlauf stepped in and took over.

Beethoven was hot. Next a few guys from the Imperial Royal Court Orchestra got him to revise his opera *Fidelio,* which the crowd loved when it premiered on May 23, 1814. This time Umlauf had told the orchestra not to pay any attention to Beethoven's conducting, but to follow him—Umlauf— instead. This seems as good a time as any to confess that when we sang "Row, Row, Row Your Boat," as a round in elementary school, I often started with the first group, got lost, and jumped ship into the second group. It feels good just to clear the air. At the same time as Beethoven's music reached great heights of popularity, Beethoven himself began a steady decline. At the premiere of *Fidelio* the crowd applauded wildly, but Beethoven had no idea until Kapellmeister Umlauf nudged him and spun him about. I'm hoping I've received ovations I wasn't aware of.

Sadly, the old note-taker made it easier to be his fan than his friend in the end. As his health deteriorated, he was often convinced that people were trying to cheat him. His friendship with Maelzel dissolved into a legal battle over money, or the rights to his *Battle* Symphony, or something. Other friends complained that they were sick of Beethoven speaking rudely to them. When Thomas E gets mad at me, he sometimes yells, "You bastard!"

I tell him he hasn't written enough successful symphonies to get away with that. His unpredictable rages are troubling, but I don't care about the word *bastard.* Children born out of wedlock are no longer considered pariahs anyway, so can't we take *bastard* off the offensive word list? I think we all know and love some wonderful bastards. I hope the bastards themselves organize to get their word off the list. There's every chance that someday, in the not too distant future, the people of the United States of America will elect a bastard president.

Beethoven's brother, Caspar Carl, died of pneumonia on November 15, 1815. Unfortunately for everyone involved, Caspar Carl had written a will naming Ludwig the guardian of his nine-year-old son, Karl. Just before he died, Caspar Carl amended his will with a codicil stating that he did not want his son taken from the boy's mother, Joanna. He said he wanted them to raise Karl together. Right away, Beethoven went to court to get sole custody of his nephew, and in the years that followed they fought over poor Karl and became more miserable. The court first put Karl with Ludwig, then back with his mother, then back with Ludwig.

The great composer finally got popped for his *von* deception when he tried to go to the court for the nobility and, of course, couldn't prove that he was from nobility. Someone finally told the girl at basketball camp that my name wasn't Janet, so I can appreciate how bad Ludwig van Beethoven must have felt when everyone found out he wasn't Ludwig *von* Beethoven and he had to go to common people's court. I'll bet Dick Van Dyke made *vons* pretend they were *vans*. I'd much rather be a descendant of the guy who danced with the penguins in *Mary Poppins* than of royalty any day.

Beethoven had kind of lived a lie his whole life, because his father had said he was two years younger than he actually was, to make his early talent seem even more remarkable. My parents did the same for me, but they only changed the month.

A friend of mine recently told me that her family had gotten a sad blow when they found out her ninety-four-year-old mother only had six months to live. Of course, it's sad to lose someone you love at any point, but if you're expecting a lot more years out of your ninety-something loved ones, you're probably setting yourself up for a fall. I don't want to seem coldhearted, but scuba gear would probably not be a good birthday gift for your favorite ninety-four-year-old, and lifetime club memberships are not much of a bargain by that point.

Anyways, miserable they were. Karl kept sneaking back to his mother, Beethoven was alternately kind and cruel to Joanna, Karl both threatened and attempted suicide, Beethoven threatened to just plain die. That kind of behavior nowadays would get the composer another *Oprah* offer, if not his own show.

I had a wonderful high school teacher who told me once that he would never kill himself because he was so anxious to find out what happens. I think he thought that there were revelations to come. He had a heart attack and died in his sleep fairly young. As far as I know, he had no revelations. Beethoven seems to have had none. I think there's stuff we'll just never know. I've watched thousands of hours of *Perry Mason* and I still don't know why Della laughs at the end of each episode. Paul, Della, and Perry sit around at the end, rehashing how Perry unraveled the crime. Sometimes the traumatized defendant sits with them. Once the mystery has been explained, someone makes a comment and Della laughs. What is Della laughing at? Why is a pencil eraser so small, and the lead, with which I can make so many mistakes, so long? There's stuff we'll just never know, whether death cruelly snatches us at the early age of ninety-four or whether we languish into antiquity.

Beethoven died a disgusting death. There were days of diarrhea, vomiting, swelling, and draining. He was probably a lot like my cat Scout in the end, without the convenience of clumping litter. Dynise Balcavage actually says, in *Ludwig Van Beethoven: Composer,* that Ludwig's nephew Karl "forgot his own worries and cared for his uncle . . . giving him enemas, and entertaining him." Let all who read this know that when I am on my deathbed, I only want to be entertained. I'm embroidering a sampler of those words to be hung by my bed for the forgetful caregiver. Sanctity of life or no, after reading about Beethoven's death, I'm taking the black capsule if I get diarrhea for more than one day.

His last words were in response to four bottles of wine that got delivered. He said, "Pity, pity too late." If someone brings me wine on my deathbed, I'll say, "No, thank you. I have random drug and alcohol testing tomorrow." The truth is, I don't want a new bunny just before I die.

Beethoven died on March 26, 1827. The great master's last composition was the string quartet in B-flat, op. 130, which shows that, right to the bitter end, he couldn't name a song to save his life.

7

Sitting Bull: A Great Warrior and a
Heck of a Ping-Pong Player

His satiny jet black hair flying loose on one side and bound in a braid on the other, Sitting Bull galloped across the Great Plains leading his band of Hunkpapa warriors. He was a wise man who became the spiritual light of his people, guiding them and giving them hope. In the end, when the American government had taken from the Indians almost everything they could, Sitting Bull gave his life in an effort to protect their religious freedom. My mother used to put one ponytail coming out the side of my head.

Sitting Bull was a Teton Lakota Indian. The Lakota were divided into several tribes, and the tribes were divided into family groups. Sitting Bull belonged to the Icira band of the Hunkpapa tribe. My mother told me we were descendants of two different lines of Indians, including Cherokee, but we've got to be pretty watered down by now. There's no evidence of Native American heritage in my life, except I don't do so well with the firewater, and in one summer's synchronized swimming show at the Sudbury Swim and Tennis Club, we did a routine to the song "Cherokee Nation" by Paul Revere and the Raiders. I think I felt it more than the others. None of us could float, so the coach had us wear tights with Styrofoam shoved down the back of the legs. Our heads kept sinking, but our legs were high atop the water. The kids with good abs could do floating sit-ups. Synchronized swimming is in the Olympics now, but they test for Styrofoam.

I let my kids watch some summer Olympics, because I wanted them to see the positive side of drugs. I thought the athletics were just amazing, but the interviews were less than scintillating. Why would anyone talk to a weightlifter unless they wanted something heavy moved? It's not a great interview. There's not much strategy involved.

"What were you trying to do in that first qualifying round?"

"Lift."

"Fascinating. And in the finals?"

"I lifted."

"Really . . . and did you carry your own luggage from the airport? Not that those weightlifter tank suits could be that heavy . . . Anyway, boy, that's quite a face you made, lifting that thousand-pounder. Did you ever pull a cheek muscle doing that? Okay, let's go back down to the floor and watch the Polish team chalk up."

It's not the fault of the athletes. They've spent their lives developing muscles, not conversational skills, and besides, the interview topics are limiting. I saw the poor woman who won the 400-meter hurdles talking to a toothy, microphone-waggling interviewer. The runner's heart was still visibly jumping in and out of her uniform; she had just won her race and now she was stuck trying to answer such inspiring questions as "What were you thinking?"

We know what she was thinking. She was thinking, "Run!" because anybody thinking anything more creative than that didn't win. The people thinking, "So, this is Greece . . . I thought it'd be more slippery. What a strange name for a country . . . Look at all those people watching. They seem to be looking ahead of me. I wonder what they're looking at. Boy, I'll have to jump higher next time. I almost crashed into that thing. I wish they'd get those out of here. Someone might get hurt." They're not in the winner's circle.

Sitting Bull's father was Returns Again. He got this name because whenever he had finished a battle, he ran back to wreak more havoc on his opponent. I could be called Returns Again because of how many times I get out to the car, realize I forgot something, and have to go back in the house. It's just as well that I had to sell all of my Disney animation cels when I went broke. Almost every square inch of my walls has become covered with behavior charts and reminders:

"Bring ice skates and bathing suits."

"Bring damp cloth."

"Put Band-Aids in glove compartment."

"Sign Alley's water-consumption log for PE."

"Sign permission slip."

"Sign permission slip."

"Sign permission slip."

I've got to be the most permissive parent who ever lived. I've signed a thousand permission slips. I had to sign a permission slip for Alley to go on her fifth-grade camping trip that I had paid for, in installments I could barely afford, for a year.

Permission? Yeah, she not only has permission, she's going no matter what. After I paid for the fifth-grade camping trip, I'd make her go if I had to postpone her surgery. They also sent home a "waiver" I had to sign for her fifth-grade camping trip that said I understood the trip involved some risk, and that if she got hurt or killed I wouldn't be that upset. Done.

Toshia had a field-trip permission slip one time that I told her I wouldn't sign because of some behavior problems she was having, and when I went to the middle school to read to her English class, they told me she was away on the field trip with the science class. She told the teacher who was collecting the permission slips on the bus that I had signed it, but that it accidentally got erased, and the teacher let her on. With that kind of tight security, why even have the permission slip? Why not just let her drive the bus?

"My mom says I can go, and that I can drive the bus if I'm careful . . . A license? Oh, uhm, yeah, I have a license, but I left it in my pants in my bedroom in the White House. My mom said she'd bring it, but she's busy meeting with the cabinet right now, so don't call."

When I talked to Toshia about it, I explained the importance of trust in relationships with friends, teachers, and family, and how the value of that trust can't be traded for anything. I said, "In order to be willing to sell your integrity for a trip on a bus, you must have been going someplace really special, someplace worth jeopardizing your connections to the people you love. Where did you go?"

I swear to you, she looked at me with a straight face and said, "The sewage treatment plant."

I've never made the mistake of thinking I'm good at raising children. I'm just doing it. I love my children and I'll just do my best and not cede a drop of responsibility to anybody else, but prior to hearing her answer I thought I had some general understanding of human behavior. Now I'm not even sure I know what hole the food goes in. Just goes to show you something, doesn't it?

In Alley's sixth-grade PE class, her homework was to keep a log of how much water she drank. She drank a lot. She has the hall passes to show for it, too. She probably missed half of her academic day trotting back and forth to the bathroom, but she got an A in Hydration. I think schools are beginning to panic over the awful health costs of the obesity epidemic, and they're just coming up with wacky ideas. Taco Bell still owns and operates the school lunch program, but middle schoolers have to write down how much water they drank, and get it signed. Given the empty coffers of California public schools, they've decided to just throw water at the problem.

Returns Again changed his own name to Sitting Bull after a bull buffalo talked to him by the fireside one night. Indians were renamed throughout their lives, based on defining experiences or qualities they had. I wish I had known that when I got my cats. I only have ten because I had ten good cat names. If I had had just one cat with ten names, my life would have been a lot more productive. It'd just be me and my oldest cat Urinates Wherever. And the possibilities for name changes for my children and me are without limits.

Returns Again became Sitting Bull, and his son, who eventually became Sitting Bull, started out named Slow. Slow was the fastest runner among the Hunkpapa boys. So Slow was not slow. It's a little like Fuzzy Wuzzy having no hair. He was called Slow because he would slowly deliberate over a decision and then stick to it.

If our family had lived with the Hunkpapas, Toshia would have been named Slow. There would have been a lot of confusion, with more than one Slow. We'd have had to use initials to keep it straight. Toshia would have been Slow P. Slow P. would have made the other Slow look even faster. Slow P. is slow. Part of the reason we don't have a traditional Thanksgiving dinner is that Toshia doesn't finish breakfast in time. She eats her toast into the shape of a turkey that day. She's unbelievable. She tilts her head back with half a cup of milk, works her esophagus up and down for five minutes, and puts a full cup of milk back down on the table. She makes the illusionist David Copperfield look like a birthday party clown.

Sitting Bull told a reporter that somebody told him he had been born on the Missouri River. He didn't remember who told him. Nobody knows exactly when he was born. They say it was likely that his mother, Holy Door, gave birth to him in the 1830s. He was born into a tribe of nomadic warriors. They followed the buffalo, and they fought with about twenty-six different tribes. They fought over land, over horse theft, to show bravery, in endless retaliation, and because they didn't have a good organized sports program. Thomas E's preschool teacher used to tell me that sports were the answer to his terrible tantrum problem. I'd do anything to help Thomas E stop those tantrums. He takes gymnastics three days a week, plus swimming lessons and hockey. It hasn't stopped his tantrums, but now he can have them in water, on ice, and up-side down.

When Slow was a baby, he was carried around in a cradle board, an early Snugli. Now they have such high-tech baby conveyances. You can put the baby in the bucket thing that clicks into the car seat, click it onto the stroller, then attach it to the front of the refrigerator, where the baby can feed from a convenient tube, and then you can put it on some suction cups in the bathtub and hose the baby off. It's possible now to never even touch the baby.

Lakota parents didn't baby-proof the tipi. They thought it was better to let the babies figure stuff out for themselves by getting hurt, instead of having to chase them around, shooing them away from household dangers. They didn't even keep them from the fire. It sounds brilliant, but I think my son Doesn't Get It would have gone up like kindling. Our sliding electric van door is broken, and I have repeatedly told Doesn't Get It not to push the door with his fingers wrapped around the edge. So, naturally, we get out of the van in a parking garage and No Ears wraps his hand around the edge of the door and slides it. I even shouted for him to let go, but the door shut and latched with his thumb in it before I could grab him. It was awful. Driving Me to an Early Grave was screaming with his thumb in the door, and the door was all the way shut. I was afraid that if I pushed the remote-control door opening button, the door would recoil and squish his thumb more before open-ing. I had no choice. He had an entire van on the end of his thumb.

I pushed the button and it opened. Van-on-Thumb was

screaming, "I'm dying!" So I grabbed him up in my arms, yelled to Slow P. and Puts Up With a Lot to hurry, and did a *Kramer vs. Kramer* run through the street, not to a hospital, but to a Mexican restaurant and bar that's always kind of noisy anyway. His thumb was huge. I ran in and asked for a bag of ice and a Shirley Temple. He seemed to recover much sooner than I would've thought, so I wondered how badly he was really hurt. It occurred to me to compare his uninjured thumb with his van-toting thumb. His uninjured thumb was huge, too. I never knew. It's a good thing little Van-on-Thumb never went missing, because his mother, Doesn't Notice Her Kids' Extremities, couldn't have given a detailed description of him. They are seriously fat thumbs. If he gives a movie two thumbs up, it's gotta be a masterpiece, because it takes some effort just to get them up.

Bravery, fortitude, generosity, and wisdom were as important to the Lakota then as showing their navels and having really cool cell phones are to middle-school girls now. The Lakota considered it shameful to have a lot of stuff. It was important to give your stuff away in order to be generous, but of course you had to have had some stuff to do that. Horses, for example, were often given as gifts, but if you already had some and then someone gave you some, it could look bad, so you'd need to give some away. It was a little bit like playing Old Maid, I imagine, trying to pass it and not be caught with it. The Lakota Indians were probably the first people to use the phrase "No, no, I insist."

It reminds me a bit of AA. One of the basic ideas of AA is that, in order to feel better yourself, you must help someone else. I have no argument with the wisdom of that philosophy on some level, but within the confines of a small AA meeting hall, that's a lot of self-serving helpfulness bouncing around like a Superball.

"How are you?"

"No, how are *you*?"

"No, really, how are you?"

"I asked first."

If someone's life doesn't suck right then, how can anyone feel good?

The little kids often went to listen to the camp storyteller, who wove Lakota values into stories and proverbs that he told verbally because bumper stickers pulled out the horses' hair. He used to say stuff like, "A Lakota may lie once, but after that no one will believe him." My daughter Toshia believes that, although that may be true, the first one to get to a million lies receives a valuable prize. We'll find out soon. The storyteller wouldn't have had a shot at a little parable getting through to Toshia. Her middle school has "Character Counts" posters all over the hall walls. Toshia steals them, rolls them up, and smokes them.

Sitting Bull's sister Good Feather learned to do all of the girl jobs, like tanning buffalo hides, putting the tipi up and down, and sewing and cooking. Historians seem to go way out of their way to try to say that the Lakota were not sexist, as if any group back then, other than mermaids, didn't suffer from that. Sitting Bull and his cohorts used to mock the U.S. soldiers by telling them not to bring any women to fight them. Not that I wish women to be pierced with bullets, spears, and arrows. I don't think it's a good idea for anyone, but it's clear that those who did garnered greater honor in history. No one ever went out in a blaze of glory tanning hides. I don't think they ever had a ceremony to honor an outstanding tipi packer, no matter how tightly they rolled it. I wonder if they ever had the tipi almost up before remembering they broke a pole last summer.

Horses were an invaluable part of Native American life. The Spanish conquistadors brought them horses in the 1520s, and the idea of riding them around to fight with each other took off like the hula hoop. Indians were farmers before they had horses, because running after buffalo on foot, yelling, "Come here, I want to eat you," had proven unsuccessful. Horses were also used for toting a family's belongings when they traveled. They dragged stuff on a kind of a litter. Before horses provided this service, dogs did it, but of course, their carrying capacity was smaller, so families had to have less stuff. Horses made Hummels possible. Transportation was greatly improved by horses, but women had to dust more.

We'd live sparsely if we relied on my dog Cal to carry our belongings. He eats my underwear when I'm in the shower. That may be how the Indians ended up with the revealing breechcloth fashion that dangles loosely before their loins. It used to wrap around the whole lower body, but the dogs got to it on moving day. I wonder if there was ever a breechcloth with a drawstring curtain, something a little Frederick's of Hollywood.

When Sitting Bull was Slow, his father taught him all about horses. He had him up on a horse when he was very young, and he could shinny up a horse's leg and mount it by the time he was three. He'd have been a master horseman by the time he was four if the car seat hadn't kept falling off. He had his own horse to care for when he was five, and was given charge of the family horses when he was seven. Yes, but did he know his shapes? When Thomas E was two, he knew the name of every piece of construction equipment there is. Because he was a ward of the court before I had adopted him, he was "tested" at age two to see if he needed some sort of therapeutic service. I sat with him while a lady asked him to put little blocks in a cup and stuff like that. As part of her information gathering, she asked me if he knew his shapes. "I do," I assured her, but she insisted on knowing if he did. I felt like such a bad mother—and this was a couple of years before I really was. I really didn't know if he knew shapes. I understand that they need some common standard to measure development by, so that they can help someone early on if they need it, so I don't think there's anything wrong with the question. It's just that he and I had never talked about shapes. He was barely two and he knew *cherry picker, hobknocker, excavator,* and *stabilizers.* I felt confident that, in a pinch, he'd pick up *square* and *circle.* Besides, maybe I baby him, but if he ever says to me, "Mom, what is that closed figure whose points are all equidistant from its center?" I'll tell him.

The chief benefit of the horse was in battle. The Indians could charge into arrows, gunfire, and cannon fire on horseback. Sometimes they'd hang off the side of the horse at a gallop to shield themselves. My only real knowledge about horses comes from *The Horse in the Gray Flannel Suit,* a Disney movie starring Dean Jones. Kurt Russell's picture is on the spine of the videotape, which is kind of misleading since he is only in it for a little bit. It's a Dean Jones vehicle.

When Alley was around two, she loved cold water. I don't know how I ever learned this, but at the end of her bath or shower she used to beg me to run the cold water on her. She couldn't pronounce "on," so she always said, "hawn," and we used to add a *y* to lots of words. So, at the end of a bath or shower, she'd yell, "Coldy hawn! Coldy hawn!" I took her with me to *The Tonight Show* when I was on with Kurt Russell. My dressing room was right next to his, and when we stepped in and little Alley saw that there was a shower, she started squealing with delight, "Coldy hawn, coldy hawn!" which made me laugh really hard. I've always wondered if Kurt Russell heard us and if he thought we were making fun of his partner. If anybody who knows Kurt Russell reads this book, I'd be grateful if they'd straighten that out with him.

The Lakota were amazing horsemen. Sometimes, when their horses got shot out from under them, they'd just commandeer another and charge that horse into the fray. I don't know how you train an animal to do that. My dog, Full of Cats and Underwear, won't go out when it rains, and when I say "Sit" when we're walking, he crouches because he doesn't like to put his butt on the sidewalk.

Slow was an impressive learner. He often distinguished himself in the games the boys played that were designed to make them good warriors. They learned to shoot arrows with precision, knock one another off horses, deflect arrows with shields, steal horses, and bash in dead skulls with rocks without getting grossed out. I imagine that Sitting Bull Sr. taught his son well, but when I used to watch my son's after-school kindergarten boys' soccer class, I often thought, as I watched them rolling around on top of one another nowhere near a ball, that it'd be easier to teach them to be warriors than to teach them not to. I must tell Thomas E to "be gentle" with people a thousand times a day. I got hurt playing chess with him. How much easier it would be, instead of saying, "Ask your friend nicely to share the toy. No grabbing," to yell, "Take his head off, honey!"

Slow became an excellent buffalo hunter, too, but they're big and easier to find than a small jar of peanut butter at the back of a dark cabinet. The Lakota did that cool thing where, although they ate the buffalo, they thanked it first. Pop-Tarts don't really lend themselves to that kind of spirituality, but I admire it in the Lakota. Slow bagged a buffalo on his first time out. Hunting skills were, of course, important to a man, but in their culture, bravery was what made him a man. They were constantly proving their bravery, admiring one another's bravery, and bragging about their own bravery. Slow belonged to two or three clubs in his youth and adulthood, for which the requirement for membership was just plain being brave. I assume they met with the lights out. That'd weed out an impostor or two, including me.

Toshia was in the knitting club at school for a while. I think she was drummed out for not taking the oath. Stealing horses was considered an extremely brave act, because if you were caught you'd be killed. All of the Plains Indians stole horses from one another. There must have been a certain number of horses that rotated. Time-share horses. It was important to risk being killed because, in addition to the fact that it impressed everybody else, it was a drag to live a long time. A person's body started to fall apart in old age, and their teeth fell out.

I went to a new dentist on my last checkup, and the waiting area was packed with older people. The new-patient form I had to fill out included the question: "Do you want to keep your teeth?" I didn't even have to mull it over. I checked Yes, circled it, highlighted it, left a toothmark in it, and reminded the dentist. I even tied a little floss around his finger. The visit must take a little longer if you want to keep your teeth. You could tell the people who checked No. They were in and out in a jiff, and left with Sugar Daddy candy in their mouths.

When a Lakota boy was approaching manhood, he sought guidance through a vision quest. First a holy man helped the boy purify his body in a sweat lodge for several days while praying to Wakan Tanka, who was the Great Spirit or Great Mystery who created everything. He then went off alone, maybe on a hill somewhere, and sat on a buffalo robe in moccasins and breechcloth, praying, smoking a pipe, fasting, and remaining awake until he had a vision. The vision was private and very personal. It told him who he was and what he was to do. Whatever spoke to him—wind, grass, trees, bugs, animals, anything I guess—would be his protector. It gave him rules for living. No one knows specifically about Slow's vision quest, they just assume he had one, especially because he became a very holy man. He was a Wichasha Wakan, which is a person who got important messages through their dreams.

After his vision quest, Slow kept a satchel of magical belongings that he believed gave him a leg up in seeing the future.

Honestly, I'm just telling you what I've read, while trying really hard not to plagiarize. I don't understand the Hunkpapa religion any better than I do any other. A Jehovah's Witness friend of mine showed me a pamphlet with a picture of all sorts of wild animals and people sitting together peacefully, and told me that this was what life would be like for Jehovah's Witnesses soon, once everyone else got some sort of fires-of-hell comeuppance for not joining up. I looked at the picture. I saw a giant cleaning project. It's a good thing that bears shit in the woods, because it's in the woods. I'd like to pet a lion as much as the next guy, but if there's one thing my life experience has shown me, it's that where there's petting, there's lint lifting, shoveling, sifting, waste disposal, and disinfecting. The Jehovah's Witnesses' vision of the future doesn't seem to address that. Atheists have a glorious vision of the future, which includes never having to deal with waste products again.

I was raised in the Methodist Church. We were regular churchgoers in the early part of my life. I went to Sunday school and Vacation Bible School. I never read the Bible cover to cover, but I've read parts of it and have always thought I gathered the broad strokes, but a few years ago I heard Jim Lehrer say that a box had been found in the Middle East that they believed contained the bones of Jesus' brother, Saint James.

Gee, I had no idea that Jesus even had a brother. He must have been a younger brother, he's not on the Christmas card. Boy, that must've sucked, to be Jesus' younger brother. Who's ever gonna believe Jesus' younger brother? "Mom, Jesus hit me!"

And, of course, if they had the same teachers in school, James couldn't help paling in comparison.

"Mary and Joseph, thank you for coming in. Jesus was always such a wonderful student, but Jimmy . . . does some acting out. Oh, by the way, do thank Jesus for me for the myrrh he brought over on teacher appreciation day."

I haven't read what the Lakota smoked in the pipe during their vision quests, but I imagine what was in the pipe could have had a big impact on the vision. There must also have been at least one guy who sat cold, hungry, and tired on a cliff, smoking a pipe for a few days, who finally faked it:

"Whoa, what a vision! Yessiree, Bob, I had a vision! I had to come down from the cliff just to get away from the noise. The grass was talking, the rocks, the twigs, the wind. My breechcloth wouldn't shut up. It was unbelievable. How long was I up there? A month? Oh, only a moon. Well, I'm starved. What's to eat? Wait, let me use my new powers and guess. Buffalo?"

Young women didn't do vision quests. I guess they didn't feel they needed nature's counsel. What was an eagle going to say to a woman? "Pack the heavy stuff on the bottom."

Lots of animals talked to Slow. This was an important and valued gift he had throughout his life. When he was fifteen, according to *The Lance and the Shield* by Robert M. Utley, he found a wolf impaled by two arrows. "Boy," said the animal, "if you will relieve me, your name shall be great." My cat Smike once got her head stuck in the handle of a shopping bag. I managed to get scissors between her neck and the handle, but before I could squeeze them to cut, she shredded me with her claws and tore off around the house with the bag flopping and the scissors snapping maniacally. I had thought she said my name would be great if I helped her, but apparently I misunderstood.

What she really said was, "Touch me and I'll scratch the shit out of you." She tended to slur her words.

I think I misunderstood what my dog, Mouth Full of Skivvies, said when I met him at the pet store. I realize now that what he said was, "If you're so screwed up that you take me home, you're gonna end up in jail in about a month." I thought he said, "Say, good looking, could you throw me that ball?" I feel so silly now. I have a way with animals, all right. My cat Hep spends most of her day hiding, but she comes to me every night when I lie down to read to Alley. She digs her claws into my neck and meows nervously over Nancy Drew. She is generally quite perceptive. She even answers questions for people on my website, but she doesn't seem to notice a pattern to the Nancy Drew Stories; each one seems to upset her as much as the last. I tell her, "Hepcat, we're only on the twelfth Nancy Drew and there's fifty of them. I think she recovers from this blow to her head as well as she did the other eleven." She also comes out early each morning to watch me tear my hair out while Toshia does exercises and I try to figure out whether or not she's faking on them. Hep loves a mystery.

I was once stalked by an opossum. I used to sleep on the floor just inside the bay window of my single-story house, and late one night I distinctly heard footsteps outside the window. I was frozen with fear. I lay awake all night, scared out of my wits. It happened again the next night, and again the next. During the day I kept going outside to peer through my own windows and see what kind of view someone could have. I even taped paper to the windows. I never wanted to call the cops, because I'd watched too many cop shows when I was a kid where the criminal gets agitated when his helpless female victim calls the cops, and he grabs her from behind as he says, "You called the cops, didn't you?" Remember *Mannix*? That guy sure could run in shiny shoes. His secretary got kidnapped every few episodes. Her name was Peggy. She was African American, which was a big breakthrough for television because it was still awfully white back then. Peggy kept getting kidnapped, though, which I don't think was such a good representation. Private detective Joe Mannix would come back from lunch and Peggy would be missing again. It happened so often that right beside the in-basket on her desk she had a basket labeled RANSOM NOTE HERE. He always had to get her back, because she was one of only two black women on television. Still, by about midseason he seemed to be getting annoyed with her.

"Peggy, you wanna check the peephole before you open the door? And how about you don't order out anymore?" You can't really blame him. He got knocked out with the butt of a pistol every few episodes. He came to on the couch, rubbing his head, with the screen all blurry, so many times he started to get grumpy. I always thought he should have had a protective metal plate installed on the back of his head. Anyway, one night, when I heard footsteps outside my window, I couldn't take it anymore and I called the security company. They watched the front of my house for a while and called me to tell me a giant opossum was running back and forth in front of my window. I'm pretty sure he was peering in as well. You know how they are.

To prepare their sons to be warriors and overcome their fear of dead bodies, the Lakota would drag a dead body or two through camp after a battle and encourage the children to hack them up and smash their skulls with rocks.

On the plane with me the other day was a guy with his wife and little girl, and before we had even begun to taxi, he kept saying to his kid, who had seemed perfectly happy, "Honey, are you afraid to fly up in the plane? If you get scared, Mommy and Daddy will hold your hand. Are you scared?"

I have flown with my kids many times. Unless you tell them, they don't even know if they're up or down. However, if I suggest to them the idea that it's scary, they'll buy it quite willingly. The guy was trying to be extra caring, and he wouldn't stop.

"Is it the wing flaps, honey, are you afraid the wing flaps won't go down? Are you worried about the unlikely event of a water landing? Are you scared that you'll need oxygen and your mask won't come down? Is that it? You know, honey, many children die in their sleep. Why don't you take a little nap? Daddy's here."

Lakota boys used to sneak off in small groups to get experience killing people. It makes graffiti seem out-and-out charitable. I don't mind the act of graffiti as much as I mind the poor quality of it. Some of these guys need writers. I saw "Cindy Stinks" spray-painted on a rock face way up over a freeway once. Was it art? Was it literature? I've thought about it more than I ever thought about *Long Day's Journey into Night,* but still. It must have taken such skill and effort to get up onto that rock face—and that's what they chose to write? "Cindy Stinks?" Cindy must really emit a powerful odor. Of course, if she stinks so badly that we need to be warned about it, wouldn't Cindy's scent give her away without someone risking their life on an overpass to give us a heads-up?

At fourteen, Slow snuck off to join the Hunkpapa warriors'

raid on a band of Crow. His father was among the group, and they had been preparing to go for a couple of days. Fighting required lots of powerful "medicine" in the form of rituals that gave them protection. Their shields were made of buffalo hide and decorated with beads, feathers, and painted symbols. They painted themselves and painted their horses. I understand the idea of it, because I've been using the same mascara before I perform for at least five years. I think the container has been empty for the last three years, but I can't tell my little jokes without running the empty mascara wand across my eyelashes. If I had a horse, I'd do his. The world was full of signs for the Lakota. A warrior could turn back and go home from a battle with no shame because a cricket told him to. Thomas E sure doesn't have a lick of Lakota in him. He doesn't stop doing something even when I grab him by the shoulders, look him right in the eye, and yell, "Stop!" A cricket could never get through to him. I tell Toshia and Thomas E that neither one of them will ever be able to drive a car because the Department of Transportation doesn't put four stop signs before each place you're supposed to stop.

The scouts, who were a day or so ahead, spotted some Crow hunters and signaled. Sitting Bull's warriors got ready. Following the lead of a warrior named Good Voiced Elk, they took cover and waited to take the Crow by surprise. Slow charged out early and the others were forced to follow, because it's hard to conceal a horse painted bright red with a lightning bolt on its butt for very long. The Crow were taken by surprise nonetheless. Slow took off after a Crow with a lame horse, knocked the guy down as he aimed an arrow at him, and shouted with pride in his victory. Another Hunkpapa warrior came over and finished the guy off. Lots and lots of Crow got killed in the ensuing battle, but the Plains Indians never killed all of their opponents. It was partly so that the story of their conquest could be spread by the survivors. And the other reason was . . . I have no idea. They had some funky rules. Scalping was okay and chopping up a victim was okay, but not both. They did believe in an afterlife, although I haven't read where it took place, but whatever shape your body was left in, it was supposed to stay that way for eternity. Which makes killing yourself over a bad haircut seem an even more futile idea. Anyway, at some point in the fight a leader would yell to wrap it up and they'd ride away. There were actually no chiefs in the tribe. Leadership was organic. Anybody could decide to go have a battle, but only a respected warrior with powerful medicine would be followed.

When the war party came back to the village from smacking down the Crow, they were met with celebration and great emotion by their people. The warriors carried scalps to show what a good job they had done. This was still before stickers. Slow's father, Sitting Bull, was tremendously proud of his son. For his first time Slow had done something called "counting coup," which meant tagging a dangerous enemy in battle and getting away without getting hurt. For this he received a coup feather. The big headdresses that one might order from a costume catalog are replicas of those made from a warrior's collected coup feathers. Sitting Bull ended up with thirty. Slow's father additionally celebrated his son's achievement by giving away some horses and presenting Slow with a new horse that he paraded the boy around on in front of the tribe. And that's not all. He gave him a lance, a shield, and the most important gift he could bestow: his name. Slow became Sitting Bull, and Sitting Bull became Jumping Bull. If I ever again encounter the basketball camp girl who thought my name was Janet, I'll tell her that I was temporarily Janet after Janet Leigh bequeathed me her name in honor of a particularly successful shower I once took. When I met Paula Prentiss, we hugged spontaneously based on the closeness we felt from having been in the same crossword puzzle clue so many times.

The new Sitting Bull made quite a name for himself as a warrior. He led the way in battle after battle. He would charge in, yelling that he was Sitting Bull. Probably, with all of the name changes, his victims were grateful for the introduction. It's probably hard to flee your fastest when you have to keep looking back at your assailant, trying to identify him: "I know this guy. Where the hell do I know him from?" His success as a warrior gained him membership to the Kit Fox and Strong Heart clubs. The warriors in Sitting Bull's club were responsible for protecting the camp and managing the hunt. I've always lived in fear of getting confused and confessing that I am an alcoholic at the AAA.

Sitting Bull had five wives altogether. Hunkpapa warriors had lots of wives, because when you divided the women into the men, there was a remainder. Besides which the wives' responsibilities were so burdensome they often asked their husbands to take another. I imagine families with nine wives often begged the husband for gloves, hats, and uniforms, but I have no proof of that. If I served buffalo meat for every meal, I'd need two or three more wives to share the work as well, not to cook and serve, but to get the whiny kids out of my way at the fire while I distributed the slabs. "Buffalo again? We always have buffalo. How come we always have buffalo? I'm starving. I'm not gonna eat buffalo and you can't make me."

Everything I've read about Sitting Bull's life has stressed that the Lakota didn't yell at their kids. It feels, as I'm reading it, that it's directed right at me. The Lakota didn't yell at their kids, Paula. Do you, loser? In fact, I do. I get a little stressed out. I don't know how the Indian mothers remained so patient. Maybe they never spent fifteen minutes trying to figure out which end of the new kitchen trash bag opens so they could sift the kitty-litter boxes. Maybe it's easier for everyone to just know they're gonna have buffalo for dinner.

I am so sick of the "What are we having?" question. Alley, my cooperative child, has the nerve to open the freezer door and stare in after I've already started making dinner. That's like asking to see a menu after you order. Besides, you don't need to look in our freezer to know what's in there. I tell her, "Close that door. You know what's in there. There's only two things. The junk we had last night and the junk you don't like." Little Doesn't Get It hammers me every night with, "Can I have cereal for dinner?" I tell him no, he needs to have the macaroni and cheese with a side of canned peaches that I know how to make. He always asks, "Why?" and I say, "Because, because . . . because . . . don't ask me, shit, I don't know. That's why."

Sitting Bull's first wife, Light Hair, died and he married Snow On Her and Scarlet Woman, but they didn't share nicely and he threw out Snow On Her. I'm sure polygamy has its strong points, but it's got to be a hard match to find. It's like flying to a destination. Every time you connect, you divide in half your chances of getting where you're going on time. It's one thing to find that special someone who likes holding hands, walking in the rain, sharing secrets. It's a bit harder to find another someone special who likes holding the left hand, walking in the rain, and listening to two people whisper.

When I was eighteen I had a crush on a guy who had a suit. He looked so handsome and I didn't know anybody else who owned a suit, and rightly guessed that I wouldn't for a long time. Deep down, I knew a suit was a flimsy basis for a relationship, but he also had a tie. He invited me to his place once. It turned out he was apartment-sitting and had borrowed the suit.

In the sixth grade, Rob Summers "asked me out." That's a phrase we used in the sixth grade, although in the sixth grade we didn't actually go out, as in on a date. It was more of an honorary type thing. In fact, I don't think I was ever even alone with Rob Summers. It wasn't Rob's idea, either. It didn't have to be, I watched *Room 222* and had a lot of modern ideas. I threatened him physically and finally he "asked me out," which consisted of giving me a heavy silver ring with a peace sign on it, which, I just now realized, may have been just to remind me not to hurt him. Scarlet Woman died, and later on Sitting Bull married Four Robes and her sister, Seen by Her Nation, who may have taken that name the day the tipi flaps blew open during her birdbath.

Sitting Bull took a bullet in the foot when he squared off with a Crow chief in a one-on-one fight in 1856. The Crow chief called him out while their two groups of warriors stood facing each other. Sitting Bull ran at the Crow chief. The Crow chief ran at Sitting Bull. They both fired their muskets. Sitting Bull got hit in the foot. The Crow chief got hit in the stomach, and then Sitting Bull stabbed him. The Crow chief died and Sitting Bull limped for the rest of his life.

The success of Sitting Bull in this battle proved a good occasion for a Sun Dance. I love to give parties for any reason. The party is always much the same. We play Ping-Pong, eat, drink, and have an inflatable bouncer—not a guy to throw people out, how effective would an inflatable one be?—but a large, air-filled structure for the children to jump on. The Sun Dance was the holiest of holy Lakota ceremonies. They felt that their bodies were the only thing they had that did not already belong to Wakan Tanka, so they offered the Great Spirit their skin and their blood in this ceremony. The participants had slits cut in their backs and chests by holy men who threaded skewers through the slits, then tied the skewers to heavy buffalo skulls and to a forked cottonwood tree that had been cut down and placed in the center of the ceremony. The Sun Dancers, with their hands and feet painted red and blue, stared into the sun, chanting prayers for the protection of their tribe, and danced. They believed that all good things came through pain. I'm not sure they were wrong, either, I'm just not sure I need good things that badly. How about I just get an occasional cat scratch and I just have medium things? Jack La Lanne kind of had a modified Lakota philosophy.

When I lived in San Francisco and used to stay up all night, I'd try to pay for my sins by watching Joanie Greggains's workout show on TV. At 5:00 a.m. I wasn't committed, though.

Paula Poundstone

During the commercial breaks she told the viewers to keep going and I'd hide behind the television hoping she couldn't see that I was slacking. I've always wanted to have my own radio workout show. I'd be to physical fitness what Edgar Bergen was to ventriloquism. I could implore, "Come on! Kick it out! Homestretch! Be all you can be!" while I sat in a chair tossing back malted milk balls.

Sitting Bull had fifteen children. He raised his sister's boy, One Bull, and spared a boy from an enemy's family that they killed, and raised him as a younger brother. It says a tremendous amount about the depth of the idea that they were supposed to off one another that even the little boy, whose family Sitting Bull's warrior buddies killed, thought Sitting Bull was a pretty good guy for sparing him. If a group of people killed your whole family, I would think you'd be left with a bad taste in your mouth where that group was concerned. I won't drive on the street where my children were in foster care. Killing members of an enemy tribe, however, was so just what you did, that the boy didn't seem to hold it against them. I feel so petty. On the other hand, maybe the Hunkpapas happened to break into the family's tipi just after the parents told the boy he couldn't have a new horse and that he had to share his body paint with his brother, and so the murder of his family and the new living arrangement were a dream come true for him.

I think most days Toshia would seethe with jealousy if she heard that story. She'd spend the rest of her life trying to think of excuses for us to swing by the Hunkpapas and piss them off. "Mom, for my history project we have to steal a Lakota horse . . . and it's due tomorrow." I remember waking my mother on a school morning, just before I went to the bus stop, saying, "Mom, it's the school play today, and I'm supposed to be a carrot. Can you get up and make my costume?"

I know my mother used to hope that someday I would experience some of the frustration she had in raising me. I've been paid back in spades. "Mom, my science project is due today and I need to buy a poster board and I need your spleen and we're out of staples."

"Toshia, it's really hard to get you a poster board at the last minute."

"She just told us today."

I found Toshia's report card in her pants pocket when I was putting the laundry pile in the washing machine, because not only was she not going to show it to me, she was going to ruin a whole load of laundry with it. She had turned a D-minus into a D-plus by putting a vertical line through the minus sign. I wasn't so much upset with her as I was fascinated. I said, "Exactly how different was my reaction going to be to a D-minus?" I showed her how to make a D into a B and asked that, in the future, she aim higher and have a little self-respect.

Sitting Bull's father, Jumping Bull, was killed when a band of Crow attacked them. In the midst of the battle, Jumping Bull, who felt himself aging and didn't want to deteriorate slowly and burden his family, purposely charged after a fierce young fighter so he could die with honor on the battlefield. Some of Sitting Bull's friends killed Jumping Bull's killer in retaliation, and then Sitting Bull chopped him up into little bits and spread him all around, which is another good argument for making sure your wishes for your final arrangements are well known. My parents used to keep their will in the butter compartment in the refrigerator. It used to bum us out when we made toast. The Lakota took some of the Crow women prisoners, and some thought they should kill them to further avenge Jumping Bull's death, but Sitting Bull insisted they be sent home. His compassion toward these women was striking to his fellow tribesmen, but any number of dead enemies must have been yelling, "No fair." Maybe he cheered up when he looked on the bright side and realized Jumping Bull's name was available for use now. Sitting Bull's adopted brother became Jumping Bull.

Lewis and Clark met some Lakota on their expedition between 1804 and 1806 and did not say positive things about them in their report to the President upon their return. They said the Lakota would need to be killed off in order to have a successful expansion. So the expansion began. In fairness to the white people at the time, let me just say that white people need to be spread out. I've lived among them all of my life. Even white people don't like to be that close to white people.

The Lakota had some experience of white people already, from the handful of trading posts that made their way to the Great Plains along the Missouri River. The whites traded iron home improvements like pots, axes, needles, arrowheads and bullets, plus beads and whiskey, for the Lakotas' buffalo hides. The traders were able to make really great deals for themselves when trading whiskey. The more whiskey they traded, the more lopsided the deals became. Blow me away. Some Indians lost sight of their earth's stewardship responsibilities in their efforts to grab more whiskey, slaughtering buffalo to trade instead of living gratefully by the grace of the animal's sacrifice.

One of the greatest shames of my life, and there have been many, is that I got drunk at a big Hollywood fundraiser for the Natural Resources Defense Council and said something positive about Styrofoam. I was shunned immediately. No one from there has ever spoken to me again. I carry extra luggage when I travel, so that I can bring home my recyclables. I make my children bring home their Ziploc baggies from their lunch boxes so I can rinse them for reuse. When I'm low on self-esteem, I peek into my neighbors' trash cans in the alley to assure myself that we have less trash than they do. We visit the recycling center for the sheer joy of it. I wash and dry my aluminum foil, but one night of drunken babbling about the upside of rain-forest depletion and the silver cloud of an oil spill or two, and I'm an untouchable.

During the first half of the 1800s, the settler traffic through the Oregon Trail went from a negligible trickle to a steady stream of covered wagons, boots, bonnets, and Bibles. Sometimes five hundred wagons would plod by Fort Laramie in a day. Lots of the pioneers were looking for gold, and those who weren't were hoping to sell stuff to those who were—frontier freshener, grass-stain remover, bonnet stiffener, "Wagons Ho" T-shirts, and the like. If there was that much traffic, surely one or two people weren't actually headed west, but just hadn't been able to find an exit to turn around. The whites and Native Americans didn't make sense to one another. There were some instances of friendly relations, but generally the whites thought the Indians were dirty savages who stood in the way of some good billboard locations, and the Indians saw the whites as unsightly, disease-carrying, hairy interlopers who scared off the buffalo and therefore threatened their future.

Native Americans didn't have much body hair. I was on *The Tonight Show* with ZZ Top once. It must have been in the mid-1980s, when they were big, thanks to MTV. MTV always gets blamed for people having short attention spans. I don't think that's fair. I think it was the View-Master. So I was on *The Tonight Show* for my first time and ZZ Top were also guests. I wasn't very good, but it was hard to be funny on *The Tonight Show* on one's first time back then. The pressure was so great. It didn't even feel like I was there to entertain, it was more like counting coup. People were often curious about the feather I wore on subsequent shows. Meanwhile, the show itself was no longer the "star-making machine" it had been, and if it was, surely it would have malfunctioned when I used it. I'm not good with machines. I went on *The Tonight Show* and Ellen DeGeneres became an overnight success. I was beside myself with nerves by the time I came off.

For a comic on *The Tonight Show,* sitting on the couch was an enormous deal. Comics didn't get to sit on the couch and talk to Johnny their first time unless Johnny really liked them—or they ran out of time to bring on the next guest. I knew a comic who purposely filibustered once so that they ran out of time for the next guest and he got to sit on the couch and people who didn't know any better thought he got to sit on the couch because Johnny liked him. Johnny figured it out after that, and if they ran out of time with a comic on the show, from then on Johnny would have a crew guy come out and talk about what it was like to work there, or show bloopers or something. I don't even own a couch out of fear I'd never be funny enough to sit on it. I think we were the only guests who were treated that way. The writers got to sit down. The woman who wrote a book about holiday decorating with frog spawn got to sit down, but the comics got a commemorative wave from Johnny.

Needless to say, I told my jokes and got a wave. I came off and changed clothes while ZZ Top played. The show ended as I stepped out of the dressing room. Crew people were wheeling ZZ Top's equipment offstage, and a hairy bearded guy in a hat said, "Nice job." I hadn't watched ZZ Top, but I wanted to be polite, so I said, "You guys were good, too." And the hairy bearded guy said, "No, no, it's me," and began to frantically peel off his mustache. I stared for the longest time, having no idea who "me" was. It turned out it was Carson. When the show came back from a commercial after ZZ Top performed, he had dressed up as a ZZ Top guy as a joke and to make sure there'd be no time for me to go to the couch.

In August 1851 the government invited lots of Great Plains tribes to sign the Treaty of Horse Creek, over near Horse Creek. The treaty required the Indians to corral themselves onto a smaller portion of the map, to stop fighting each other, and to allow the unsightly, disease-carrying, hairy interlopers safe passage on the Oregon Trail. They would receive $50,000 from the government in trade goods each year for a decade. The treaty didn't work. Every time I make a deal with my son, No Frustration Tolerance, about curbing his tantrums, it backfires. If I tell him he can earn points for doing a good job and he doesn't do a good job, he has tantrums over not earning the points. He'll never do well on game shows. I've told him he'd better get used to paying for his own cruises and household appliances.

He gets mad when I count. He'll never be an astronaut. He'd blast off before the spaceship did. I offer him prizes for doing a good job, but he throws tantrums because the prize isn't good enough. I also don't think I bow low enough when I present it. I think getting through breakfast without screaming deserves a punchball or some fake teeth, maybe even a congratulatory pat on the head. He wants a Game Boy. Once I was so whipped I actually said, "All right, if you can go until Friday with no tantrums, I'll get you a Game Boy."

"How many days is that?" he asked.

"Well, today is Monday, then there's Tuesday, Wednesday, Thursday, and Friday. That's five."

Then he yelled, "But we already did those days."

The main subject of the first few years of school is the calendar. Every day they go over that calendar. The teacher says, "Who can tell me what day it is?" And half the class raises their hands. Then she really throws them a curve by asking what day yesterday was. That's their history class. Thomas E doesn't have a clue what day it is, what time it is, or even what season it is. He's a great reader, he's got an inquiring scientific mind, he's excellent at math, and he's a wonderful artist, but he's flunking calendar. He couldn't get discharged from a nursing home right now.

Neither side kept the terms of the treaty. The Lakota couldn't, really. They had a police force of sorts for hunting, but they weren't governed. By this time Sitting Bull was one of several respected leaders, but he couldn't promise the compliance of all of the young warriors in the tribe who sought their manhood in battle, even if he'd wanted to. He was a fierce warrior and people sought his opinion and counsel, but he couldn't tell people what to do.

Some girls in Thomas E's class sought my counsel on the schoolyard once. I was on my way to pick him up and two girls ran up to me and said, "Thomas E's mom, Thomas E is mean to us. He bosses us and he makes fart noises with his armpit while the teacher is talking." I listened with concern and then, speaking slowly, bringing all of my wisdom to bear, I said, "Try living with him."

The United States government couldn't keep the treaty for two reasons. First, Wal-Marts are huge and it wouldn't do to have buffalo blocking the parking, no matter what savages they had promised; and, second, if they kept this treaty, people would expect the U.S. government to keep all of their treaties. It's hard to tell whether a Wal-Mart is a good thing or a bad thing for a community. When they move in, they put a lot of little businesses under, but if they're offering cheaper prices, isn't that a good thing?

I must say Wal-Mart ads make me a bit suspicious, though. They never say, "Hey, we've got school supplies cheap, come buy them." Their ads are always odd testimonials by well-lit employees about how happy they are working there. I saw one with a great-looking guy in a wheelchair, with a blue vest and a name tag, rolling around performing acts of customer service with a big huge smile on his face. The commercial showed him chucking a little kid on the cheek, getting something down from the bottom shelf, and wheeling an old lady's packages out to the parking lot, with products in his hair. At the end his voice comes over his smiling face and says, "Sometimes things happen for a reason."

I find this stomach-turning. Maybe I'm interpreting it wrong, but it sounds to me like they're saying that this guy was disabled so that he could be happy working at the Wal-Mart. O-o-h, so there *is* a grand plan. I went to the Wal-Mart near my house and I asked, "Is the wheelchair guy here today?" They didn't even know what I was talking about. The closest I could come was the woman clerk who rang up my purchases, who was missing a front tooth. She didn't seem too happy, though. It was as though she hadn't yet realized that these things happen for a reason.

The government had built forts all over the plains and loaded them up with soldiers. So, for the next few decades, Native Americans fought with each other the same as always, but they fought the soldiers of the U.S. government for their lives, livelihood, and way of life. The U.S. government continued to show early symptoms of urban sprawl. Although trading posts continued to sell the Indians ammunition, the soldiers had bigger, better, and more. They fought and fought and fought. I could tell you names and dates of battles, but the story is much the same in all of them. The soldiers built more forts. The Indians hated the forts and raided them. The soldiers attacked the Indians. The Indians attacked the wagon trains. The soldiers attacked the Indians. The whole story could be told with hand puppets or a felt board.

Sitting Bull and his Hunkpapa warriors didn't actually mix it up with the soldiers until July 28, 1864, near the Killdeer Mountains, where they fought bravely, but they got routed. One of the Indians who came to fight that day was a disabled guy named Man Who Never Walked. He brought himself on a litter dragged behind a horse that he steered, so that he could be killed honorably in battle. If he could have just hung on another

130 years, he could have been happy at the Wal-Mart. Man
Who Never Walked. That's quite a name, huh? Nowadays he'd
never be called Man Who Never Walked. We view people with
disabilities differently now. Now he'd be called Man Who We
Stare At and Quickly Look Away and Assume He's Courageous.

Toshia and I were once walking my dog Drags Me Down
the Street, and I had just reminded Toshia to lift her leg with
her leg muscles instead of by rocking from side to side, when a
woman coming in the other direction said, "God bless you, I'm
so proud of you," as she walked by. Even Toshia didn't quite
know what to make of it. What did she mean she was proud of
her, never mind the "God bless you"? Proud of what? How does
that lady know whether Toshia is doing a good job or a bad job?
Just because she wears leg braces? How does she know how disabled she is? How does she know that Toshia hadn't just said to
me, "Mom, there's a girl at school who walks all fucked up like
this," and then purposely dragged her feet?

I do believe that it takes a village to raise a child, but that
doesn't mean the uninformed village tinker should just butt in
where not invited. I swear, when people say intrusive, conde-
scending things to Toshia, especially when it undercuts what I
just said to her, I'm going to start turning to her and saying,
"Toshia, honey, if you don't give that little girl back her braces
and get to track practice, I am going to be very upset with you."
A guy in a mall once walked up to Toshia and gave her a dollar.
The other two kids started dragging their feet. Man Who Never
Walked was killed in battle. Sitting Bull's uncle, Four Horns,
was shot in the back in the same battle, and Sitting Bull and
White Bull grabbed him and patched him up.

Although torture does not appear to have been a frequent practice among the Indians of the Great Plains, soldiers and settlers believed they were torturers and struck deals with one another to avoid capture. Thomas E once asked me if I would give his bones to the dog when he dies. It's amazing that there were some Americans who called for peaceful solutions to dealing with the Indians. Newspapers enjoyed selling papers with headlines screaming of "Massacres" and "Murdering Savages." Not surprisingly, there was no balance in the telling of the tale. If CNN had covered the Indian Wars, the Native Americans would have been wiped out.

When CNN covers something live, you can hear the disappointment in the anchor's voice that it's not worse than it is. I happened to have CNN on for company in a hotel room one day when they chose to cover an L.A. car chase. I think we invented the televised car chase here in L.A. We've put in miked toll roads with special camera lighting and makeup mirrors. There's a guy with a boom mike at the turnaround near each tollbooth. Why would a car chase in L.A. be national news? I think I was in Birmingham when I saw it. It would have to cause a hell of a traffic jam for it to make any difference to anyone in Birmingham. The car chase was the dullest thing I've ever seen on a screen, and my junior high home-ec teacher showed us a film about cranberries. The camera followed the cop car following the lawbreaker's car while the CNN anchorperson speculated about what might have been happening—as if the viewers didn't know how to speculate without professional help. They thought there were hostages in the car, so the cops got a hostage negotiator and CNN got him on the phone to bring more color to their informative coverage. It did, too. It made it so relevant that when the car turned east I started yelling, "He's headed this way," down the hotel hallway. The maid dove for cover behind the linens cart.

Unfortunately, as soon as they got the hostage negotiator on the phone, the driver gave himself up quietly. The newswoman sounded like she was at the second house with nobody home while trick-or-treating. She practically snapped her fingers and said, "Aww." There was an awkward moment, and then she made a professional broadcaster recovery by asking the guy what would have happened if the driver hadn't given up.

"Could he have been blown to bits at any point during the show, uh, I mean unfolding news event?"

"That's hard to say. No, I don't think so."

"What, if I may ask, could have been the scope of this tragedy if the car had been full of passengers?"

"Well, of course, we don't want to lose any lives, ma'am, but it is a small car, ma'am."

"Yes, but what if it was full, like a clown car? They can fit a lot of clowns in those little cars."

"Yes, ma'am, well, I have to get back to the station now."

"Right, thank you for being with us. That was the LAPD's chief hostage negotiator, helping us understand today's tragedy, and reminding us how lucky we are to have our nation's clowns safe tonight—or are they? We'll be right back."

I always wondered how a hostage negotiator trains. They have to start somewhere, but do they start right in with a life-and-death situation? You can tell the rookies. They're the guys who yell, "Pretty please," into the bullhorn. Alley's teacher

Ms. Gibson used to keep the whole class after school every day. It was so annoying. Hostage negotiators could train by talking the kids out of Ms. Gibson's class on time.

"Ms. Gibson, I want to help you, but let's get some of those kids out of there. Could we just let the students out who have siblings in other schools? How about that, Ms. Gibson? Let's work together on this, Ms. Gibson."

I've always wanted to be a hostage. My abductor would be so disappointed. I already owe so many people money, no one would pay ransom for me at this point. It's just not cost-effective. I'd love to be videotaped begging for my life. I'd do a lot of retakes.

"Can't we try that again? My hair was sticking up."

I could use a good tape for movie auditions.

The Treaty of Fort Laramie in 1868 was the beginning of the peaceful solution. Unfortunately, even those with the Indians' interests at heart saw quashing their culture and replacing it with "American" culture as the only way to assist them. The government created reservations for the Native Americans, who could now get food and supplies through government offices called "agencies." They offered Sitting Bull's people this great deal on the Great Sioux Reservation. They even left them a territory they could continue to hunt in until they were ready to grow up and be farmers. They invited a bunch of tribes to sign the treaty, or "touch the pen," as they called it. By 1869 most Lakota had gone to the reservation to live like free-range chickens.

Red Cloud, the Oglala chief, became a reservation Indian. He decided that the dominance of the white people was inevitable. He thought it wisest and safest for his family and his people to try to adapt. Sitting Bull insisted he would rather die than live according to the white man's bidding, and continued his raids on their forts. Although a member of the Oglala Lakota tribe, Crazy Horse stayed away from the reservation as well, and became good friends with Sitting Bull. The various bands of Indians that remained free were drawn together by the news of Custer's devastating attack on a band of Cheyenne, which included killing women and children before torching their village.

The Hunkpapa, Blackfeet, Miniconjou, Sans Arc, Oglala, and Cheyenne who still wanted to put up a fight elected Sitting Bull to be their head war chief, which they decided the changing face of their world made necessary. It was a scary time for the newly banded group of Indians, and some even talked of quitting. So, as Stanley Vestal reported in *Sitting Bull: The Champion of the Sioux,* Sitting Bull rode around the camps singing a song he had composed to pump up his warriors.

> *You tribes, what are you saying?*
> *I have been a war chief.*
> *All the same, I'm still living.*

I don't know what tune it was set to, and maybe I'm spoiled, having had "Billy, Don't Be a Hero" stuck in my head for a few years, but I think Sitting Bull was overrated as a lyricist. Maybe there were really good hand gestures.

Not surprisingly, Sitting Bull proved himself a brave leader and an inspiration to his fellow warriors. When his judgment and leadership were challenged by a medicine man during the battle of Arrow Creek against the Seventh Cavalry, he seated himself calmly within the range of Custer's riflemen and slowly smoked a pipe. He invited the other young warriors to join him, and some were brave enough to do so. The bullets continued to fly. Someone's horse even got shot right in front of the smokers. One of the warriors who took Sitting Bull's dare said that the other warriors puffed away quickly, but Sitting Bull looked out-and-out relaxed. It showed up the soldiers and cleared up any lingering doubt there may have been within the medicine man, or any others that he led, as to who was the bravest in battle, and therefore worthiest to lead.

Miss Coonley, my third-grade teacher, used to yell at us from her desk to get to work on our workbooks, and she would point her finger to emphasize what she was saying and then leave the finger pointing and go back to correcting papers. She'd leave her finger there for a really long time. If someone made a noise, it would turn slowly toward them like a weather vane on a mostly still day. It may still be there now. It left quite an impression.

I loved it when Miss Coonley had yard duty. She was a great swing-pusher on the playground. She had powerful upper arms from long hours of pointing. Her push was smooth and she had good follow-through. There are lots of commercials for pharmaceutical products now with an older woman pushing an older man on a swing. Do older gentlemen like that? We've never had to wait our turn for a swing at the park behind an old guy.

"Excuse me, sir, my daughter has been waiting quite a while for the swing. Do you need help getting down? The slide is empty." The entire time they show the older woman pushing the older man, there's a voice talking quite fast, listing the potential side effects of Pharmaphetahoodaneen, but never any mention of why one might take it to begin with. What hideous disease could one be suffering from that makes it worth risking everything this cure could cause? "Could cause hair loss, could cause dry skin, could cause blemishes, could cause memory loss, could cause paralysis, could cause loss of limbs, could cause weightlessness, could cause pregnancy, could cause hallucinations, could cause financial instability. Not recommended for use during a person's lifetime." They say it all so dispassionately, as if any of those things are a reasonable price to pay. They never do testimonial ads with these drugs.

"Thanks to Pharmaphetahoodaneen my skin is smooth and clear, and they say the incontinence will dissipate within a year of the last dosage. For my skin, it's worth it! When I am able to leave the house again, I'll have that peaches-and-cream complexion . . . uh, hold on a minute. I'll be right back. Just the mention of peaches makes my stomach . . . uhm, I gotta go."

"Debilitating depression affects millions of Americans, so why can't I join them for a couple of months while I lose weight thanks to Pharmaphetahoodaneen!"

"Vertigo is a small price to pay for a natural head of hair."

The construction of the railroad had been cutting the Great Plains Indians' grass for quite a while, but the country's financial woes stopped it in its tracks for a time. The Indians may have thought they had scared the railroad companies off, but they were glad to be rid of them for any reason, as they were unaware that future advertising for Good & Plenty candy hinged on a thriving railroad industry. I try not even to think what would have become of the Boxcar Children without it. The United States' economy was suffering badly. Banks closed, un-employment soared, people rioted, and George Bailey wasn't there to save the day. I'm a million dollars in debt now, and it's not that bad. I actually felt lighter when I hit seven-digit debt. If I were $100,000 in debt, I'd be working my ass off right now because I'd have a shot at paying it off, but once you get to a million, you relax into it a bit.

President Grant was sure that gold would revive the econ-omy. I know nothing about economics, but I'm going to guess that a nugget or two wouldn't do my account any harm, either. Custer was sent with 1,200 men to fight, study, map, and mine the Black Hills, which are at the border of what's now South Dakota and Wyoming. He returned with a favorable report about the ease of driving off the Indians to scoop up the gold. The search for the shiny stuff brought swarms of prospectors to make a mess of the Black Hills, which were sacred land on the Great Sioux Reservation established by the Fort Laramie Treaty.

The Lakota killed lots and lots of gold prospectors, who continued to feel that that was a small price to pay to dig for gold. After they'd already let the cat out of the bag about the gold, the army tried to get the prospectors back out of the Black Hills. Not an easy trick, of course. I know because my cat Hep has ear mites. President Grant then tried to buy the property, to avoid bloodshed. The subject divided the Lakota community, but they did not sell, which, of course, annoyed the government. So, the hunting tribes were all required by the government to move onto the reservation by January 31, 1876, or be treated as enemies of the United States. Sitting Bull blew them off.

After a terribly harsh winter, Sitting Bull rallied the remaining free bands to war on the soldiers. Some people, including Red Cloud's son, Jack Red Cloud, even left the reservation to join them. Angry about the white man's abuse of the Black Hills, lots of warriors heeded the call. Sitting Bull had a lot of people counting on his strength, wisdom, and leadership now, so he sought guidance from his spirit-helpers on a hilltop where he prayed, slept, and dreamed. He believed his dream told, symbolically, of the coming of the soldiers. He told his people all about the dream and then held a very dramatic Sun Dance. After fasting, dancing, and remaining awake for a day, he sacrificed his flesh to Wakan Tanka. While he sat on the ground surrounded by his followers, his adopted brother Jumping Bull cut holes in his skin, removing fifty small pieces of flesh from his wrist to his shoulder blade with an awl and a blade, and then did it again on the other side. Sitting Bull bled profusely, but showed no sign of his pain. He prayed and prayed to Wakan Tanka to have mercy on his people.

I've never heard anyone say that someone had good plastic surgery, so why is it such a popular thing to do? Remember that lady who tried to make herself look like a lion? Why would a doctor agree to that? I always wondered if he told her to look at some magazines in the waiting room to get some ideas, forgetting that there were some copies of *Ranger Rick* out there. If he'd had a *Highlights* in his waiting room, she might have ended up looking like Tommy Timbertoes.

Sitting Bull was, of course, temporarily unable to fight, so it was Crazy Horse who commanded the warriors when they took on Brigadier General George Crook and his 1,500 soldiers. The Lakota and Cheyenne warriors rode in with about the same number, and both sides lost about ten men. Poor Jack Red Cloud freaked out when his horse was shot, and he didn't do all of the right brave things. He returned to the reservation with his tail between his legs. It must have felt especially bad, since he went to fight against his father's counsel.

My kids are not carbon copies of me, that's for sure. Alley once asked me to help her study for a science test. I said, "Sure, honey, have you got a test tomorrow?" She said, "No, next week." I said, "What the hell are you doing studying now? The morning of the test isn't good enough? You want to remember it, don't you?" She sure didn't learn that from me or Slow P.

That battle, the Battle of the Rosebud, didn't fit what he had seen in his dream, so Sitting Bull knew that a bigger fight lay ahead. It was the Battle of the Little Bighorn. Colonel George Custer led the Seventh Cavalry in this, the most famous failure in U.S. military history. Just to clear up the record on a less important topic, I didn't work while I was in rehab from late May until December 15, 2001. When circle time was finally over, I went back to work, partly because, like so many of us, I needed food and enjoy a place to live. I also had Pamela's intervention to pony up for. It makes so much sense to me, but I can't tell you how many people, even though it's been years since my unfortunate sabbatical, have come up to me after shows, told me how funny I was, warmly shaken my hand, and told me with a nod and a face full of sympathy that they're glad I'm back. When I thank them and tell them I didn't work only from May until December of 2001 and have been back for years, they withdraw their hands and that look of sympathy fades, as if, unless I'm just now crawling out of the devastation of my personal failure and humiliation, I should have gotten a lot funnier by now. It's like responding, "Then could you return the five bucks you owe me?" when someone tells you their tumor is benign. Although it was the army who came after the Indians, and Sitting Bull just stayed around to shout encouragement, the newspapers blamed Sitting Bull.

Now the soldiers just kept coming. Sitting Bull at one point had someone write a note for him to Colonel Miles, one of the Lakotas' many soldier adversaries, whom the Lakota called "Bear Coat." In his note to Colonel Miles he said straight out, "You scare all the buffalo away. I want to hunt in this place. I want you to turn back from here. If you don't, I will fight you." This was before they had that festive metallic confetti stuff people sometimes put in envelopes. Otherwise Colonel Miles would have torn open the missive and colorful little bow-and-arrow shapes would have fallen out all over the plains, maybe even a little scalp shape. Have you ever gotten mail with that annoying junk in there? It has no real function and it spills all over the place. I've opened invitations only to have the rug showered with metallic confetti, and then I couldn't possibly go to the party because I have to stay home and vacuum. I'd rather get a bill.

More and more soldiers were sent to deal with the "hostile" Indians and avenge Custer. They burned lodges and killed women and children. More and more Indians made reservations on the reservation. The large band of Indians that had joined together was forced to break up.

The Lakota crossed the border into Canada. The Canadian Mounties were willing to keep the U.S. soldiers away from

Sitting Bull and his fellow exiles, but only on the condition that they obey Canadian law, which meant no stealing and no fighting. Sitting Bull agreed. He dealt directly with Major James Morrow Walsh, who had an honest, straightforward approach that Sitting Bull liked. Why are Canadians always so much nicer than Americans? We're only across a border from each other. We see mostly the same violent movies and television, but they don't have a fraction of the gun crimes we have. They even cross the street more safely. How do they do it? They should be great role models, yet even though they're our closest neighbors, we know nothing about them.

I was nineteen or twenty the first time I went to Canada. I took a Greyhound bus trip to see what comedy clubs were like in other cities. I don't think I had ever even heard of customs at that time, so the idea that I would need government-issued work papers just to audition in a club had certainly never occurred to me. I used to wear a red satin baseball jacket over a faded red hooded sweatshirt, over a brown sweater, over a T-shirt, over a turtleneck. I carefully selected the T-shirt from an assortment of T-shirts each day, so I could look my very best. I wore street shoes and carried a yellow backpack with Double Stuf Oreos and a notebook inside, and my sneakers dangling by their laces from a strap. So, when the bus stopped at the Canadian customs office, I went in with everyone else, and I don't know what box I checked on my form, but I got taken into a room and interrogated by the only angry Canadian I've ever seen. He was likely an immigrant. I tried to explain what a comedy club was, and he kept shouting at me that I was a stripper and that if I tried to work in Canada I would be deported.

One thing we now know about Canadians for sure is that they have no standards at all when it comes to their strippers. I could have stripped for hours and never gotten down to skin.

Years later, once my stripping career had gotten up a head of steam, I was working in Canada and I read a newspaper article about a guy there who shot someone who laughed at him when he was singing in a karaoke bar. We have probably had hundreds of those incidents in the United States, it's just that they are so ordinary, one might not even make the paper, unless it was a music trade paper that specifically covered karaoke shootings, and even then it wouldn't have stood out unless it was the cover story on the "easy listening shooting" page. A shooting during a Carpenters song might draw some interest owing to the cruel irony of being blown away during "We've Only Just Begun."

In Canada, for whatever freaky reason, they don't shoot at each other the way we do. They don't tote guns casually. So this guy must have actually thought it through before he left the house. He came home from work, looking forward to a night at the karaoke bar. He quickly showered and changed to evening wear, double-checked that he had some cash and ID in his pocket so he could drink, and then thought, "I haven't been hitting those high notes so good lately, maybe I should pack some heat," grabbed his gun, and headed out.

Sitting Bull and his Lakota were suffering dismally. Under pressure from the American government, the Canadian government began to sour on the exiles. Buffalo became sparse, and disease and starvation crippled the spirits of the once-proud tribe. Even the horses got skinny. In 1880 many of Sitting Bull's closest allies headed for the hated U.S. Indian agencies and life on the reservation, including Jumping Bull.

Sitting Bull's wife had twins in 1880, which added to his burden during this increasingly lean time. So, on July 12, 1881, Sitting Bull and 187 of his people headed out to turn themselves in. A week later they shuffled into Fort Buford, dusty, tired, ragged, and hungry. Sitting Bull had a bandage around his head, obscuring his eyes, which were badly infected. I pass a 3 Day Blinds store on my way to the airport. I used to misread it as the 3 Days Blind store, and I always wondered who would pay for that.

Life on the reservation was demeaning for Sitting Bull. Most of his people still treated him as their chief, but some had been lured away; some even policed for the agency, and the government was anxious to undermine his influence upon those who still supported him. They moved him from agency to agency, kept him under guard during a two-year imprisonment at Fort Randall, then finally moved him back to the Standing Rock agency, supervised by the Bureau of Indian Affairs in the Department of the Interior.

The end of Sitting Bull's life was just plain weird. He was allowed, under the careful supervision of his captor and nemesis, Major James McLaughlin, to perform for a season with Buffalo Bill Cody's Wild West Show, which included a reenactment of Custer's Last Stand. He was paraded around a lot. Most people found him charming, and then he went back to being a public enemy.

I'm starting to feel the anxiety of ending this book. I've never been a good closer. I just don't end well. I might just leave a couple of blank pages and you can conclude things for yourself. I think, if I ever write a daily reflections book, page one will say, "Don't reflect too much," and page two will suggest, "Skip day three."

Don't you find that the happier the kid looks on the box, the more disappointing is the toy inside? Back at Standing Rock, the powers that be were intent on "Americanizing" their captive savages. Many of the children were put in suits and sent to Indian school, whose number-one course of study appears to have been Becoming White People 101.

When they tried to coerce the Indians to sign a treaty giving up more land, Sitting Bull fought against it. Interestingly, however, the last battle of his life was over religion. Missionaries frequently descended upon the Indians with the persistent belief that freedom of religion meant freedom to practice the religion of the missionaries. I saw a billboard in Oregon once that said THE WAGES OF SIN ARE DEATH, but of course, with taxes taken out it'd just be kind of a tired feeling. I hate the new trend of clever sayings on the signboards outside churches. They used to bear quotes from the scriptures, but now the source is often unclear. I've seen stuff like GOD WANTS YOU TO WATCH THE GAME WITH HIM THIS SUNDAY and HAVE YOU PRAYED TODAY? JESUS WANTS TO KNOW "WHA'Z UP?"

A guy named Kicking Bear introduced the Ghost Dance religion to the Lakota. It's based on what the Great Spirit told a medicine man, Wakova, when, during a high fever, his spirit left his body and went somewhere beyond the stars, where he saw the dead ancestors looking good. When Wakova woke up, he told everyone the good news about what awaited them. The only catch was, the believers had to dance. This ray of hope for the Indian spread like smallpox. As luck would have it, the Great Spirit also threw the "Ghost Shirt" into the bargain. To the casual observer, it's just a white shirt with a lot of decorations on it, but the newly converted Ghost Dancers, desperate as they were, accepted the belief that the Ghost Shirt was magically impenetrable by bullets. So they danced.

Some ballet school in Santa Monica used to have a program in which, during one school day each week, they gave all of the third graders at our school a dance class. It was called "Dance for All." At the end of the program they had a presentation for the parents. Of course, at the end of the presentation, the teacher approached the parents of the children who seemed to have a "special talent" and signed them up for pricey ballet classes. I was one of a handful of parents there. It started out pretty well. The kids all sat in a circle, stretching with the teacher, and she talked about the importance of good posture. I sat up tall. She had taught them the names of some muscle groups, so she quizzed them verbally and they only giggled briefly over gluteus maximus. They did a couple of little dances. So far, so good. Then the teacher, Ms. Gluteus Maximus, I think her name was, said they were going to do the "friendship dance" where they all hold hands and sidestep in a circle, but first . . . she asked Toshia to take her place. Toshia proudly loped into the middle on her crutches and stood there. The wide circle of children gathered around her, the music started, and they sidestepped. I raised my hand really high and shouted that I had a question. Somewhere Miss Coonley's finger probably turned toward me. When the music stopped and the

teacher called on me, I said, "Why isn't Toshia part of the dance? She can sidestep." With a big phony smile, the teacher explained, "Toshia is a very important part of the dance. She shows us where the center is!" I stood up, took a chair, placed it in the center, and walked Toshia to a place in the circle, where she performed brilliantly. Nureyev never did such a sidestep. If the class had been called "Dance for Everyone but Toshia," I would have sat quietly and taken my lumps, but how dare they call it "Dance for All" and leave someone out?

Apparently just picking the name of a dance class is somewhat challenging. Alley used to take a jazz dance class taught by a woman from the Middle East. A lot of the girls in the class had Middle Eastern backgrounds, which was great, but when I went to the recital they had elaborate costumes with veils and kept doing belly dances. Don't get me wrong, I've nothing against belly dances. It's just that it wasn't jazz. It's as if you went to hear an evening of Beethoven at the symphony and they only played Helen Reddy hits. I love Helen Reddy. I still get a chill from the lyrics "Living in a world of make-believe—well, maybe . . ." from "Angie Baby," but, if you had bought the ticket expecting to hear Beethoven, it could be jarring, that's all.

So the Lakota danced the Ghost Dance and they danced the Ghost Dance and they danced the Ghost Dance. Sitting Bull did not dance, but he encouraged others to do so, and it made the Indian Affairs people very nervous. They supposedly had some boneheaded idea that the Lakota were dancing to prepare for a rebellion. They wanted Sitting Bull to put a stop to it, and when he wouldn't, his detractors convinced people in Washington, D.C., that he was a negative force among his

beloved Lakota. The missionaries had made no headway, and the American government thought what it always thinks but never says, which is, "If they'd just settle down and be Christians, everything would be so lovely."

Boy, they're at it again in Kansas, insisting on teaching "intelligent design," aka the biblical story of creation, in public schools. Now that they've finally swept that pesky separation-of-church-and-state thing out of the way, they can really beef up our science programs. Next they'll have a science class where students don't actually study science at all, but rather the science teacher ties each student into a burlap sack and throws him or her into a pool and the students that God thinks are good science students float to the top and get an A, and for the really poor science students who sink and drown, God's hands are tied. It's called "intelligent flotationism."

Toshia had a history test on the Constitution, and when I pointed out to her that she needed to actually read it, she balked and said, "There's a lot of shit in there."

"Yeah," I said, "and some of it's some pretty good shit. We just haven't achieved it all yet."

I was explaining to Alley one day that, as atheists, we welcome learning about many different religions because it helps us understand the world, but that our beliefs are as valuable as anybody else's and that teaching religion in public school is not something that we would want. I explained that we respect other people's beliefs and that, for a lot of people, religion helps them organize their lives and know what to do. "People often get to an age where they are plagued by the question 'Why am I here?'" I said, and she replied, "You're here to make people

laugh." I said, "Thank you, honey, but I think you're forgetting about cleaning up the cat vomit, wiping off the door handles, and my invaluable work with the crevice tool." Oh yes, my death will leave a gaping hole.

They made a plan to arrest Sitting Bull. He had predicted a while ago through a dream that he would be killed by his own people, and in fact it was a group of Lakota police (no longer his followers because of years of efforts by the government to divide them) who was sent to bring him in. Forty-two of them went to his cabin in the middle of the night with backup troops to protect them. Some of Sitting Bull's supporters joined him. He refused to go. Both sides got angry and agitated. Some of them shot those, and some of those shot them. Sitting Bull was shot in the chest and they smashed his head to a pulp. Linus and Sally sat in the pumpkin patch waiting for the Great Pumpkin all night, certainly an offbeat belief, and no one arrested them. Sitting Bull's young son, Crow Foot, begged for mercy and they shot him and threw his body out the door. The shirts didn't work.

When Alley was about three, we were rocking in the rocking chair and, as she so often did, she brought up the subject of death. Maybe I rocked too fast. I said, "Honey, it's just the circle of life. Everybody is born. You can't find anybody who wasn't. Just ask them. And everybody dies. It's a big world, it happens every second." To illustrate my point, I snapped my fingers and said, "Right that second, somebody was born." I snapped again. "And right that second, somebody died. Hopefully you do the best you can and do some good in between your snaps." She sat up in my lap, gave a faint little snap (the best her little fingers

could do), and said, "Right that second, someone fell in love."
Am I the luckiest woman in the world or what? I have three
great kids, and not one of them is at risk of inheriting my pot
belly. I still don't understand where Alley got that thing about
studying a week ahead of time.

I read a biography of Sojourner Truth, hoping to include
her in this book, but this particular biographer came to the
conclusion that much of what we know about Sojourner Truth
isn't true. I have long suspected that that was going to turn out
to be the case with most, if not all, of recorded history. That's
why I started skipping history class in high school. Who knows
what's true? Biographers in the old days focused on the heroic
qualities of their subjects, whether they were real or not. They
don't do that anymore. Here's hoping that if my story ever gets
told, it gets told the old-fashioned way.

Well, I don't know, I guess that's it. What are you gonna do
now? I'll miss you. I'll be around if you need me. Boy, this is
awkward.